MANSIONS
of the HEART

MANSIONS of the HEART

Exploring the Seven Stages of Spiritual Growth

R. Thomas Ashbrook

Foreword by
Eugene H. Peterson

JOSSEY-BASS
A Wiley Imprint
www.josseybass.com

Published by Jossey-Bass
A Wiley Imprint
989 Market Street, San Francisco, CA 94103-1741—www.josseybass.com

Library of Congress Cataloging-in-Publication Data
Ashbrook, R. Thomas, date
    Mansions of the heart : exploring the seven stages of spiritual growth / R. Thomas Ashbrook.
      p. cm.
    Includes index.
    ISBN 978-0-470-45472-5
      1. Spiritual formation.   2. Teresa, of Avila, Saint, 1515–1582. Moradas.   I. Title.
BV4511.A84   2009
248.4—dc22

                                                   2009026349

Printed in the United States of America
FIRST EDITION
HB Printing   10 9 8 7 6 5 4 3 2 1

CONTENTS

FOREWORD

Eugene H. Peterson

WHILE I WAS IN SEMINARY IN TRAINING TO BE A PASTOR, I was immersed in the Bible (a good thing), provided with an extensive familiarity in the theological thinking of Luther, Calvin, and others (also a good thing), but learned virtually nothing regarding the on-the-ground living of the Christian life and what was actually involved in following Jesus over a lifetime in the cultural conditions of America.

When I became a pastor, I was grateful for the training I had received in the Bible, the authoritative text for the Christian life. And I appreciated the careful instruction in theology, right thinking about the Christian life. But it wasn't long before I realized that my professors had left me pretty much on my own when it came to matters of the soul, caring for the unique and eternal souls that were entrusted to me.

I felt adequately prepared to teach the truth of God, what to believe. I was well schooled in guiding people in moral and ethical matters, how to behave before God. But when it came to relationship with God, *being* with God, *listening to* and *answering* God, I found that I was reduced to what I had learned rather piecemeal on my own, supplemented by a few slogans and anecdotes I had picked up from others. It wasn't enough. I knew I needed help.

Help came through a friend who introduced me to Teresa of Avila and John of the Cross, two masters of the spiritual life, masters in understanding the soul and the nature of prayer. I had never heard of either one. They lived in Spain in the same century in which my theological masters, Martin Luther and John Calvin, were doing their work a thousand or so miles to the north in Germany and Switzerland.

Tom Ashbrook wrote this book that you hold in your hands to do for you what my friend did for me fifty years ago—to introduce you to these two companions who knew, practiced and wrote on the spiritual life with insight and passion. I am so glad that he wrote this book. His work could not be more timely. There is an enormous interest in spiritual formation these days, interest in growing up in Christ, living up to the "measure of the stature of the fullness of Christ." All of us need all the help we can get. Tom Ashbrook's *Mansions of the Heart* immerses us in this old but wonderfully contemporary holy wisdom. It is a gift to the Christian community. Take and read.

There is far more to the Christian life than getting it right. There is *living* it right. Learning the truth of God, the gospel, the Scriptures involves understanding words, concepts, history. But living it means working and praying ourselves through a world of deception, of doubt and suffering, a world of rejections and betrayal and idolatry.

Listening to sermons, reading books, and participating in a worshiping community prepare the altar. Spiritual transformation takes place when we gather the stuff of our ordinary lives—our parents and children, our spouses and friends, our workplaces and fellow workers, our dreams and fantasies, our attachments, our easily accessible gratifications, our habit of depersonalizing intimate relations, and our commodification of living truths into idolatries—take all of this and place it on the altar of refining fire—our God is a consuming fire!—and finding it all redeemed for a life of holiness.

Many of us (most of us?) know more about Scripture and truth than we do about souls and prayer. But souls and prayer require an equivalent demand on our attention as do Scripture and truth. And not just in bits and pieces—something comprehensive. Ashbrook leads us carefully and patiently into the rich praying company of Teresa and John.

Teresa and John are theologians every bit as "theological" as Luther and Calvin. But they use a very different language. Teresa told stories; her *Interior Castle*, the basic text of this book, is one of her best. John wrote poems; many consider him Spain's major poet. They are saturated in the same Scriptures as their contemporaries to the north of Spain and as theologically astute. But they, instead of arguing and defining and interpreting, express and witness and insist on the presence of God no matter how we feel about it, or if we feel anything at all. Luther and Calvin try to make the truth clear, which they do wonderfully. Teresa and John try to deal honestly and discerningly with the experience of God when it isn't plain, insisting that there are necessary obscurities and shadows to be embraced if we are to grow into mature holiness. We cannot have God on our terms, domesticated to our requirements, reduced to our ideas of what we think God should be doing. Prayer is an immersion in the way God is present with us whether we understand or like it or not. *This*, they are saying, is what it is like to live a life of faith and love, to pray, to be detached from a life of self, and become souls free for God and one another.

My learning of the Christian life, along with that of most of my friends, had pivoted on Martin Luther and John Calvin, brilliant and comprehensive thinkers, writers, and exegetes of Scripture. They taught me to think largely and passionately about God and the Scriptures. For them, reforming the Christian life was primarily (but not entirely) a matter of recovering right thinking, understanding doctrine, interpreting Scripture. Teresa and John worked from the other end. They took up matters of the soul, reforming Christian living by taking seriously the life of prayer and recovering the ways of prayer. They gave themselves to discerning the illusions and pitfalls that interfere with receiving what God is giving and reducing prayer to a self-help project with little concern for relationship and love, adoration and mystery.

I have come to visualize Luther and Calvin as mountain people, scaling the heights, taking in the horizon. And I have come to appreciate Teresa and John as valley people, tilling the soil, going to the market, cooking meals. They draw me into honoring the dignity of souls at work and play, returning me daily to the sweet mysteries of prayer.

PREFACE

MANSIONS OF THE HEART EMERGED OUT OF CONFUSION and frustration, mine and maybe yours. As a pastor, and then a spiritual formation teacher, coach, church consultant, and spiritual director, I have seen two converging movements that God means for good but that are giving many of us real headaches. A lot of us are recognizing that we need to pay much more attention to our own spiritual growth and that of maturing Christians. We look at the amazing lives of followers of Jesus in the Gospels and Epistles, and then we look at our own lives and churches and wonder what's going wrong. We know there has to be more. Although many of us have been hot after the discipleship of new Christians, the tendency of our church programming has been to stop there and leave the ongoing discipleship of maturing Christians to hit-or-miss circumstance. Sometimes we realize our lack of spiritual growth through our unfulfilled longings, and sometimes only because our spiritual immaturity gets us into trouble. Either way, we end up frustrated and confused.

Another movement has to do with our growing realization that the church has to become outwardly focused. Many of us are reclaiming our missional responsibility to move into the culture around us with the love of Jesus, but we are also realizing that it takes increasing spiritual maturity for followers of Jesus to really be salt and light in our neighborhoods and the dark places of the world. So, even though we sense what Jesus would have us do, we are frustrated by our inability, personally and as a community, to follow Him in spiritual authority and power.

As we try to address this need for greater spiritual maturity, again we find ourselves confused. There seems to be a lot of stumbling about as we try to pursue spiritual growth personally, and in our churches. Many of us don't seem to have a real handle on the goal of our spiritual journey or how to cooperate with God in the process. We continue to crank out spiritual practices that might once have helped us but now seem empty. In an effort to move forward in our relationship with God, we may try to add a few spiritual disciplines for our hurried lives, stir in a conference or two on prayer or spiritual formation, and sprinkle with a few readings from the latest self-help books. Confusion and frustration often result, however, as we realize that not much is changing. What should we expect to happen, and how do we connect with God in the process? Many maturing Christians, feeling this frustration and confusion, either give up on their own spiritual growth or give up on their church for not meeting their needs, or both.

Mansions of the Heart begins with my personal story of frustration and confusion and the discovery that there is more to the Christian life than building a successful church. Although I fully confessed that Jesus is head of the church and I wanted to follow His leading, I came face to face with the realization that my love for God was mostly about my needs and what I could get out of Him. In prayer, I presumptuously tried to tell God what to do, when to do it, and how to fix my church (and the universe, for that matter). I realized that if Jesus were to really lead my life and church, then I would have to move beyond trying to figure out "What would Jesus do?" and start really listening and responding to God. That would take a whole new kind of relationship. In the following years, Jesus took this first-born, Type A engineer-turned-pastor on a wondrous and sometimes terrifying adventure of discovery.

I found that this generation is not the first to experience this frustration and confusion. Our Christian ancestors studied Scripture and their own experiences and provided a roadmap for our journey of spiritual growth that can help us understand where God is taking us, where we are in the process, and how to cooperate with rather than frustrate what God is doing in our hearts. Early in my spiritual formation journey, I discovered Teresa of Avila and found that her *Interior Castle* provided an amazing description of our journey with Jesus into the heart of the Father, through the work of the Holy Spirit. Her seven phases of growth described how God desires to move us into deeper relationship with the Trinity and cooperation with His mission to the world. Her insights brought wonderful clarity to my own journey as it has done for others through the centuries. *Mansions of the Heat* attempts to address our difficulties in spiritual growth, describe this roadmap, and suggest how we can move forward in our personal and corporate spiritual journey. It describes seven wonderful phases of spiritual growth through which the Holy Spirit leads us toward an amazing and loving intimacy with God. The tragic fact is, however, that most of our churches disciple people less than half the way.

It is my prayer that *Mansions of the Heart* will speak to followers of Jesus who want more in their relationship with their Lord and Savior, people who are longing for a new intimacy with God and want to discover how to walk with Jesus, hand in hand, rather than stumble along some distance behind. I am also writing for those who God has called to shepherd His people, leaders who are responsible to foster an environment in the church community that encourages the spiritual formation of its members. It is not easy to make course corrections in churches with longstanding traditions, so *Mansions of the Heart* makes some suggestions about how we might proceed to help the church become all that the Lord has called her to be: the very loving presence of Jesus in a lost and dying world.

It is my prayer that *Mansions of the Heart* will be an opportunity for Jesus to meet you in new ways, enable you to live in His love more profoundly, and follow Him more closely into the wonderful destiny God has for you. The "mansions" you will read about have many doors within them, doors to a new and wonderful life with our Lord. Jesus is inviting you to open the one before you and explore the rooms of love beyond.

> Behold, I stand at the door and knock; if anyone hears My voice
> and opens the door, I will come in to him and will dine with
> him, and he with Me. He who overcomes, I will grant to him to
> sit down with Me on My throne, as I also overcame and sat down
> with My Father on His throne. He who has an ear, let him hear
> what the Spirit says to the churches
>
> —REVELATION 3:20–22

ACKNOWLEDGMENTS

A HOST OF FELLOW TRAVELERS WEAVE A TAPESTRY THAT SERVES as the context and the resource out of which any author is able to speak. In my case, the foundational fabric was woven by a man who met me in my darkest place of despair, hopelessness, and blindness. This man has walked with me ever since and led me, through the inner working of the Holy Spirit, into the loving and forgiving arms of my Heavenly Father. This man, my dearest friend, bears the scars of my sin and stupidity, and His sacrifice still permeates every fiber of my being. Jesus.

For *Mansions of the Heart* to emerge, Jesus wove into the tapestry the beauty and color of more people than I can possibly mention here. The influence of a few, however, has been profound. My wife, Charlotte, has lived out the loving presence of Jesus in ways that have always encouraged and supported my spiritual journey. Many times she has left the safe and familiar to join me in His sometimes scary invitations. Her bright colors and designs shine through any page of this work that truly honors Jesus.

For the three-dimensional depth of this tapestry, God used a monk named Brother Boniface. Bon taught me to "be still and know God," then simply to "be still," and finally to just "be," in the loving intimacy of God the Father, Son, and Holy Spirit. Bon not only introduced me to Teresa of Avila but showed me what the seventh mansion looks like. Our friendship was always an experience of Jesus, and I will be eternally grateful to him for calling out the monk within me.

I speak a lot in *Mansions of the Heart* about community. It is truly the community that God has built around me over the years that has enabled me to follow Jesus and complete this manuscript. Dr. Chuck Conniry, vice president and dean of George Fox Evangelical Seminary, encouraged and supported me as I tried to "systematize" the mystical writings of Teresa of Avila into a paradigm for spiritual formation. Chris Lyons lovingly badgered me to convert my doctor of ministry dissertation into something more readable and available to a wider audience. *Imago Christi* helped me field-test its premises and truths as together we prayed for and discovered deeper intimacy with the Trinity, and then attempted to encourage others into that same discovery. My brothers and sisters in *Imago Christi* provided the consistent pattern of love, forgiveness, and commitment within this emerging tapestry.

As *Mansions of the Heart* began to take shape, Mike Klassen, Chris Lyons, Bill O'Byrne, Jeremy Stefano, LaVahn Ferré, and Arlene Kampe read, edited, and reread endless versions, helping me discover how to communicate better what God had laid upon my heart. The advice and coaching of Greg Johnson, my literary agent, and the staff at Jossey-Bass have added joy as well as expertise to the emerging image of this woven work of God.

For you all, I am so grateful that you followed Jesus' lead and touched my life in transforming ways. May the fabric of our lives forever honor and love the One who calls us onward into the mansions of His love.

MANSIONS
of the HEART

CHAPTER I

Is This All There Is?

But now, O LORD, You are our Father, We are the clay, and You our potter; and all of us are the work of Your hand.

—ISAIAH 64:8

THE JOURNEY WITH JESUS: MY JOURNEY QUESTIONS SURFACED in the most unlikely way—in a Quonset hut and a chicken coop, with a tall thin monk who talked about listening to God. It happened during the years when I pastored a Lutheran church in the Salt Lake City area. Not aware of any spiritual growth questions in me, I visited this Trappist monastery only because I heard they had quiet guest rooms where I could get away to study and work. Holy Trinity Abbey lies in a beautiful mountain valley, with eighteen hundred acres of prime farm and pasture land that the monks work to support themselves. The lush green fields are surrounded with high, snow-capped mountain peaks. The vistas were breathtaking, but I was a little disappointed with the facility: simple Quonset hut buildings, with foam insulation on the outside, placed in a quadrangle. The simplicity, silence, and smell of cows were later to become a hint of the kinds of transformations that the Lord had planned for me. But at this point, I just wanted to be alone and work.

The guest master, Father Emmanuel, showed me to my tiny room: a single bed, dresser, chair, desk, and a coat hook.

1

Nothing fancy, for sure. At supper, I asked Father Emmanuel if I could worship with the monks, having no idea what I was asking. Only occasionally did a visiting Catholic priest chant the psalms with the monks, much less a Protestant—and a Lutheran at that! He explained, to my surprise, that the monks worshiped seven times a day, starting at 3:30AM. Was I really up for this?

That evening, Father Emmanuel ushered me past large wooden gates, into the two-story Quonset church, around rough wooden churchlike pews and into an area where rows of individual stalls were set facing each other, just before and perpendicular to the altar; two rows on the right, and two rows on the left. "I'll seat you next to Brother Boniface; he likes guests," whispered Father Emmanuel.

Here sat an "elderly" man, skinny, with bright blue eyes and a warm smile. Boniface's job was to show me what to read or sing or say and whether to sit or stand, at the appropriate time during the worship. It was a strange experience indeed. The Gregorian chanting of the psalms, reading from Scripture, and times of silence and prayer had a solemnity and the taste of mystery that was not typical of my church or the ones I had attended. As my day-and-a-half retreat progressed, I was struck by the deep sense of God's presence in the worship with the monks, in the solitude of my room, and in my walks in the surrounding hills.

What amazed me most was the nearly palpable love of Christ that I felt in standing next to Brother Boniface in "choir" (which is shorthand for the worship times or Offices). It was particularly unusual because there were none of the normal ways of communicating such love. The monks were in church to worship God, not to visit or fellowship. They didn't exchange words, or even glances if they could help it. Boniface winked at me once as he came to his stall, but never a word. Yet there was something intriguing, and I decided to come back to the monastery again.

A month or two later, I scheduled another visit. Again, I sat next to Brother Boniface in choir, seven times a day. Again, I felt that love. Finally, I couldn't help myself. I broke the rules and whispered to him at the end of choir, "I need to speak to you." He whispered back, "Eight-thirty, chicken coop," and walked off. I was dumbfounded. Was that AM or PM? Where was the chicken coop?

That evening, I confessed to Father Emmanuel my breach of silence with Brother Boniface and asked for some guidance. It turned out that Boniface took care of the chickens, and he finished his chores about 8:30AM. The next morning I was there.

The chicken coop turned out to be a huge barn that housed three thousand chickens in a fully automated egg operation. I found Brother Boniface, dressed in ragged overalls covering his monk habit, just finishing the candling of the eggs. After I had waited a few minutes, this tall thin monk came over to me, dropped to his knees, and asked for my blessing. Again dumbfounded, I muttered some sort of prayer for him. When he arose, I introduced myself and explained that I had felt the love of Jesus in him and wanted to meet him. As we walked out of the chicken coop and onto the road, he responded, "Oh, I felt the love of Jesus in you too, and wanted to meet you as well, but the Lord told me to wait until you asked."

Now, some folks talk like that, hearing God and all, but you wonder whether or not God really told them anything. I sensed that Brother Boniface, however, had asked God about meeting me, and that God in fact told him to wait. It caught my attention. How I longed for a relationship like that with God. My soul yearned to feel God's presence and hear His voice of guidance and instruction. Little did I realize that it was for this previously unrecognized yearning, my heart's desire that God had brought me to Holy Trinity Abbey and to Brother Boniface. We walked and talked some, and I was determined to return again.

During the third visit some months later, I found myself weeping almost constantly. To my embarrassment, I snuffled and sniffed through choir, alone in my room, or walking in the hills around the monastery. Strangely, the tears didn't seem to be connected with any particular emotion. A Scripture verse, a flower, or nothing at all could set me off. When it was my scheduled time to leave, I called my wife, Charlotte, and said, "I don't know what is going on, but whatever God is doing, it isn't done yet, and I'm not ready to come home." Then, and since, I have realized how wonderfully blessed I am by a wife who trusts me to God. A day or so later, I talked again to Father Emmanuel, telling him about my almost constant tears. What did it mean? After some quiet reflection, he responded, "Tom,

I think Jesus may be calling you closer to His heart. Just listen and do what He says." Listen? How do I do that? God was not in the habit of speaking out loud to me or giving me writing on the wall.

Later I asked Brother Boniface about listening to God. He responded, "Well, that's what prayer is all about. Certainly, what God has to say to us is more important than what we have to say to God; He already knows what we need." Again, his words rang with experience and spiritual authority, not mere platitudes he read somewhere. I realized that, beyond the printed words of Scripture, I had no idea of how to "listen to God." Furthermore, my prayers weren't really about listening, but about telling God what to do and when to do it, as if He didn't already know.

As I reflected, it seemed my spiritual life had been this steady plodding, and I now I was mounting the crest of a hill to see a phenomenal vista ahead of me; one I had never guessed existed, a relationship with God in which I could hear His voice. I had further to go in my spiritual growth than I could have imagined. But there was a sense of hope, and even excitement, and adventure, as I glimpsed the life God wants for me. I recalled Paul's prayer for us in Ephesians:

> . . . that He would grant you, according to the riches of His glory, to be strengthened with power through His Spirit in the inner man, so that Christ may dwell in your hearts through faith; and that you, being rooted and grounded in love, may be able to comprehend with all the saints what is the breadth and length and height and depth, and to know the love of Christ which surpasses knowledge, that you may be filled up to all the fullness of God.
>
> —EPHESIANS 3:16–19

Really Knowing God

I realized that I wanted much more than to hear God's voice of instruction and to follow Him. I wanted to really know Him, to experience His love so profoundly that it would push out my own self-hatred and enable me to truly love those around me.

At first I visited the monastery a few days every couple of months; then it became three days a month, and later four week-long retreats a year. During my retreats, I would meet each day with "Bon." We would talk about our spiritual lives, particularly about prayer. It became increasingly apparent to me that there was quite a different quality to Brother Boniface's prayer life (really a life of prayer) than I had been exposed to before. Since my adult conversion, I had been taught that prayer was talking to God; for Brother Boniface, it was more listening to God, enjoying God.

My new thirst for God created a new problem, however. Where could I learn about how to listen to God and experience Him? I had been involved in the Charismatic Movement, which certainly was experiential. But the emphasis on the spiritual gifts focused on "doing for God." I hungered for deeper insight and experience into "being with God."

I had come to understand the importance of ministering in the power of the Holy Spirit, beyond the abilities of our human gifting. But it had also become increasingly clear to me that it was necessary to minister responsively, that is to say, in response to the particular way in which Jesus leads, as a sheep hears and follows his Shepherd. I saw that church programs and strategies were often, if not always, inadequate in their ability to enable us to follow Christ through the intricacies of our rapidly changing world. The phrase "What would Jesus do?" would not cut it. How could I possibly know beyond the bounds of basic morality or imitation of what I read in the Scriptures?

If I were to follow Jesus, in actuality I must follow Him the way He follows the Father: "Truly, truly, I say to you, the Son can do nothing of Himself, unless it is something He sees the Father doing; for whatever the Father does, these things the Son also does in like manner" (John 5:19). On the Mount of Transfiguration, God told Peter, James, and John to listen to Jesus (cf. Matt. 17:5; Mark 9:7). God's word to us is still the same today. This encounter with a monk who spent his life listening to God made me realize that I was being called to serve God on a whole new level. This new level was not about greater skills, but about an intimacy with God that would enable me to hear His voice and truly come to know Him in the process. This new life would require a new me. It would take a transformation of my heart from a headstrong pastor who tried to earn self-esteem through performance, to a receptive and free follower of Jesus. The Potter faced major work with this lump of clay.

I found encouragement among the monks and participation in an international movement called Renovaré.[1] Renovaré, led by Richard Foster, hosted conferences all over the country, with speakers such as Dallas Willard and Eugene Peterson. Through these writers and their books, spiritual disciplines became a new part of my experience. With some of my friends, I started a Renovaré covenant group, where we read certain spiritual classics, shared our spiritual experience, and prayed for one another's spiritual growth. I began reading the mystics, the Desert Fathers, the Church Fathers, and many contemporary writers on prayer and the spiritual life. As I began experimenting with Christian meditation and contemplation, I found that God entered the prayer closet of my heart with words, thoughts, feelings, and most profoundly, a sweet silence.

What is more, I found that the qualitative nature of my relationship with God began to change radically. I was growing spiritually and relationally, not just at an intellectual level. The ongoing experience raised even more questions for me about what the process of spiritual growth or formation is all about, and my reading began to expand. My life began to explode with the awareness of God's presence. As I learned to become attentive to the presence of God in my "prayer closet," I found that my heart also spotted Him in daily life. I remember climbing Mt. Timpanogos, just south of Salt Lake City, with my boys. We were camped near Emerald Lake at about ten thousand feet. Early in the morning, I suddenly awoke, as if beckoned. I pulled on my coat and crawled out of the tent to meet the frosty morning, just before sunrise. I walked to a rock at the water's edge, sat down, prayed, and waited for the sunrise. As the first rays of the sun hit my face, I heard loud noises all around me. I slowly opened my eyes to see beautiful long-horned mountain goats coming to the water to drink. Seemingly unnoticed, I sat perfectly still as they came within a few feet of me. The sight was awesome, and I felt privileged to be so close to these rarely seen creatures, usually glimpsed high on some distant cliff. As I sat still on my rock in the sun, God seemed to say, "I made them for you to enjoy, because I love you." The rest of the climb seemed like a walk in a mystical garden, planted and cultured just for me; the Gardner was climbing with me.

The Call to Follow Jesus Specifically

During these same years, the call to listen to God and follow him spilled over into my church and ministry. In the midst of a struggle among our staff and elders to know God's direction on a specific issue, we retreated to the monastery for four days to listen to God and to one another. We each started out on various sides of the issue. However, after four days, God had miraculously brought us absolutely to one mind. We wrote a document entitled "Reflections from the Abbey," which we brought back to our elders with an explanation of what God had done. It began a change in the way we led that is still foundational for that congregation today.

About the same time, I began hearing about pastor friends who were seeing "spiritual directors." Spiritual direction was something new to me. I learned that a spiritual director is trained to understand the Christian life and listen to God in the context of listening to other people. Reflective questions help the directee discern God's hand in the circumstances they discuss. These Protestant pastors sought out mostly Catholic monks and nuns to talk with about their lives. As I inquired about their experience of spiritual direction, I found two things. First, these spiritual direction conversations seemed generally helpful. Second, it appeared there were only a few cases where the direction or focus of those conversations was the same. Many had a decidedly psychological bent to them. Some included discussion of spiritual disciplines, but not all. One common theme was the directees' deep hunger to move forward spiritually. Most of the men and women I talked to were like me: they yearned for a greater experience of the reality of God and a more complete integration of their faith in everyday life. They wanted to become "spiritually mature."

But the strange thing was that few of them agreed on what being spiritually mature meant. Some said that maturity was becoming holier. Some talked about character. Others said it was about leading a healthier lifestyle. For some, spiritual growth was about becoming more useful to God, better disciples, preachers, evangelists. Most had no idea about where their spiritual growth was headed at all. They sought spiritual direction for a time, but most stopped for a variety of reasons. There was little talk of the completion of some process or the reaching of some goal.

My heart shouted, "What is spiritual growth really all about?"

I remember reading Thomas Dubay in *Fire Within*, where he explains that the most significant spiritual growth is often discerned by the believer as backsliding.[2] That's exactly how I felt: always fighting backsliding. As I learned more, I realized I often wrongly interpreted my spiritual experiences, assuming that because I was confused or discouraged something must be amiss. But by what criteria should I understand what God is doing in me?

As I explored further, I found that the same spiritual hunger I was experiencing was far-reaching in other Christians as well. Christian colleges, seminaries, and specialized institutes around the country had recently begun offering courses in spiritual formation and certificates in spiritual direction. But as I reviewed many of these programs, their curricula indicated what I had already discovered: there was little consensus on either the method or the goal of spiritual formation.

This fuzziness and confusion reflected what I've always felt about the Christian education curriculum of my denomination. It included lots of good material about the Bible, Christian morality, and Christian doctrine and theology, but it did not describe the Christian journey's method or goal. I realized that if we took much of our discipleship teaching literally, we could well believe that the Christian life is simply about conversion, biblical knowledge, morals, witnessing to one's faith, and, for a few, work on a church committee. The implication is that once these basics are under control, life will fall into place and all will go well.

But what I saw with my colleagues and parishioners was that "reality" eventually hit. The spiritual journey is just not that simple; life often gets more difficult, not simpler, and is seldom under control. This shallow view of the Christian life is finally pretty boring, and our experience is often filled with all sorts of trial and pain. I saw that many people with this simplistic understanding eventually become disillusioned and leave their church. Others become critical of their pastors and church programs because they are not "getting fed." A few search for a more meaningful relationship with Jesus. But what is that more meaningful relationship, and how do you and I find it?

In my present role as a spiritual formation coach and leader of *Imago Christi*, I have found that missionaries, pastors, and serious followers of Jesus in many places in the world are asking the same questions.[3] For example, I have been coaching spiritual formation for a number of pastors and missionaries through a Protestant form of the Spiritual Exercises of St. Ignatius.[4] One man wrote to me, "Every few years there is another 'bestseller' that touts yet another new program for successful ministry. I am tired of rotating programs that ultimately seem to leave me and my church right where we started. I want to find out what Jesus wants to do, and do it." In a later journal he confessed, "I've realized that I am on the edge of burnout. If Jesus doesn't set the agenda and provide the strength, I won't survive here." Maybe you've felt the same way.

Tired and discouraged, Christians are asking questions: "How does a person grow spiritually? Why are the old discipleship programs of Bible study, doctrine, and evangelism training not transforming wounded people into empowered warriors for Christ? Why am I so bored with church?" I have come to see that the answer lies in what we are now calling "spiritual formation."

Spiritual Formation and Traditional Views of Discipleship

"Wait a minute," you may be saying. "What about all the 'discipleship' programs that have been part of church life for generations? How are they different from what you're calling 'spiritual formation'?" It's a good question.

The word *disciple* should have a far greater meaning than it often has. Our limited view of discipleship has meant being a student of God, "doing" the right things such as daily Bible reading and memorization, praying for others, practicing moral behavior and witnessing, attending a local church, believing the right things, and maybe for the really serious undertaking a short-term missions trip. We talk about a "personal relationship with Jesus Christ," but more often than not we just teach people how to work for a God up in the sky. We can imply that these practices are all there is to the spiritual life. The question remains: Does that kind of discipleship produce the kind of personal transformation needed to live meaningfully and dynamically in the world today? When we're really honest, we have to answer no. There has to be more.

Richard Peace, professor of evangelism and spiritual formation at Fuller Theological Seminary, comments on the failure of many ministries to effect genuine spiritual growth:

> The inherent promise in all this was that if we persevered, we would grow. And this was our goal—to grow in the Christian life. We really did want to be like Jesus. The problem was that things never quite turned out as expected. Sure, we got to know a lot of Scripture and we were active in ministry of sorts, but change in our core personality came so slowly, if at all. What was wrong with our spiritual pursuits that the growth we sought eluded us or, at least, took so long?[5]

Maybe like me, you feel that you have persevered and the promised growth never came. The more I found my own unrest resonating with others, the more I wanted to pursue a new understanding of hearing Jesus, knowing Jesus, and following Jesus in a way that was deeper than traditional views of discipleship I'd been exposed to. I not only wanted to work for the Boss, I longed to get to know Him.

My marginal involvement in the Charismatic Movement slightly expanded my traditional understanding of discipleship by bringing a new sense of the imminent power and presence of the Holy Spirit and His ability to touch, heal, and empower ministry. But despite the possible addition of spiritual gifts to the basic discipleship curriculum, the understanding of spiritual growth did not change.

Another emphasis arose among leadership development circles, in the eighties, called "character development." It was based largely on creating a greater understanding of the moral mandates of Scripture and used accountability relationships to impose those mandates.[6] Unfortunately, we can mandate Christ-like character all we want. Sin is still an obstacle we cannot overpower. What we need is transformation.

In the nineties, the Holy Spirit began to move in new ways and many serious followers of Jesus began to rediscover classical forms of spirituality. Richard Foster's *Celebration of Discipline*[7] opened doors to classical works such as Teresa of Avila's *Interior Castle*[8] and Thomas à Kempis's *The Imitation of Christ*.[9] Contemporary writers such as Henri Nouwen and Thomas Merton further described, in modern terms, the life of prayer and intimacy with God in ways that were more palatable for Protestants as well as Catholics.

And so the term *spiritual formation* slowly became preferred to "discipleship," in many circles. Peace describes the difference: "The same hunger prevailed as has always been present within evangelical circles: the hunger for transformation into the image of Christ. But now the path to such transformation came by way of the exercise of ancient spiritual practices."[10]

Spiritual formation does indeed have a deeper dimension than discipleship. James Houston, founder and professor of spiritual formation at Regent College in Vancouver, B.C., defines Christian spirituality as "the state of a deep relationship to God."[11] So we could say that *spiritual formation* spans the whole of the Christian life, while the term *discipleship* has been used to relate primarily to the early spiritual growth years. But the problem is that although the old discipleship term had a concrete meaning (there are books and tracts and curricula), spiritual formation became a general and elusive term. Discipleship was aimed at equipping the believer for ministry. Character development worked at Christian integrity and behavior. Ongoing spiritual formation targets much more: lifelong transformation of the whole person into the image of Christ, in the context of a deep relationship with God.

What Is the Goal of Spiritual Formation?

This is another good question. The goal still seems fuzzy when you read much of the literature to date. What is it about the "image of Christ" we are after in spiritual formation? What is the process through which this happens? What is the difference between a "deep" relationship with God and one that is shallow? Careful not to get labeled or boxed into a narrow understanding or regimen; many contemporary spiritual formation writers advocate that we practice "a little of this and a little of that." For example, Peace concludes, "So, in place of a single model, I suspect that in the new millennium we will see a blending of approaches. I can imagine an evangelical bookshelf containing . . . [a list of books from varied traditions]."[12]

The trouble is that in the effort to be inclusive and holistic, there has been little clarity about either the goal or the process of spiritual formation. Will an eclectic library and a dabbling in the spiritual disciplines accomplish true transformation within us? I think we need much more. We'll see later that God's goal for us is simply a restored relationship of love with God through Jesus Christ. It is so deceptively simple that it's often overlooked.

The problem facing all Christians today is that the process of the spiritual life is not clearly understood or taught in most of our churches and seminaries. Followers of Jesus are left without clear reference points for spiritual maturity or processes to aid progress in their spiritual journey. No wonder so many Christians feel ambivalent about church. They often find that church attendance does not really make a difference. A recent study by Willow Creek Church documented the disparity between going to church activities and spiritual growth. It shockingly demonstrated that there was, in fact, no correlation between participation in the ministries of the churches surveyed and personal spiritual growth.[13] Christians who desire to grow into spiritual maturity desperately need materials to help describe our overall journey with Jesus so that we can find ourselves in process, and discover how better to cooperate with God as He leads and transforms our lives.

A Roadmap for Ongoing Spiritual Transformation

But there is good news! We've all longed for a description for lifelong spiritual transformation, a roadmap for our growing relationship with God. We want this roadmap to have sufficient detail that we can locate ourselves in the spiritual journey, and learn how to cooperate with God as He leads us forward in Christian maturity.

Once we have such a spiritual formation roadmap, with the characteristics of each stage of growth, we can develop a "mapping tool," which will help us locate ourselves in process. The mist of confusion about our ongoing life with Jesus can clear as we celebrate His work within our hearts. Think how such a roadmap and assessment tool could assist you personally. It could also be a wonderful tool for churches, Christian colleges, and seminaries to help them design spiritual formation programs and ministries that help followers of Jesus become mature disciples for Christ and bring health and vitality to the church. A roadmap for our spiritual formation does exist. In fact, it's been around for centuries. Teresa of Avila's Seven Mansions provide a wonderful description that we'll explore in depth in Chapter Three.

So, get ready for an adventure of discovery. We will explore Teresa of Avila's seven phases of spiritual transformation as an ancient yet timeless roadmap to help us understand our journey. What follows could revolutionize your walk with Jesus, as it has mine. The following chapters will guide you through a personal discovery, as you view your life experiences and your relationship with God in the context of the various stages of this roadmap.

I encourage you preachers and teachers to read not only with your analytical prowess but also with your heart. Read not just to glean information, but slowly as an opportunity to recall memories, reflect personally, and hear from God. Let *Mansions of the Heart* be an adventure of new discoveries as you listen to the heart of God, not just about the subject of spiritual formation for your church but for you personally. We cannot lead where we have not gone before, so let this reading in some way become a journey forward.

If you have had a hunger to "hear" the voice of Jesus and help others do the same, if you thirst for intimacy with God as I do, and need a spiritual perspective from which to truly follow Jesus, then read on with the confidence that God has something in store for you. Jesus promises: "Blessed are those who hunger and thirst for righteousness, for they will be filled" (Matt. 5:6). The Potter is waiting. Here is how we will proceed.

Chapter Two addresses common myths that lead us down dead-end roads that get us stuck in our spiritual growth. We'll find there is one road that leads to an adventurous life with Jesus and accomplishes all we may have searched for on dead-end roads.

In Chapter Three, we delve deeper into this apparent absence of a model for lifelong spiritual transformation, and we will see that not only don't we have a commonly accepted road-map, we often don't even agree on the destination. We will discover that an ancient treasure map exists to help us understand our journey.

Chapters Four through Eleven launch us into the phases of spiritual formation. The first phase begins with a description of the new believer who comes to personal faith in Christ as Lord and Savior. The final phase describes life in unity with the Trinity, and a wonderful season of inner peace in loving God and others. In each phase, you will be able to see part of your own journey and that of those around you. As you find the phase with which you most identify in this season of your walk with Jesus, you can use the "Keys to Growth" in that phase and the ones right around it to become more intentional about your own cooperation with God's amazing work in your life.

In Chapter Nine, we take a "time out" to discuss one of the great mysteries of the Christian life: the Dark Nights of the Soul. Although we all know that there are times of discouragement in our lives, it is often inadvertently taught that as we grow spiritually, the terrain becomes more level and happier. In fact, our most intense struggles with spiritual growth often come in the later phases. We will look at John of the Cross's teaching about these Dark Nights that come in the more mature years of our Christian journey.

In Chapter Twelve, we will look at our individual differences in how each of us grows in our relationship with God. We have explored a specific roadmap for the spiritual journey, but it is important to understand that we are all different and God's movement in our lives reflects our uniqueness.

In Chapter Thirteen, we'll speculate about how wonderful it would be to have a community of fellow travelers with us in our spiritual formation journey. This chapter explores how you can help your church take specific actions to form itself in ways that empower spiritual growth from prebeliever to aging saint, releasing the full power of the Body of Christ to a hungry and thirsty world.

Chapter Fourteen explores your opportunity to be part of one of the most amazing seasons in history. God is doing a new thing in our time! You are not alone in your quest. Chapter Fourteen paints the picture of the adventure awaiting you as you let Jesus mold you into the beautiful daughter or son you were created to be. Your spiritual formation is the key to a world-wide movement of the Holy Spirit to form the church as she has never yet been formed, to make the Bride beautiful for her Bridegroom, and to let the whole world know the love and saving power of Christ.

I first wrote these words, sitting in my little room at the monastery in Utah, twenty-five years from where I started my story. Brother Boniface was then eighty-seven years old and still radiated the love of Christ.[14] At dinner that night, one of the guests exclaimed, "You know, all the monks love God, but you can just see it in Brother Boniface!" I nodded agreement as gratitude flooded my heart. I am now busier than ever with teaching and coaching, but silence and simplicity have become the bedrock of my relationship with God and the way I listen to His heart. The smell of farm manure that initially turned my nose has become symbolic of the stinky places in my life that God wants to bless and heal and empower.

It is my prayer that you and I might so live in the radiance of God's love that others can be blessed in sensing Jesus in us. In knowing us, they will want to journey on—on into love, into the heart of the Father, hand in hand with Jesus, His Son, aflame with love, to the utter joy of the Holy Spirit. You're about to embark on a journey of discovery that, if you are listening to God, will change your life.

REFLECTION

- What has God used, most powerfully, to increase your hunger and thirst for spiritual growth?
- When you think of the "ultimate" in a relationship with Jesus, what things come to mind?
- What might backsliding look and feel like in your spiritual journey?
- What frustrates you most about your own spiritual growth?

CHAPTER 2

Common Myths That Lead Down Dead-End Roads

*Enter through the narrow gate; for the gate is wide
and the way is broad that leads to destruction, and
there are many who enter through it. For the gate is
small and the way is narrow that leads to life, and
there are few who find it.*

—MATTHEW 7:13–14

YES, WE ALL WANT A JOURNEY OF DISCOVERY that will change
our lives, but many of us are not experiencing it. Ever feel stuck
in your relationship with God? Worse, do you feel as if you are
going in the wrong direction? It could be true.

You and I are being spiritually formed every day. But is it
the kind of "formation" we really want? Our environment works
overtime to form us into its image; we're transformed every day,
oftentimes, for the worse. You see, everyone is on a spiritual formation journey. We don't live in a neutral world, with church or
God as our only spiritual influence. We are bombarded by influences—some good and many bad—constantly seeking to form
us into the world's mold. Just turn on the TV and watch for the
worldview being taught, or the values portrayed as normal, or
the images of false happiness, meaning, purpose, and so on. This
negative spiritual formation is always working on us. Statistics tell

us that this negative formation is actually quite successful with many Christians. Unfortunately, we Christians have about the same rates of divorce, addiction, and other problems as the rest of the population.

To counter this influence, many serious followers of Jesus make intentional efforts to avoid negative influences and focus on Scripture, church, acts of kindness, and so on. We work at being more loving, serving God better, praying more faithfully, and working more at church. But the sad truth is that many of us still find little success. We feel stuck in our relationship with God. Our spiritual formation efforts feel more like a dead-end road leading to disappointment rather than increasing closeness to God. A recent conversation illustrates the situation.

Roxanna and other friends were at our house for dinner. Over dessert, she shared her story. Growing up Christian, she was usually the first one to volunteer for various jobs at church. She believed that serving others would bring her closer to Jesus. For a time, teaching the Bible to kids did help make the life of Jesus more real to her. More than that, it was exhilarating to see new faith blossom in her kids. But Roxanna had some real struggles in her faith related to unanswered prayers and the dryness of her daily quiet time, struggles that faithful church service didn't seem to address. Church had become just the same curriculum, the same sermons, and polite people—none of which addressed her deep hunger to know more of God. So Roxanna figured that a good walk on Sunday mornings might do her just about as much good, and many times it did. But inside, she was deeply discouraged about her relationship with God.

Roxanna had worked hard to grow in her faith and become the kind of person who could please God. But she felt like a failure, stuck at what appeared to be a failure in the spiritual growth path she had taken. But then, she didn't have anything with which to compare her experience. She was stalled, and all her efforts now seemed like a dead-end road.

Roxanna is not alone. Maybe you feel that way. I'm sure that at the least you know someone who is.

For example, recent studies, published in Willow Creek's book *Reveal*, show that this feeling of being stuck and dissatisfied is very common among maturing believers.[1] Willow Creek's research, in its church network of thousands, shows that 63 percent of the most active and committed church members are so discouraged with church and its ability to support their faith that they are considering leaving their church.

How do people get so discouraged? Being dissatisfied with our spiritual growth is often the result of believing myths about relating to Jesus that lead us down dead-end roads. I know from personal experience.

In the early days of my Christian walk, I assumed that God was out to make me a better layman in my church, and later a better pastor, husband, and father. This would all be great, but I longed for more than that. I wanted to grow in my faith. Like Roxanna, there were too many nagging doubts in me, not so much about the truths of the Christianity but about trusting God in actual situations.

I grew up in a home where an "I love you" was not necessarily associated with an "I'll be there for you." My father's struggle with alcoholism, and my parents' failed marriage, left me with fearing failure and lacking any inner certainty that love and faithfulness were connected. Maybe this was as much a matter of counseling as spiritual growth, but it certainly affected my relationship with God in a negative way. I didn't like distrusting "Someone" who I was supposed to love. Did God's plan for me include fixing my heart so that I could love Him without reservation, or was He only interested in my performance? My guess is that this is, or has been, a question for you as well.

My problem was that I had not yet realized that God's goal for my life was simply a love relationship with Him; I didn't know what it was. As I continued my reading in the area of spiritual formation, I was frustrated to find that a clear goal for our spiritual journey was seldom offered, or I found that there were significant differences when goals were discussed. Our spiritual journey has to be more than random help from God as we go through life. God must have a purpose, a goal, and a destiny for us all. God said to Jeremiah, and to us, "For I know the plans that I have for you, declares the LORD, plans for welfare and not for calamity, to give you a future and a hope" (Jer. 29:11–14). The apostle Paul said, "I press on toward the goal for the prize of the upward call of God in Christ Jesus" (Phil. 3:14). So, what is the goal—the upward call to what?

Ultimately, we know that the Scriptures must show us the goal of our "training in righteousness." The trouble is, however, that we can find a number of biblical goals for our life with Jesus. We're called to love God, follow Jesus, love our neighbor, and stay away from a host of things. The goal we choose as the primary one becomes the lens through which we see and interpret the person of God and our spiritual experience. To make matters worse, traditions tend to emphasize the goals that have been important in their own movement. To oversimplify, for example, if you were raised Roman Catholic, faithfulness with Holy Communion was probably stressed; for Methodists, it may have been correct behavior; for Lutherans and Presbyterians, it could have been correct theology; and for Evangelical churches it could have been bringing others to faith in Christ.

If we are convinced God is up to one thing in our lives, then we will interpret our experience from this perspective. Roxanna thought that serving others would produce a deep relationship with God within her. When it didn't seem to be happening, she quit church, feeling frustrated and hurt. When God didn't make me into the perfect husband, father, and pastor I wanted to be, I was confused and angry.

We were both traveling down roads that ended in anxiety and failure. Maybe this has happened to you. Let's look at some of the myths that get us stuck, roads that seem to be following Jesus but result only in disappointment.

Myths of the Dead-End Roads

God Simply Wants Me to Be Holy

The *Holiness Goal* contends that God's primary purpose in our lives is to create increasing virtue within us, until we are holy in the same way that Christ is holy. Key words within this potential goal of spiritual transformation are character, sanctification, godliness, fruits of the Spirit, and of course holiness. The center of spiritual growth, from the Holiness Goal perspective, is us—our attitudes, our feelings, and most of all our behavior.

God's work in us is directed toward stamping out sinful tendencies and behavior so that we may fully reflect the character of God Himself. There are certainly scriptural foundations for the importance of holiness in our lives. "Be perfect as God is perfect" is an example (Matt. 5:48).

Maybe you've understood God's call to live a holy life as the primary goal of your spiritual growth. It is true that we all need a greater degree of holiness in our lives. As we mentioned in Chapter One, researchers find that incidents of divorce, alcoholism, abuse, and so on are about the same for those calling themselves Christian as for the general population.[2]

So what makes "holiness" a mythical goal as God's primary purpose in our lives? There are at least two things that make it a dead end. First, we never get there; the goal is always moving ahead of us. We find only relative success, at best. Yes, maybe we can make some progress in our ways of relating to other people, at least better than So-and-So. The second dead-end nature of holiness as the goal of our relationship with Jesus is that the "target" grows infinitely harder to hit. The great saints of biblical times and throughout history tell us that the more we grow in our relationship with God, the more we realize how truly holy God is and how deep our sin runs, in comparison. So the apostle Paul could say, "I am the chief of sinners" (1 Tim. 1:15). Or, in Romans 7:15–16, "For what I am doing, I do not understand; for I am not practicing what I would like to do, but I am doing the very thing I hate." Ever feel that way?

No matter how hard we try, we never get there, or even close. Using the lens of holiness, we may well feel like Jesus, the Holy One, is simply a judge of our ungodliness and far removed. Holiness is a great virtue, but as a goal for God's work within us it's a dead end.

God Wants Me to Be a Better Worker

This *Usefulness Goal* of spiritual growth is like the Holiness Goal because it also focuses on us, our behavior. Usefulness is associated with our ability to serve God faithfully. God's purpose in our lives, from this perspective, is our performance in ministry, formal or informal. Whereas holiness is about a state of "being" for God, service is about effective "doing" for God. If God rids us of character flaws, it is so that we can do the work of ministry. Key words for this focus include witness, justice, compassion, discipleship, service, spiritual gifts, calling, and so forth. Proponents for the Usefulness Goal of spiritual growth may focus on effectiveness, excellence, contribution, and finishing well.

Of course, the call to serve God as a faithful disciple is consistent throughout Scripture. Jesus' famous command to "follow me and I will make you fishers of men," is central to our understanding of what it means to be a disciple of Jesus (cf. Matt. 4:19). The ability to serve God has always been seen as a part of Christian development and discipleship throughout the history of the church. However, Western civilization's growing fixation with accomplishment has brought productivity to the place of primacy. Success and accomplishment have become the goals in almost every aspect of life and culture. Our objectives in the spiritual life may well have been formed by culture.

Like the Holiness Goal, the dead end we hit with this spiritual formation goal is that we never get there. No matter how much we work for the Lord or how good we may get at it, effective service is always relative. We may be doing more and better than some of the folks around us, but there is always someone to show us we could be making greater sacrifice, having greater impact, or serving God better. If the mythical goal of effective service is our lens, it may feel to us as though Jesus is marching on further ahead of us, ever more distant and possibly ever more demanding. We may salve our feelings of discouragement by falling into bed at night exhausted, saying to ourselves that surely God couldn't expect anything more. Like holiness, our usefulness to Jesus is certainly important, but when made the principal goal of our relationship with God it becomes a dead-end road of failure and discouragement. When we stop and think about it, we all want more in our relationship with Jesus than just working for Him.

God Wants Me to Be Whole

Personal wholeness is a third mythical goal of spiritual growth. The Wholeness Goal can be described as wellness and balance in the whole person, mind, body, and spirit. As with holiness and service, we are the focus. This goal has become particularly prominent with the increasing influence of modern psychology in pastoral care and counseling and through the healing movement. Possibly, as a counterbalance to our Western workaholism extremes, emphasis on personal balance of mind, body, and spirit has also become a theme in today's secular marketplace. Key words for the Wholeness Goal might include balance, boundaries, peace, health, serenity, healing, and so on.

There are numerous places in the Scriptures that reveal the importance of our spiritual, physical, and mental health and balance. The apostle Paul teaches, "But we urge you, brethren, to excel still more, and to make it your ambition to lead a quiet life and attend to your own business and work with your hands, just as we commanded you, so that you will behave properly toward outsiders and not be in any need" (1 Thess. 4:10b–12). A number of modern authors encourage us to resist our world's obsession with success and accomplishment and focus more on the balanced life, on the health of the soul.

The Wholeness Goal leads to a dead end because it is far beyond our control, and only relatively attainable, if at all. For example, every apostle lived a life of extremes, difficulty, and sacrifice. They all suffered martyrdom. Even John died alone, exiled on Patmos. History is filled with followers of Jesus who have had to bear great illness and poverty, far from what we might call a balanced life.

Although we may find seasons of relative wholeness, its "happiness" dimension may be more an American illusion, a myth, than a biblical goal for our lives. Our sinful nature and external circumstances are ready at any instant to turn a peaceful country lane into a dead-end road of disappointment and disillusionment.

So far, we have seen three potential goals for spiritual growth, all with genuine biblical foundations. Holiness, service, and wholeness are part of God's plan for our lives at some level, and certainly they can be evidence of spiritual growth. But can we say that any one is the ultimate or final goal for God's relationship with us? At the end, each of these goals poses the same questions: "Why aren't things working out like I expected? What's wrong with God? What's wrong with me?"

I Only Need a New Understanding with God

"If I only understood . . ." One of the great gifts of the Protestant Reformation is the insistence that we should have access to the Bible, in our own language, and be able to understand the clear teachings of Scripture. The Reformers reclaimed the truths of a Christ-centered theology emphasizing salvation by grace through faith. Over the years, new denominations and church groups formed around particular theological perspectives. Emphasis on teaching sermons and Christian education supported this movement.

Although our theology said that we are saved by grace, emphasis on correct understanding often subtly taught that we are saved by what we know, by "correct theology." Over the years, authors have written thousands of books trying to help us get it right. The subtle and mythical assumption was that if we only understood, really understood, then our lives would change and spiritual growth would occur.

In so much of the modern spiritual formation literature, there is an underlying assumption that "enlightened understanding" is the key to spiritual growth. If we could just "understand" the truths of Scripture and how to live the Christian life, then our lives would automatically align with God's will. Although it is certainly true that lack of understanding and misinformed theology can get us into trouble and prevent us from moving in the right direction, the opposite is not necessarily true.

We are our own best test case to critique the truth or falsehood that correct understanding results in a transformed life. How much of what you know are you able to put into practice? Can you honestly say that inadequacies in your relationship with God are simply lack of understanding? In a sermon some years ago, I asked the congregation what turned out to be a question that was humbling for me. I called for a show of hands of people whose lives had been significantly changed by listening to a sermon. I gave them permission to be honest, and the one or two hands that went up told the story. Although sermons may have been helpful in supporting ongoing spiritual growth, testimonies of spiritual growth were seldom keyed to some new insight, but rather to experiences with God that came through community, prayer, and life events.

Even worse, we all have seen situations where the desire for knowledge or understanding is really a selfish quest to control our own lives and try to do what only God can do.

So, you may ask, "If enlightened understanding is not the key, why are you writing this book?" This is an important question. I don't believe for a moment that reading what I am writing will bring you an inch closer to Jesus or change your spiritual growth. What will bring profound change and spiritual growth is your personal experience with God, as you walk the lifelong transformation journey described in the following pages.

It Just Happens

Does God work in a consistent way in our lives, or does He just bail us out here and there? I have talked to so many people who are confused about their ongoing relationship with God. They don't know whether to rejoice in what is happening in their lives or to despair. What seemed simple in the beginning is now much more complex. When we review the spiritual growth literature, however, we find confusion about not only the goal but the process as well.

For example, many spiritual formation writers seem to suggest that spiritual growth will happen if we just take the spiritual disciplines seriously. All we need to do is practice prayer or solitude or fasting, and good things will happen. But is our spiritual formation so controllable, or random? In the same way that God designed how we develop physically, isn't it probable that He designed us to develop spiritually in some predictable way as well?

If we are to cooperate with God in this business of spiritual growth, we also need to understand the process, the landscape of the journey. We need markers that can help interpret our experience in light of what God is doing in us. We need a roadmap for spiritual formation that can help us identify our relative position in our journey.

The True Road to Living in the Love of God

We've seen that holiness, service, wholeness, and enlightened understanding wind up being dead-end roads when we try to make them *the* goal of our spiritual growth. Let's go on, then, and look at the real goal: a *Love Relationship with God.* Why should our love relationship with God be our foundational goal, rather than merely the means to some greater end? Even though some of you may not need convincing, I hope that a review will help you confirm that a "restored relationship of love with God through Jesus Christ" is more than a means to another end; it is the primary and foundational goal of spiritual growth.

A scan of the Scriptures reveals the simple, but often overlooked, truth. God created us, redeemed us, and leads us because He loves us. A love relationship with God has been absolutely foundational in our Old Testament history with God, from the creation story to Moses and the covenant with God's chosen people, through the prophets and the Psalms. It continues in the teachings of Jesus and the apostles. The centrality of living in God's love and loving Him in return was the heartbeat of the Desert and Church Fathers and Mothers, the Reformers, and many Christian authors and church leaders today.

God has not loved us so that we can accomplish one thing or another, but for our own sake and His. Although the focus of the other potential goals is self, the focus of this goal is God Himself. What a wonderful realization to know that God does not have an ulterior motive in His relationship with us. Loving intimacy with God in Christ has profoundly transforming effects on every aspect of our lives. Jesus died on the cross to redeem us in God's love, not just to save us for heaven, fix us, deploy us, or shape us up.

Followers of Jesus have emphasized such love passages as John 3:16: "For God so loved the world that He gave His own begotten Son that whoever believes in Him shall not perish, but have eternal life." When Jesus was asked about the most important thing we can do, He responded with the greatest commandment: "You shall love the Lord your God with all your heart, and with all your soul, and with all your mind" (Matt. 22:37–38).

It is clear in Scripture that God's ultimate goal for your life is for you to live fully and freely in His love, and to respond by loving Him as well. He has no ulterior motives; He just wants you to be His son, daughter, friend, co-worker in love.

All Goals Come out of the "One"

Despite the overwhelming evidence of this love relationship as the foundational goal for spiritual formation, we must still take seriously the importance of the other potential goals. Let's look at each in the light of this love relationship with God in Christ.

Why, then, is love for God a more basic spiritual growth goal than holiness? Scripture makes it clear that holiness is the product of a loving relationship with God; we cannot attain it by our own effort. Romans 8 is one of Scripture's clearest teachings on this point. The Spirit of God gives life; the law's demands only condemn us (cf. Rom. 8:1f). In Romans 12, Paul teaches that our holiness comes from an inner transformation emerging out of a surrendered relationship with God in Christ (cf. Rom. 12:1f). Holiness is a result of transforming intimacy with the Trinity, and a secondary goal rather than a primary one.

How about serving God as a disciple? Again, the New Testament tells us it's impossible to serve God through our own effort; it is the result of knowing Him personally. Jesus teaches, in John 14 and 16, that the disciples will be able to serve Him only through the Holy Spirit. In fact, Jesus explains that even He can do nothing of His own without the participation of the Father (cf. John 5:30). In John 15:5, Jesus is clear when He says that a relationship with Him enables service: "Apart from Me [an intimate relationship], you can do nothing." Jesus' words to Peter after his betrayal make the point crystal clear: "Do you love me? . . . then shepherd my sheep" (John 21:15–17). Like holiness, we see that service is certainly an important product of spiritual growth, but secondary to, dependent on, and a result of a relationship of love with God through Christ.

Finally, how does the Wholeness Goal of spiritual transformation relate to a love relationship with God? Scripture is clear that wholeness in life, though desirable, is an attitude of the heart and the result of the work of God's love. James's teaching about healing is a good example of the dynamics of this relationship. After the command to pray for healing, he says, "the prayer of a righteous man will accomplish much" (cf. James 5:16). From a New Testament perspective, we understand that righteousness is in fact a relationship with God through faith in Christ. We also have to be careful not to see wholeness as a denial of the reality of suffering in the Christian experience. Jesus made it clear that His life would include suffering (cf. Matt. 17:12; Luke 9:22). The apostles understood that suffering, for the sake of the Gospel, was also a part of discipleship (cf. Acts 5:41; Phil. 1:29). We have to understand wholeness in the context of relationship to God in Christ, not just the pleasantness of the conditions of our lives. Therefore wholeness, understood properly, is certainly a desirable by-product of spiritual growth, but one secondary to and dependent on a love relationship with God.

We can see overwhelming biblical evidence that points to love as the goal for our spiritual journey. The other worthy goals are a natural outworking of that primary loving relationship. Love is not incidental to the spiritual journey. Love is not simply a means to a greater goal. Love is the essence of our relationship with God and its goal. From a biblical perspective, a loving relationship with God produces the fruits of holiness, service, and wholeness.

Our understanding of the Trinity can offer another perspective on the primacy of the love goal. Trinitarian theologians show that we must view our knowledge of God, and the church and the Christian life as well, through the lens of the relational nature of God. Trinitarian Theology argues that the essence of God's nature involves loving relationship, as modeled by the love shared of God the Father, Son, and Holy Spirit. We are invited into this relationship through faith in Christ. Jesus' famous prayer for the church in John 17 demonstrates this perspective. He prays for unity among believers grounded in the love that exists through the indwelling Father, Son, and Holy Spirit.

Now, you may be thinking that "love" as a goal for spiritual formation is no different from the other potential goals in that we can never fully attain it. We can never be fully holy, perfectly serve Jesus, or become fully whole. Can we ever fully love God, either? It's an important point, one that is essential to our ongoing discovery. Living fully in God's love *for us* is the goal, not our perfect love for Him. God's love for us is a gift, received fully in Christ's lordship in our lives. Our love for God is the product of simply receiving His love in faith: "We love because He first loved us" (1 John 4:19). This applies to love of neighbor as well as love for God. The goal of spiritual formation is a loving intimacy with God; it is about what God is doing, not what we can accomplish. Love for God and for neighbor is a natural result.

Is Loving God Really Enough?

Though we may make a convincing argument for the love goal, it's often another thing for us to fully accept it at a personal level. Western culture and many others tend to value productivity above all else, despite the current trends in the West to substitute pleasure as the fundamental goal of life. A knee-jerk reaction to this discussion about God's goal for your life may be to wonder if love is really enough.

I have to admit, this has been exactly my struggle. My own background set the stage. Growing up in a family always on the edge of poverty engrained in me the importance of making a good living, working hard to ensure the necessary provisions for life, and of course my needed level of perceived worth. My training as an engineer and management consultant reinforced the belief that everything needs to have a worthwhile use, a productive end. Although it's easy for me intellectually to affirm the necessity, even centrality, of a love relationship with God, I can too readily place more value in the "practical" results of the relationship. I find that many of the people I have coached and worked with have the same problem. In their minds, God's love is certainly important, and even critical, but when you get down to how they really feel, the real deal is what happens as a result.

God has used my relationship with my wife, Charlotte, and my children to help me see beyond my productivity worldview. How tragic it would be if I were to love Charlotte for what I could get out of her or what we could accomplish together. What would I do to my kids if I communicated that I cared about them primarily so that they would do the right things or accomplish some great task?

No, what they need from me, and what I need from them, is to know and experience a love that is not contingent on, or tied to, outcomes. Jesus told us, "Love one another as I have loved you" (John 13:34). Jesus loves us because it's His nature to love; He loves the whole world, even those who despise Him.

Yet I have found that understanding this truth, and living it out, are two different things. Too many times, in my frustration at not "hearing" God in prayer (for some "productive" purpose), He has had to say to me, "Tom, you mean I'm not enough for you?" I was embarrassed to admit this was exactly how I felt. I didn't just want to be with God and love Him; I wanted something out of Him and when I didn't get it I was grumpy. I've found that I am not the only person who has this struggle.

Priorities of God's Calling

I've found it useful to distinguish two levels of God's call to relationship with Him relating to the being and doing, the loving and serving aspects of our relationship with Jesus.

First-Order Calling: In the first-order calling, Jesus calls us into a personal relationship of love with God. He invites us into a relationship that will enable us to "Love the Lord your God with all your heart, and with all your soul, and with all your mind" (Matt. 22:37).

Second-Order Calling: Jesus then calls us to "follow me" (cf. Matt. 4:19). Our ability to follow and serve Jesus is dependent on the depth of our relationship with Him.

Unfortunately, because our culture values doing over being, we often give more attention to our second-order calling than to the first. We assume our love for Jesus and focus on serving Him. It almost becomes a norm for our church culture. In my role as a pastor, I have often had people come to me and ask how I was doing. What we both knew they meant was, "How's your ministry doing?" Seldom are we asked about our love relationship with Jesus. It may be that Jesus' admonitions to the church of Ephesus are important words to us today.

You have persevered and have endured hardships for my name, and have not grown weary.

Yet I hold this against you: You have forsaken your first love. Remember the height from which you have fallen! Repent and do

the things you did at first. If you do not repent, I will come to you
and remove your lampstand from its place.

—REVELATION 2:3–5 (NIV)

It's easy for any of us, in any time in history, to confuse our
callings and put our second-order calling before our first-
order calling.

Is Spiritual Formation Only an Inward Journey?

In considering love as the goal of my relationship with God, I've
also struggled with the fear of "navel gazing." Because of my own
background, evangelism is a huge priority and value for me. Is
there a danger we can get so inwardly focused on our relationship with God that we forget the Great Commission to evangelize and disciple new believers? Does a focus on living in a love
relationship with God leave out the poor, lost, and marginalized?
It's an important question and one we need to take seriously. We
are all well aware of the human tendency to become selfish and
self-focused.

We need to start by asking, "What motivates our efforts to
evangelize those who don't know Jesus? What prompts us to feed
the hungry, care for the mentally handicapped, homeless, and
poor?" It could just be humanism. At some level, all human cultures have compassion for the "poor." Because we are created in
the image and likeness of God, it is natural for us to be moved
by the needs of others. At the same time, we often see the over-
riding manifestation of sin, which makes us selfish and hardens
our hearts against the suffering of those around us.

But Scripture tells us that our care for the suffering (spiritually and physically) is intended to be more than human compassion; it is the work of God in and through us. It was God's love
for us all that prompted the coming of Jesus: "For God so loved
the world that He gave His only begotten son" (John 3:16). Jesus
says to us that He sends us in the same way the Father sent Him.
It is not some obligation to save the lost that is the true motivator of evangelism, but the love of God working in our hearts,
transforming us from the mold of the world and the deformation
of sin.

We are set free by God's love to love our neighbor: "We love because He first loved us" (1 John 4:19). The rule or law is not successful in making us love our neighbor; a transformed heart filled with the love of God enables us to love and empowers the action that carries it out. An authentic love relationship with God will always result in love for neighbor. Evangelism is simply the outpouring of God's love through us to others who also need to know His love. A love relationship with God not only does not leave out evangelism and good works, but it is ultimately what causes them.

Spiritual Formation

Now that we've gained some clarity on God's goal for our lives with Him, we can define the term *spiritual formation*:

> The process that takes place in us, as the life of the Spirit of God transforms our life through deepening love and intimacy with Father, Son, and Holy Spirit, remaking us in the likeness of Jesus Christ, in His love for the Father and the world.

God transforms our hearts so that we are able to live in His love in greater degrees of intimacy. In this nearness to Jesus, our very being becomes more like that of Jesus and we are able to relate to the Father and the Holy Spirit increasingly as Jesus does. In this relationship, the fruits and gifts of the Holy Spirit are made manifest, and we are able to follow Jesus into our world, in ways that bring blessings to others and glory to God. But one essential question remains.

How Does It Happen?

In a recent conversation over coffee, an older couple shared with me their frustration with church and with their spiritual journey in general. "All we hear about is what we're supposed to be doing better, not what is really important." "What's that?" I asked. "God!" they responded immediately. They had, at one time or another, done about every job in the church and were now leading a Bible study for couples. Although they did not use the words "process of spiritual formation," it was clear they were starving for something that would address their relationship with God in a deeper way, not just what they could do for Him. "What you want to happen in church is to know God's love more deeply and to love Him more fully," I suggested. The woman's eyes filled with tears, and her husband stared at me. "How does that happen?" he whispered.

Even though we're satisfied that "a relationship of love with God in Christ" is the best biblically, theologically, and historically based goal for spiritual growth, you and I would ask the same question as the couple: "How does that happen?" How does our relationship of love with God in Christ deepen? How do we cooperate with God in His wonderful work in us?

This haunting question is not unlike the question that you and I, and countless other Christians, are asking. We may well have seen progress in our lives in the areas of holiness, service, and wholeness, but there remains a longing, a hunger that will not leave us. This quest for something more drives us to discover more about how God works in our lives, about how spiritual formation actually happens. Let's continue our quest.

REFLECTION

- Which of the dead-end roads of holiness, service, wholeness, or enlightened understanding have you been most tempted to pursue? What was your result?

- What is it that makes it hard for you to really accept personally that God's goal for you is simply a deepening love relationship?

- As we look for a roadmap into the heart of God's love, consider what you might do to bring another person into a loving relationship with you.

CHAPTER 3

Your Journey into the Love of God

In My Father's house are many dwelling places;
if it were not so, I would have told you; for I go to
prepare a place for you. If I go and prepare a place
for you, I will come again and receive you to Myself,
that where I am, there you may be also.

—JOHN 14:2–3

ONE MORNING WHEN I DROPPED OFF MY TEENAGE SON at school, we had one of those "Why can't I do that?" discussions. As I drove off, I reflected about his immaturity. Then the thought came to me that he really wasn't supposed to be mature yet; he was still growing up. In an instant God put the thought in my mind, "And so are you, Tom, spiritually." I laughed out loud. How wonderful that God loves and accepts me "in process," and how grateful I was that I knew something about my son's developmental phases so I could love and accept him in process, as well. At times all of us have wished we had a roadmap for our spiritual development, so that we'd have some perspective about where we are and where we are going. Fortunately, we do.

It would be so simple if there were one Scripture passage that would give us such a map. Even though the Bible is the source of everything we need to understand about our spiritual growth, there are many passages addressing spiritual formation. Here are some key passages:

- Ephesians 3:14–19 tells us that God's goal in our lives is an internal relationship of love, which comes through truly knowing Jesus personally.
- Romans 12:2 and 2 Corinthians 3:18 tell us that our spiritual formation in this love relationship is an ongoing, lifelong process of surrender.
- 1 John 2:12–13 and Hebrews 5:13–6:1 show us that our spiritual growth is progressive and developmental.
- In 1 Thessalonians 5:23, we see that God forms us in His image in a personal way that makes us uniquely who we are.
- Ephesians 4:1–16 shows us that our spiritual growth is integrally tied to our life in community, where God works through others to speak to us and develop our gifts.

No one of these passages is a complete description of the spiritual growth process, but together they do give us guidance as we look for a model that encompasses the teachings of Scripture about spiritual formation; we need a model or paradigm that is ongoing, progressive, personal, and communal in nature, and that moves toward an increasing intimacy with the Trinity through an experiential relationship.

Any complete description of the Christian spiritual growth model must encompass these values:

- Biblically faithful to the clear teaching of Scripture (cf. 2 Tim. 3:16)
- Historically validated through many years of experience
- Sufficiently descriptive to understand its elements, and see ourselves in its phases
- Developmentally sensitive to recognize our own human maturation
- Universally applicable so that it relates to people of all cultures and conditions

We might surmise that there are a number of models for our spiritual growth journey.[1] However, the best pathway I've found for describing this deepening love relationship with God comes from one of Christian history's most respected spiritual writers. In the middle of the Spanish Inquisition, an exceedingly tumultuous time in Christian history, God birthed a unique and courageous woman who loved Jesus so much she was willing to risk her life to help others love Him too. After years of bringing people to Christ and helping them mature in their faith, Teresa of Avila wrote down the most amazing description of seven phases in which we grow more and more deeply in God's love, a love that results in loving our neighbor. The Seven Mansions of Teresa of Avila's Interior Castle meet all our criteria.[2] She describes a spiritual formation journey that is biblically faithful, validated by its use over a long period of history, sufficiently descriptive for us to understand its phases such that we can see our own experience, consistent with normal human development, and applicable to us all of us regardless of our cultural setting.

John of the Cross offers an additional and vital piece of the roadmap with his teachings about the Dark Nights of the Soul.

Before concentrating on the Seven Mansions of the Interior Castle, let's place Teresa of Avila into an historical context, for her significance in understanding her writings. (A good history of both figures can be found in the introductions to their collected works.)[3]

Teresa of Avila

Teresa was born on March 28, 1515, in Avila, Spain. She came from a well-to-do noble family and entered the Carmelite order on November 2, 1535. Much later, in 1555, she underwent a "second conversion" through reading the *Confessions of St. Augustine*.[4] Like many of us, Teresa grew up in a Christian home and believed in Jesus from as early as she could remember. Even as a child, she wanted to live her whole life serving God. In her time, the only way to do that was to join an order and become a nun. In reading Augustine, Teresa was filled with awe at the intimate and personal experience of God he described. She realized that religious devotion was not enough;

she longed to give her whole heart to Jesus and return the love He had lavished on her. In response to her deep surrender, God filled Teresa with a deep love for Christ. In the ensuing years, she experienced many visions of God and dreamed of a community of prayer that would truly focus on loving Him.

She felt called to give her whole life in service to Jesus, but the accommodations in the church and monastic orders to the materialistic cultural values of her time troubled her. Though certainly not part of the Reformation as we know it, Teresa was herself a reformer. She finally established a house of Reformed Carmelites (the Discalced, or Barefoot, Carmelites) that would live in strict observance of the Rule, with a singular focus on prayer and loving God and neighbor. Teresa was persecuted for her reforms, and her writings were under constant scrutiny by the Inquisition. Canonized in 1622, she was the first woman "Doctor of the Church." The "doctor" title she received indicates respect and the influence that Teresa of Avila had on the church of her time and in the ensuing years.

Although Teresa's life was filled with mystical experiences, she was not the stereotypical cloistered ivory tower hermit that comes to mind when we hear of mystics or contemplatives. When I started retreating at the Cistercian monastery, I remember thinking, sure, it's easy for you monks to have a deep prayer life and to talk of spiritual growth. I'm just too busy with the many duties of a parish pastor! Teresa of Avila's story was a good corrective for my excuses. She was a reformer and a significant leader in her own time. Her managerial duties included the overseeing and coaching of a number of monasteries, requiring a great deal of travel. In modern terms, she could be compared to a church planter, establishing new houses around the country. Teresa could have related to our busy and complex lifestyles today. Maybe for this reason, we find her description of spiritual growth practical, engaging the issues of our everyday life.

Dallas Willard said at several conferences that Teresa of Avila made one of the greatest contributions to the understanding of spiritual formation since the biblical writers. In *The Great Omission*, he writes: "The book [*Interior Castle*] provided instruction on a living relationship with God that I had found nowhere else. . . . Most of what I learned about the phenomenology of

God speaking to us, I learned from studying and putting into practice what Teresa says in Dwelling Place Six, Chapter Three. I still think it is the best treatment ever written on what it is like for God to *speak* to his children."[5]

John of the Cross

Another famous lover of Jesus offers an additional and vital piece of the roadmap with his teachings about the Dark Nights of the Soul. John of the Cross was a contemporary and associate of Teresa whose writings contribute significantly to understanding the journey of love into the heart of God.[6] His teachings about the Dark Nights of the Soul have brought vital clarity to the ongoing painful desert experiences that involve letting go of the world so that we are able to be fully embraced by Christ.

John of the Cross was born on June 24, 1542, in Fontiveros, Spain, twenty-seven years after Teresa. Unlike Teresa, John was highly educated in philosophy and theology. He met Teresa of Avila in his hometown at the celebration of his first mass; it was a meeting that was to radically change his life. He asked Teresa how he might find an order that was authentic and faithful. She said he probably would not find one but would have to start one himself. (Doesn't this sound just like young leaders of our day, who are disillusioned with the institutional church?) He later became the founder of the men's Discalced Carmelites and developed a close friendship with Teresa, who guided him in his spiritual life. It was during years of imprisonment for his reforms that John created his masterful prose treatises on mystical theology, notably *The Dark Night* and *The Ascent of Mount Carmel.*[7] He died in 1591 at the age of forty-nine.

John of the Cross was also a persecuted reformer. His spirituality, like Teresa's, was born out of God's call to restore the church to biblical and historical authenticity. Many of us today have had that same call from God, in our own time, to restore the Bride of Christ so that Christ will be renowned among the nations. We too live in a time when many churches have succumbed to cultural pressures and looked askance at the authority of Scripture. With the modern emphasis on theological distinctiveness and correctness, there has grown a corresponding skepticism about the subjective nature of spiritual experience. Many have come to believe that only "correct" theology will keep Christians on track and safe in their relationship with God. In many circles, discussion about spiritual experience or personal piety is often viewed with disdain, or even rejection. Our time is not so different from that of Teresa and John as one might think. So it's all the more important that we have clear biblically based teaching about the nature of spiritual growth, its goal, and insight into its ongoing process. Teresa's and John's teachings about spiritual formation have stood the test of time, and their writings have taken on increased interest in recent years. Teresa's description of the spiritual journey is comprehensive and offers a wonderful roadmap for our spiritual growth journey.

A Faith Shared by All Christians

For those of us who are Protestants, let me say a few words about using "Catholic" figures as secondary sources for our understanding of spiritual growth. It was a problem for me, at first. In my early visits to the Trappist monastery and in my readings of early Christian writers, I found myself stumbling over differences with my Protestant theology and practice and that of the Roman Catholic Church, particularly at the time of Teresa and John. Although I was so blessed by my retreats at the Monastery in Utah, at times I found myself questioning: "If these people are right, then why was the Reformation necessary?" We all have our theological distinctions. Yet I discovered, both in the monks of Holy Trinity Abbey and in Teresa and John, a genuine love for Jesus and an affirmation of the biblical orthodox faith shared by all Christians.

I was reminded that God has revealed His truth to His followers throughout history, quite apart from their particular denominational affiliation. We are free to learn from others without accepting everything about their theology or the church practice of their time. The Holy Spirit has been at work throughout human history, and particularly in the church, teaching us how to know and love God.

We may cherish the traditions in which we find ourselves now, but I hope that we have not stopped learning and becoming.

It sometimes takes a person from another perspective or tradition to challenge our blind spots and presuppositions. I would encourage you to view Teresa of Avila and John of the Cross simply as followers of Jesus, in the context of their place in time and history, who have something to teach us from their experience with God.

The Seven Mansions: Roadmap for a Lifelong Journey of Spiritual Transformation

Teresa's superiors asked her to write about the process of spiritual growth, as she understood and experienced it in those she oversaw. Teresa asked God how she might describe this development of a believer's spiritual life. She received a vivid picture of the soul, or the heart, as a castle made of a single diamond or clear crystal. There were many rooms in the castle, and in the center resided the "Sun" illuminating outward. The crystal castle had seven concentric groups of "dwelling places." Teresa imagined us as pilgrims, journeying through these dwellings toward our Lord. The King of Glory resided in the seventh mansion, at the center, and with great splendor illumined and adorned all the dwellings as far as the outer ring. As we grow in our spiritual relationship with Christ, we are drawn closer to this divine Sun at the center. The nearer we journey toward the center, the greater the light of God we experience. We are transformed into His likeness and enter into a deep intimacy and cooperation with the Trinity.

These groups of mansions are not in a row but are like a fruit that has layers, which must be peeled away before the center can be eaten. Although we progress generally from the outer mansions toward the center, the journey is not simply linear. We are like pilgrims with a transient home, living here, visiting there, investigating another place, and returning to our transient home again. Subtly, we may find ourselves dwelling more in a mansion closer to the center than we did previously, until it becomes our new home.

Although Teresa does not quote the fourteenth chapter of the Gospel of John, it undoubtedly influenced her imagery. Listen to Jesus' words in light of Teresa's picture, not just about heaven but also describing our relationship with Him now: "Do not let your heart be troubled; believe in God, believe also in Me. In My Father's house are many dwelling places [Mansions; KJV]; if it were not so, I would have told you; for I go to prepare a place for you. If I go and prepare a place for you, I will come again and receive you to Myself, that where I am, there you may be also" (John 14:1–3).

This passage is typically taken to describe heaven, but its characteristics are important for understanding the dynamics of the spiritual formation process.

- We are to feel peace about our journey of growth, built on faith, not performance.
- God's dwelling place for believing Christians is within us, in our heart, internal rather than external.
- Our relationship with God is a multifaceted journey.
- Jesus precedes us in our journey and personally prepares our next place of growth.
- God is proactive in our spiritual growth. He does not wait for us to discover the next step of transformation but takes the initiative and comes to us and invites us on, so that we may be together with Him, where He is.
- The goal of this lifelong pilgrimage is intimacy with God in Christ.

Our Effort and God's Grace in Growth

Remember the phrase, "Let go and let God"? Teresa of Avila presents a unique understanding of the problems we have in trying too hard. In addition to her description of the mansions of spiritual growth, Teresa is famous for explaining the changing relationship between our effort and God's grace and initiative, as we grow in intimacy with Him. She uses the analogy of watering a garden, the garden of the soul, where the water is God's grace. Teresa describes four conditions, called the "Four Waters," four ways in which the garden of our soul is "watered" by the Holy Spirit. Thomas Dubay gives a concise overview of the Four Waters analogy and its relationship to the Seven Mansions:

> The garden of the soul, she says, can be watered in several manners. The first, drawing the water up from a well by use of a bucket, entails a great deal of human effort. The second way, cranking a water wheel and having the water run through an aqueduct, involves less exertion and yields more water. The third entails far less effort, for in it the water enters the garden as by an effluence from river or stream. The fourth and final way is the best of all: as by a gentle but abundant rainfall the Lord himself waters the garden and the soul does not work at all.[8]

Teresa describes the relationship between these Four Waters and our progress through the mansions. She points out that there is a decrease in our effort and control, and an increase in divine initiative and empowerment, as we progress through the last four mansions. This is great news. Normally we would expect it to be the reverse; the more we advance, the harder we work. I cannot overstate the number of times I have heard Christians say they are already so busy and overcommitted that one additional thing is impossible ("If spiritual growth takes more work, then I guess I'm good enough").

Teresa, in fact, shows that maturing believers who just "try harder" often find that their increased efforts in the spiritual disciplines are not fruitful, and they become discouraged. When we understand Teresa's Four Waters and our relative place in the spiritual journey, we can know when godly effort should evolve into a greater yielding to God's direction and power. This is so significant to Teresa's understanding that the first three mansions are known as the "Active Mansions," and the last four are known as the "Passive or Infused Mansions"[9] (see Figure 1 later in this chapter).

Teresa describes these mansions primarily as they are reflected in our prayer life and in our relationship to others. She also includes behavioral, emotional, and spiritual transformations that take place as a result of the deepening relationship with, and of the love for, God in each mansion. This deepening intimacy with the Trinity supplies both the desire and the power that transforms and restores the image of God within us. She shows how the other "goals" of spiritual growth—holiness, service, and wholeness—flow out of this increasing union with God.

Cautions About Using a Spiritual Formation Roadmap

Anything can be misused, and we might be especially tempted to do so with a description of spiritual formation. Before we go further, let's discuss some cautions.

A Guide, Not the Rule

First, any roadmap is only that: a map, never completely descriptive, and never applicable identically for everyone. Teresa cautions us that exact descriptions are impossible because language can never fully capture the mystery of God's work.

The Whole, Not Only Parts

You may be tempted to jump to the place where you think you are, or skip the mansions that seem beyond you. Why is it important to learn about ground we may have already covered, or bother with experiences that seem way beyond us? Understanding more clearly some of the terrain we have previously traversed spiritually can shed light on where we find ourselves now. Our current growth often comes through new understanding of what God did at important times in the past. For those of us further along in the journey, clear understanding of the earlier mansions will enable us to mentor others who have not traveled as far. Teresa presupposes the criticism that it might be confusing or even discouraging for us to be exposed to description of experiences that are ahead of our level of growth and experience. On the contrary, says Teresa, it will be a great consolation to know the blessings that God has in store for us. Although we can never grow ourselves from one mansion to another, it helps to be prepared to interpret a new movement of God in our lives when it happens. Finally, because of the pilgrim nature of our spiritual journey, we do not simply progress in a straight line; we explore forward and then return to the safety of an earlier phase. Understanding all seven mansions can help us recognize both the forward and reverse excursions.

Description, Not Prescription

As Teresa says, not all believers will have every experience she describes in her writings. The experiences should therefore be used descriptively, not prescriptively, as a way of understanding something at a relatively broad level. We can discover where our experiences relate to the general description of spiritual growth, and we can become aware of experiences that other believers may have at various phases along the way. We should not look for an exact description, but a general outline to support us in interpreting our own journey.

God's Work, Not Ours

We may be tempted to treat a spiritual growth roadmap as a ladder to be climbed or a path to be mastered—something to be accomplished. However, it is the Holy Spirit that transforms us; we can never accomplish our spiritual growth by ourselves (cf. Rom. 12:1f). Similarly, we must also be careful about comparison with others or any sense of competition. God's love for each of us is complete, from before the foundation of the world (cf. Eph. 1:4), and our salvation is accomplished by God's grace, received in simple faith (cf. Eph. 2:8–9). God loves and accepts us fully, right where we are. Thus the use of a spiritual growth roadmap is not a matter of our trying to get somewhere, but rather to better understand where we are and how to cooperate with God more fully, as He develops deepening intimacy with us.

Comparing the Mansions

The Seven Mansions describe the general movement of spiritual growth from conversion to union with God. Many have loved exploring Teresa's writings but have found the mansions difficult to understand. Reading Teresa is more like having an ongoing discussion than reading a systematic work. Right in the middle of a description of one mansion, she remembers and discusses an important point in another. In my early studies of the mansions, at about the time I thought I understood what she was saying, another part of her writings would either elucidate some aspect of that mansion or make it obvious I did not really understand it at all. For my own sake, and maybe for yours, I found it helpful to systematize some information to better understand each mansion and compare it to the others. Teresa does not, for example, title the mansions but simply calls them "dwelling places." I have given them descriptive titles to assist in understanding and in making reference to a given mansion:

- Outside: Lost; not yet a Christian
- First Mansion: New beginnings
- Second Mansion: Between a rock and a hard place
- Third Mansion: Following Jesus
- Fourth Mansion: Discovering the love of Jesus
- Fifth Mansion: Longing for oneness with God
- Sixth Mansion: The passion of God's love
- Seventh Mansion: A life of love in the Trinity

Teresa understands that our spiritual formation parallels the natural human process of maturing to adulthood and then falling in love, becoming engaged, and finally getting married. Amazingly, the process she observed is simply the maturation process God designed into us—one that is common to all human beings in every culture. Scripture says that, when we receive Jesus as Lord and Savior, we are born again. We therefore need to "grow up" as a follower of Jesus, discover who the real love of our life is, and become the kind of person who can live in loving intimacy with God for the rest of our lives.

Most of the descriptions for the mansions come from Teresa's writings in *Interior Castle*, but many additional insights can be gleaned from her other writings.[10]

One of the difficulties in comparing the mansions is that they tend to differ more in the degree of a given spiritual experience than in introducing completely new experiences. For example, we experience the love of God to some extent in all the mansions, but more intensely through the fourth to seventh mansions. Similarly, all Christians pray, even many nonbelievers, but prayer changes significantly as God draws us deeper into intimacy with Him. Therefore to make comparison easier, we can identify several categories, markers, or diagnostic conditions that are present in each mansion.

Rooms Within Each Mansion

Like any map or travel guide, it will be important to use common categories. In the same way that a AAA TripTik identifies such things as major roads, minor roads, campsites, cities, food, and lodging, our spiritual formation map has several common categories to consider for each mansion. Even though Teresa does not specify these categories per se, they are nevertheless present in her discussion of the mansions. Here is another way to think about it. Remember that a given mansion is not just one large space in the castle, but a network of rooms. As we journey within a mansion, we explore these rooms, or categories, of our spiritual experience. All the mansions have the same set of rooms. We will use these specific categories, or rooms, to give a detailed description of each mansion, and to show how we experience change for each room, as we move from mansion to mansion. We must also remember that a mansion is not a milestone, but an area of growth. We can experience a range of mansions at any time in our lives. For example, we might have grown well past the doubts that plagued us when we first became a Christian. But it's probable that, when some crisis hits and our prayers don't seem to be answered, we find ourselves again plagued with doubt. In the same way, we may experience prayer exceptionally. Talking to God may be our "normal" practice of praying, but we might one day lapse into an extended time of silence, more typical of a later phase of spiritual growth. In Chapter Thirteen, we will discuss a spiritual growth mapping tool, using the uniquenesses of each mansion seen in each category or marker. This tool can assist us in locating our approximate position in the mansions' spiritual growth blueprint. The following categories, or rooms, encompass the spiritual experiences addressed by Teresa as she describes the Seven Mansions:

- "Your Heart's Desire" in relationship with God
- "Key Activities" in response to God

- "Changing Patterns of Prayer" in communication with God
- "Jesus' Initiatives" to draw us into a deeper intimacy with God
- "Schemes of the Enemy" to try to destroy our growth in God
- "Keys for Growth" that help us cooperate with God

Figure 1, then, is a visual image and overview of the progression of the mansions, from outside, through the active mansions, on through the passive mansions, to the final goal of loving spiritual union with the Trinity, in the seventh mansion.

The Wonder of Discovery

From my experience with hundreds of maturing Christians, believers who have been able to better understand their journeys with God in light of the Mansions of the Heart, I know you'll find an amazing discovery ahead of you, as we explore each mansion. You may discover that you are far more on target in your spiritual growth than you ever guessed.

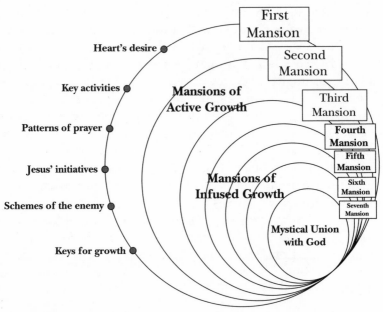

Figure 3.1 The Seven Mansions of the Interior Castle

The important focus in our discussion of the mansions is not so much a technical description of each mansion as it is an understanding of our personal journey so far. Once we see more fully what God is up to, right where we are, we will be able to understand how to cooperate with Him more fully as He continues to lead us onward.

REFLECTION

Let your reading and reflection in these chapters become an opportunity for your own spiritual growth. Be attentive to yourself and to God as you read. It may also be helpful to prepare for these chapters by reflecting and praying about your own spiritual journey "time line." Recall your spiritual experiences, both pleasant and difficult, that brought you to where you are now. Here are some aspects to consider:

- Begin with your family heritage, moving on to your first memories of God or church.
- List key events, mentors, doubting and faithful times, and milestones.
- Note how God was present, in retrospect, in major transitions, in difficult or hurtful experiences, and in your celebrations and successes.
- Describe your relationship with God at these milestones in your life.
- Then prayerfully reflect:

  - What means has God used most to get through to you?
  - In what situations do you experience God most easily?
  - When do you feel most loved by God?
  - What barriers or obstacles have tended to keep you from deeper intimacy with God?
  - What patterns in you, and in God's work in you, seem apparent?

(Continued)

This kind of personal reflection will prepare you to identify your journey in the seven mansions and locate the significant times in your life when you resided in or visited some or all of them. As you see your own journey with God through your specific history, God's grace, grandeur, and mystery will be revealed in new and wonderful ways. You will see—maybe more clearly than ever—the fulfillment of the promise that God made to you: "For I know the plans that I have for you, declares the LORD, plans for welfare and not for calamity, to give you a future and a hope" (Jer. 29:11–14).

CHAPTER 4

New Beginnings: The First Mansion

For by grace you have been saved through faith; and that not of yourselves, it is the gift of God; not as a result of works, so that no one may boast. For we are His workmanship, created in Christ Jesus for good works, which God prepared beforehand so that we would walk in them.

—Ephesians 2:7–10

REMEMBER WHEN YOU BEGAN YOUR JOURNEY WITH JESUS? Whether you grew up knowing Christ or came to know Him later in life, this new beginning, your testimony, is the most important story of your life. In the following chapters about the Seven Mansions of spiritual growth, I use two ongoing life stories to illustrate God's amazing transformation. Abigail and Michael's experiences represent composites drawn from people I know and projections based on Teresa's explanations. Although the stories are not the same as yours, you will be able to find some common themes and experiences, as we look at the six descriptors or categories we discussed in Chapter Three. Prayerfully read the stories and the reflective description. Ask the Holy Spirit not only to teach you but to bring to mind what you need to recall and reflect on. Even though you have probably grown past this first mansion, there may well be past experiences in that phase of your spiritual growth that need to be put into a new perspective.

Abigail

Abigail was about nineteen, and exciting things were happening in her faith. Growing up in a conservative church, she had always believed there was a God. She tried to live a moral life and please her parents. The family attended church regularly; she participated in her church youth group. At about ten, she had gone forward at a church service altar call. As the pastor gave the invitation, Abigail, hands sweating and heart racing, knew that Jesus was calling her to personally receive the gift of His forgiveness and love. Tears flowed as she ran back to her parents and they shared their joy together. It was a wonderful time for Abigail, as God touched her heart discernibly. Although she had always been a "good kid," now she seemed to delight in helping out at home and really looked forward to church. Her parents bought her a Bible and she read and prayed every night when she went to bed. One might correctly say that her faith was based largely on the beliefs of her parents and Christian friends, but it was a "believing" faith, nevertheless.

At eighteen, Abigail went to college. Like many of her friends, she enjoyed her new independence. A few beer parties now and then and edgy dating caused her some guilt, but nothing she couldn't handle. Her earlier religious beliefs had to be put aside a bit to adjust to her new freedoms, but a class in comparative religion was devastating for her faith. She recounted:

> I knew there were other religions and not everyone was a Christian,
> but I didn't realize that Christianity was just another religion among many!
> What makes all our beliefs and moral taboos so right? It seems like everyone
> I know believes that whatever makes a person happy and doesn't hurt
> anyone is just fine. I am beginning to think they're right; maybe church is just
> for old people, to make them comfortable. Maybe Jesus isn't the only way.

About a year later, Abigail visited the church near her school and asked to see the pastor. She shared with him that a few weeks earlier she had sat up all night with her Christian roommate. Her roommate's loving and caring friendship impressed Abigail, and this long discussion touched her in a new and uncomfortable way. What if Jesus *was* the only way? A few days later they met and talked again, and this time Abigail recommitted her life to following Jesus as Lord and Savior. She described the experience as though a huge weight of guilt had been lifted and replaced by a deep sense of peace and joy. She told the pastor she wanted to learn more about how to really follow Jesus. But, she asserted, she definitely had no interest in returning to the old "religious routines" that marked her upbringing.

The pastor introduced Abigail to some of the young adults who met weekly for Bible study and prayer, and she began attending the church more regularly. But she was busy with school, friends, and sports so there was only so much time for God.

Abigail described those months in the journal she was keeping:

> It is so wonderful to be able to come to God with everything. Wow! It is hard to believe that God himself would really care that much about me. But I can see the answers to my prayers happening right before my eyes! What I used to see as coincidence, I now see as the hand of Jesus! Although I still have to focus mostly on school and my friendships, I want to do every-thing in a way that's right and pleases God. Maybe He will help me win that cheerleading competition! The Bible study group last night was great. People are so open! I think we all want to change and be more like Jesus. I know there are some things that have to go, but I am glad God doesn't blow me off when I mess up. I need to try to pray more often, and not just about me. The Bible is still pretty boring, but maybe I just need to understand it better. I hope to be able to share my faith with some of the girls in the dorm, but right now that feels pretty scary. Thanks, God, that you've made me who I am. I really am excited about the future!

The First Mansion

Abigail was experiencing life in the first mansion. God, by His grace and power, brought her into the Interior Castle of her heart to discover His love, forgiveness, and a new depth of relationship. I am sure you can remember that season in your life. Maybe you are there now. Let's take a closer look at this first mansion experi-ence of spiritual growth and see if we can understand more about what is happening to Abigail and maybe discover more about what God has been up to in our lives. Before we do, though, it's important to hear what Teresa says about life outside the castle.

Outside: Lost, Not Yet a Christian

Although Teresa does not discuss the area outside the castle in any detail, she does say that even here the Light of God can be felt extending outward from Christians, through the Gospel as it is proclaimed and lived. Made in the image and likeness of God, the human heart hungers to be loved and accepted unconditionally. Spiritual formation begins, for better or worse, even before a person becomes a Christian. While the influences of the sin, death, and the devil attempt to increasingly warp the soul, the Holy Spirit is active, calling us through whatever means are available (cf. John 16:7–11; Joel 2:28–29). He calls ceaselessly to all human kind, through the created order, the yearnings of our hearts, and the witness of the church. When we receive God's grace through faith in Jesus, as Lord and Savior, we enter the new beginnings of the first mansion. These early experiences, both positive and negative, will greatly affect our spiritual growth later.

New Beginnings

Teresa believes that prayer, in some form, is the beginning of spiritual growth. She says, "Insofar as I can understand, the door of entry to this castle is prayer and reflection."[1] Although the Holy Spirit was wooing Abigail for many years, she entered the Christian life and the first mansion when she met God in prayer, the prayer of surrender, confession, and trust in Jesus as Lord and Savior. In the first mansion, we are just beginning to learn what it means to be *in* the world but not *of* it. Yet we're mainly focused on getting God's help to obtain the worldly pleasures we have not been able to get for ourselves. We may seek God for deliverance from the addictions or habits that have been causing us pain.

God continues to call us to Himself by responding to our calls for help. Hopefully, as new believers, we find a Christian community, are baptized, and receive instruction in the faith. But the light of Christ is still hard for us to discern. Demonic delusion and self-deception are still great. Teresa describes some of the difficulties of the first mansion:

> You must note that hardly any of the light coming from the King's royal chamber reaches these first dwelling places. Even though they are not dark and black, as when the soul is in sin, they nevertheless are in some way darkened so that the soul cannot see the light. The darkness is not caused by a flaw in the room . . . but by so many bad things like snakes and vipers and poisonous creatures that enter with the soul and don't allow it to be aware of the light. It's as if a person were to enter a place where the sun is shining but be hardly able to open his eyes because of the mud in them.[2]

C. S. Lewis, in *The Great Divorce*, describes the kinds of attachments that can remain for Christians and cloud the ability to discern good from evil, and confuse God's gifts with false securities and pleasures.[3] We observed that Abigail still saw herself as the center of the universe and defined success as becoming important, respected, and loved. It will take significant spiritual growth before she discovers that God is the Center and that she is successful because He profoundly loves her.

Let's discuss two of the many *scriptural foundations* that shed further light on our experience of the first mansion. I chose these passages because they speak to our condition of being newly saved and the corresponding contradiction of the world values still within us.

> And I, brethren, could not speak to you as to spiritual men, but as to men of flesh, as to infants in Christ. I gave you milk to drink, not solid food; for you were not yet able to receive it. Indeed, even now you are not yet able, for you are still fleshly.
>
> — 1 CORINTHIANS 3:1–3

> What is the source of quarrels and conflicts among you? Is not the source your pleasures that wage war in your members? You lust and do not have; so you commit murder. You are envious and cannot obtain; so you fight and quarrel. You do not have because you do not ask. You ask and do not receive, because you ask with wrong

motives, so that you may spend it on your pleasures. You adulteresses, do you not know that friendship with the world is hostility toward God? Therefore whoever wishes to be a friend of the world makes himself an enemy of God.

—JAMES 4:1–4

It is clear from these passages that conversion to Christ does not immediately result in a changed mind and heart. The context of these passages indicates, in fact, that the people to whom Paul and James wrote were probably not brand new believers, but still struggling with worldly issues.

We are saved by God's grace through trust in Jesus as Lord and Savior (cf. Eph. 2:8, 9; Rom. 10:8, 9), but our motivations and lifestyle have yet to be transformed. Romans 12:1f, which applies to all believers, shows that ongoing transformation must remold us from the world's likeness into the likeness of Christ. Let's see how Michael experienced the first mansion.

Michael

When Michael left rehab he was referred to a local pastor. His life of substance abuse began in his early teens, and at twenty-seven he had pretty much destroyed every relationship in his life. He had been married for a few years right out of high school, but it didn't last. With an outgoing and gregarious personality, Michael easily made friends, but many of his friendships were not healthy. He hadn't been raised in church and his parents weren't Christians. For Michael, there just never seemed to be any reason to believe in a God. Drugs, sex, and extreme sports seemed to give him all the "mystical experiences" he needed. Work was just something to pay for the fun, as long as it didn't get in fun's way. Michael had a tender heart and could easily be hurt, but a macho exterior covered it. He took great pains to maintain his polished persona. Then came the accident, arrest, jail, and rehab. Life came to a crashing halt.

The Twelve Steps of Alcoholics Anonymous in his rehabilitation program introduced Michael to the possibility that his life was out of control and that there was a "Higher Power" that could restore sanity to his life. After weeks in the rehab center, he finally broke down and in tears of anguish surrendered his life to this God he had never known. The following months were filled with heart-wrenching confessions about his life and the people he had wounded. He longed to see his parents and his former wife to try to make amends, but he knew it would take a long time before he was ready. Michael also knew he needed to live in a new way, and only God could make that possible. He began reading the Bible and praying. He'd failed so many times to stop drinking, or smoking pot, or worse; it would take a miracle for sobriety to become a reality in his life.

In the following months, Michael joined a recovery group at a local church and finally began to attend occasionally on Sunday mornings. His new friends were there for him when he was tempted, and they encouraged him to work the program. In time, Michael came to believe in Jesus as Lord. He grew to depend on Him and wanted to please Him by the way he lived.

A new job at the gym opened up opportunities to use his experience in sports, and he began feeling hopeful about the possibilities ahead. Now that he had gained sobriety and found God, he could get on with his life. Michael shared how he was feeling in a portion of a letter he wrote to his parents.

Dear Mom and Dad:
I know it's been way too long since we've seen each other or even talked or written. I know how deeply I've hurt you and I'm truly sorry. Through the rehab program I've realized what a mess I've made of my life and I really want it to be different in the future. I know this may sound crazy to you, but I have started going to church and I really believe that Jesus will help me walk the straight and narrow. I know that God has forgiven me and I want you to forgive me, if you can. I love you and I want us to have a relationship again. I also want to tell you about the way God is working in my life.
I know you don't believe in all this, but it is important for me to share it with you. Every day I read the Bible and pray for the things that are coming up. I realize that I don't have the power to stay sober or to stay out of trouble, but I trust God to guide and protect me. And guess what. He actually does! I can't say I am not tempted, and sometimes it is almost more than I can bear, but God is there. My friends really help, too. Mom, Dad, I want you to know that I am praying for you every day. I love you and hope you will forgive me. Maybe you could write back or even call.
Love, Michael

Let's look at the six "rooms" that we explore within the first mansion, the experiential categories we identified in Chapter Three. Remember that each mansion is not just one room but a whole complex of rooms in which we explore our relationship with God. These accounts of Abigail and Michael gave us an example of the first mansion season of our journey. But an analysis from these six perspectives, or sets of rooms, will enable a more detailed understanding and offer a basis of comparison with the other mansions.

"Your Heart's Desire" in Relationship with God

Our souls are now alive in Christ, by God's grace, through faith in Jesus as Lord and Savior. Our sin is forgiven through the atoning death of Jesus on the Cross. All the gifts and resources of God are now available in this restored relationship with our Savior (cf. Eph. 1:3–14). It is important here to note that our spiritual growth through the mansions is not about receiving "new" blessings from God. All the gifts of God are lavished on us at conversion. Spiritual growth is the deepening experience of God's person, and the resulting ability to live in the fullness of what has been given. However, in the first mansion our attention is still focused primarily on the things of the world as they center on us.

I remember kneeling in my college professor's living room, saying *yes* to God for the first time. I was there for one reason: getting help. A broken family, a lost girlfriend, and vocational confusion had left me depressed and lost, and I needed hope and clear direction. God was merely a means to my lifelong desire for security and happiness. Fortunately, it didn't stay that way, but as my college professor said at the time, "You have to start somewhere."

"Key Activities" in Response to God

In these early days of the first mansion, we began the task of ridding sins from our daily activities. For Teresa and the people of her day, there was a more defined sense of the meaning of sin than is often the case today. Sin was not only breaking the Ten Commandments but failure to adhere to the many details of religious practice. There has been, it seems, a full pendulum swing from that perspective.

Today's Christians, immersed in postmodern culture, often consider conduct to be sinful only if it is a gross violation of the Ten Commandments. Much of the church has stopped looking to the Bible as a guide for moral behavior. Tom Clegg, a nationally known church consultant, says that, "The belief system of a huge number of churchgoers is dangerously at odds with the faith of the first church led by Jesus' apostles and recorded in the New Testament."[4] George Barna is a Christian sociologist and researcher who has sounded the alarm about the church in America's slip toward secularism and decline. He tells us that, "Sadly, an above average acceptance of relativism among believers has occurred in the intervening years. Currently, 62 percent of all born-again adults say there is no such thing as absolute truth. Amazingly, close to half of all evangelical Christians (42 percent) also reject absolutes when it comes to truth."[5] Postmoderns tend to believe that morality is relative to a particular community, Christian or otherwise.

THE BEGINNINGS OF PRAYER

Conversation with God

When we come to Christ, we need to be taught that prayer is simply conversation with Someone who loves us. We are invited to share our hearts openly and honestly, whether or not we think it is something that God wants to hear. He knows our hearts already. This conversation can happen anytime, anyplace. This conversation, by definition, is a two-way street; God wants to "talk" to us as well. We need to learn early on that we can become attentive to how God might be speaking to us, through Scripture, Christian friends, circumstances, and His quiet whispers in our hearts.

Internal Communication

Scripture makes it clear that God comes to live within our hearts through the Holy Spirit when we receive His gift of grace and salvation.

(Continued)

We no longer believe we live in a three-layered universe: God up there, us here, and hell down there. Yet we think, talk, and—worse—pray as if that were true. We talk to God as if He were off on some mission and we have to get His attention. We talk about God "showing up." The truth is, however, that our conversation with God is within our hearts (see Col. 1:27). It is there that the Holy Spirit communes with our spirit and helps us to pray (see Rom. 8:26). Although we may be able to "talk" to a God "up there," we fail to hear His voice because it comes from within, and we expect it to come externally. It is our heart that is the real prayer closet.

Therefore in today's world, the effort to rid oneself of sin, at least initially, is often not as strong a motivation as it was in Teresa's time; we are more accepting of "whatever," and not particularly afraid of hell. However, we have learned through Scripture and the teachings of the church that it is important to love one another. Good works become more intentional and focused, arising out of our desire to please God and bless others. Most probably, our lifestyle is still largely reflective of the world's agendas. Schedules, time, and money commitments are still built around the "demands" of making a living, raising a family, and entertainment. Teresa comments:

> For even though they are very involved in the world, they have good desires and sometimes, though only once in a while, they entrust themselves to our Lord and reflect on who they are, although in a rather hurried fashion . . . but their minds are filled with business matters which ordinarily occupy them. They are so attached to these things that where their treasure lies their hearts go also (Matthew 6:21).[6]

"Changing Patterns of Prayer" in Communication with God

Because the focus of our lives, as new believers, is still the world, our prayers mostly involve requests for help with issues of life.

Prayer is discursive in nature: talking to God. Depending on the Christian tradition in which we became involved, our prayers might also include written prayers from a devotional guide, or those prayed as part of the church liturgy. Because God's love is working in our hearts, we've also begun intercessory prayers for others. Prayer times, other than in church, are usually pretty random, as the need or thought presents itself.

"Jesus' Initiatives" to Draw Us to a Deeper Intimacy with God

God is present and responding to our every initiation as new believers, giving us protection far beyond our thought or belief. The Holy Spirit continues to speak to our hearts through the reading of Scripture, church services, and encouragement from other Christians. Although God is trying to reveal Himself, in prayer and in daily life, we have not developed the ability to discern spiritually and can scarcely see His light. Teresa says of God's willingness to give us favors to reveal Himself:

> His majesty can reveal His grandeurs to whomever He wants.
> Sometimes He does so merely to show forth His glory, as He said
> of the blind man whose sight He restored when His apostles asked
> Him if the blindness resulted from the man's sins or those of his
> parents (John 9:2–3). Hence, He doesn't grant them because the
> sanctity of the recipients is greater than that of those who don't
> receive them but so that His glory may be known, as we see in
> St. Paul and the Magdalene, and that we might praise Him for
> His work in creatures.[7]

Although Teresa makes this comment in the context of her discussion of the first mansion, her insight into God's self-revelation is particularly important in understanding the increasing revelations of God throughout our lives. The graces are just that; they are not based on our merit, but on the grace and will of God, and at this stage they are given to help us—but even more, to spur us on to further growth.

"Schemes of the Enemy" to Try to Destroy Our Growth in God

Unfortunately, as we grow in the first mansion, the enemy gives us increased attention. This attack may not come right away, however. Certainly many Christians come to faith as children and live comfortably for many years in their Christian family and culture. Satan's attacks in the early years may be focused on doubts or temptations to minor rebellion. Often, however, as we enter adolescence and young adulthood the enemy turns up the fire, with delusions about how important it is to be accepted by non-Christian friends, how narrow and rigid our upbringing was, and how much pleasure could be found in the "fun" that was now being offered to us.

As we grow older, the devil attempts to reinforce our perceived importance of the world and its benefits. He also attempts to create false pride about worldly honors and aspirations. Temptations are relentless. Shame is usually a strong tactic, tempting us to feel unworthy to trust God's favor or to live in His presence, more comfortable in the world than among other Christians or at church. Adult converts are already immersed in the world's delusions, and the enemy works to keep them there. Here is how Teresa describes the devil's strategy in the first mansion:

> . . . for souls with good intentions, enter here in many ways. But since the devil always has such a bad intention, he must have in each room many legions of devils to fight off souls when they try to go from one room to the other [within a given mansion]. Since the poor soul doesn't know this, the devil plays tricks on it in a thousand ways. He is not so successful with those who have advanced closer to where the King dwells. But since in the first rooms souls are still absorbed in the world and engulfed in their pleasures and vanities, with their honors and pretenses . . . [they] don't have the strength God gave human nature in the beginning.[8]

C. S. Lewis's *The Screwtape Letters* is an excellent description of the enemy's tactics, in the early mansions. Listen to how

Screwtape, a head devil, advises his assistant, Wormwood, about strategy toward his Christian assignee. Screwtape says:

> All we can do is to encourage the humans to take the pleasures which our Enemy has produced, at times, or in ways, or in degrees, which He has forbidden. Hence we always try to work away from the natural condition of any pleasure to that in which it is least natural, least redolent of its Maker, and least pleasurable.[9]

In short, the devil reinforces the lies of the world to keep us from noticing the light of God, or seeking Him more deeply. Although we have the Holy Spirit's power to resist, few of us are taught about such warfare. The result is that we may well ascribe all these tempting thoughts to ourselves, and once the evil intentions are recognized we feel shame and guilt. We may just work harder rather than turn to God more deeply.

"Keys for Growth" That Help Us Cooperate with God

No matter where we are in our journey, Bible study is always a critical part of our spiritual growth. A growing knowledge of the Scriptures helps us develop an entirely new worldview. The Old and New Testaments describe the history of humankind's ongoing relationship with God, with many illustrations. God's interactions and responses, described in Scripture, may be important examples of what to expect of God in our present circumstances. Clear biblical teaching and understanding is essential if we are to gain greater intimacy with God. We have to know who God is before real intimacy can develop. Mistaken images and projections will distort our relationship and impede its growth. Who is God? Who am I in relationship to God? What's wrong with the universe? What has God done about it? Who is Jesus? Although intellectual understanding is not the only part of our worldview change, it is often the beginning, and essential to our ability to grasp what is happening to us. Ultimately this understanding must move to "knowing" in the biblical sense: an intimate and personal experience of the person of the One we call God.

Interaction with an authentic Christian community is essential for maturity to develop freely. It is in the presence of relationships of trust that we are able to look honestly at self, without shame or condemnation, and seek the Lord for His power to grow and change. Lewis Smedes, a popular Christian psychologist, addresses some of the aspects of healing that can happen once our shame is faced: "If you wonder where God's grace can be found, find yourself a critical friend. A friend who wants you to be as good a person as you can be, a friend who dares to confront your flaws and failures, and then accepts the whole of you in grace."[10] Far too often, the local church fails to spawn these kinds of relationships. One can quickly sense whether or not vulnerability is "appropriate" in a given church culture.

Nurturing small groups, within this larger community, offer essential relationships where we can discuss biblical principles and how they relate to this new world of experiencing God. These small groups need to be communities of safety, openness, and vulnerability, so that we can learn not only biblical truths but discover from one another how to live them out. This mutual sharing, prayer, and encouragement is critical to growth throughout our spiritual journey, but particularly important here. Irving Harris, editor emeritus of *Faith at Work* magazine, comments about the importance of this kind of group for new believers:

> Far more likely in a group than in public worship, an inquirer
> will find a handle to take hold of—the backslider a place to begin
> again. The central purpose of fellowship is to discover skill in passing faith on to others; how to witness to the problems of home and
> occupation. To see, to pray, to grow, to share, to apply—these are
> the verbs at the heart of Christian groups.[11]

Increasing self-knowledge, another important key to growth, comes through these groups and in everyday experience. Kieran Kavanaugh, one of the translators and compilers of Teresa of Avila's writings, comments on its importance, in his introduction to the first mansion:

> Their [new Christians'] need, as is true of everyone, is for self-
> knowledge and for knowledge of the beauty of the soul in grace

and the ugliness of one in sin; in a word, for some insight into
the Christian mystery of sin and grace. Self-knowledge and humility grow as the soul moves inward through the castle toward the
center.[12]

As the Holy Spirit begins to illumine our relationships with
others, insight increases about our own personality traits, character development, and perspectives on life. Humility also
increases, as we learn more about ourselves in light of our relationship with a holy God. As we become humbler, we become
more dependent on God, and the relationship deepens.

For those new Christians struggling with addictions, support groups, such as Alcoholics Anonymous, Overeaters Anonymous, and Moms Supporting Moms, are powerful tools
in the hands of the Lord.[13] Facing our fallen humanity and
our sinful nature, in contrast with the way we were created to
live in the image and likeness of God, is a continuing line of
growth throughout all the mansions. In this vein, Teresa says
that intercessors are particularly important for Christians in
the first mansion, because we do not yet know how to rely on
the power that God has given us in Christ. We're still working
hard at living the Christian life.

As new believers, we need intentionality. Remember our
discussion of Teresa's insight about the changing amount of
the effort that is required of us, as growth happens? She compared our relationship with God with a garden that continually
needs watering, and described four phases, called "Waters." In
the beginning we have to work hard, as in drawing water from
a well in a bucket and pouring a bucketful down each garden
row. She called this the First Water phase. Later our effort less-
ens, as though we now have a water wheel that can pull multiple
buckets up for us. But in this Second Water phase we still have to
work pretty hard, carrying every bucket to the garden rows. The
Third Water is likened to irrigating the garden through a chan-
nel from a nearby stream, which involves much less work. The
Fourth Water and final phase has no real work to it at all. Like
a gentle rain or spring, the Holy Spirit totally waters the garden
of our relationship with God. The first mansion is a "First Water"
time, with a great need for us to be intentional about spiritual

growth. Thomas Dubay, who titles his discussion of this mansion "First Mansions (First Water)," comments, "St. Teresa's starting point is the absolutely basic condition for a serious prayer life: an earnest, continuing effort to rid oneself of sins, imperfections and attachments."[14]

Spiritual Coaching

Let's return to Abigail and Michael in the context of spiritual coaching as they address their personal struggles to grow in their love relationship with Jesus. Have you ever had a "spiritual coach"? It's probably a new concept to most of us. A spiritual coach is more than just a Christian friend, on the one hand, yet probably not a schooled and certified spiritual director either. The spiritual growth coach is a more mature Christian who has learned the basic coaching skills of listening, asking questions, and discernment; he or she understands and has experienced personal movement through the spiritual formation journey. Coaches can relate to people who come to them, in the context of the person's relative place in the journey. Sadly, few such people have been deployed in most of our congregations.

Abigail

Some time after Abigail came to her church, her pastor introduced her to Emily, a spiritual coach. Emily was several years older than Abigail and was specifically trained by her congregation, as we described. In their initial meeting, Emily simply listened as Abigail shared the story of her growing faith. Emily realized quickly that Abigail was well into the first mansion of spiritual growth, and she listened for insight into the rooms the young woman had been exploring. She encouraged her to continue to stay close to her Christian friends in her bible study group and be regular in worship and prayer.

At first Abigail occasionally "checked in," but she knew Emily was available, whenever she felt the need. Some months later, Abigail made another appointment; she had finally become hungry for more power in her Christian life. She launched into a long litany about the ways she wanted God to bless her life. She felt frustrated that a number of her relationships were stressful and wondered why God wasn't fixing things. Most of all, Abigail was perplexed by her own inability to measure up to what she felt were God's expectations.

After listening at great length, Emily asked Abigail about her relationship with her dad and how she experienced him, growing up. As she shared, Abigail began to discover that she was projecting the demanding tendencies of her earthly father onto her Heavenly Father. Her coach took her to passages of Scripture about God's grace and forgiveness, and His willingness to pursue us and help us solely because He loves us. Then Emily asked Abigail how she spent her time and the shape of her prayer life. They explored life priorities from Abigail's perspective and speculated about how God might look at them.

Emily encouraged her and explained that the frustrating situations in her life were all places where God wanted to bless her. But for that to happen, she needed to let Jesus become first in her life—in practical ways. They prayed together for all of the areas of concern that Abigail mentioned. As she was leaving one of their sessions together, Abigail turned to her coach and said, "Wow, I can see now that I've had this whole God thing backwards. I have just wanted Him to fix my life to make it happier and more successful. I guess He wants to do that, but most of all, He just wants me to experience His love and love Him back. Guess I've got some changing to do."

Michael

Michael too was one of the fortunate few who had access to a spiritual formation coach. This coach was also an addiction survivor, who could understand some of the unique challenges Michael faced. Like Abigail and her coach, they had met occasionally from time to time, just developing a relationship of trust, something that was particularly hard for Michael. As you can guess, it was not too long before the subject of the relationship with his family came up. Together they

(Continued)

explored Scriptures that relate to forgiveness and reconciliation. Michael was freed to realize that neither his parents nor his former wife was perfect and that forgiveness had to go both ways. Yet as a believer, Michael had the responsibility to take the first steps that began right there, with prayers of repentance and forgiveness. In the following months, Michael and his coach discussed how he could move toward reconciliation, and eventually those relationships began to be restored.

In the ongoing coaching sessions, it became apparent that a major motivator for Michael was success. First he wanted to be successful at sobriety. Then he wanted to be a successful athlete, a successful physical trainer, successful socially with lots of friends, and—what haunted him most—successful at finding a new mate. Michael and his coach explored passages of Scripture relating to God's desire to bless him and give him good gifts. They also explored passages that addressed sacrificial living and the need to love our neighbor. Michael's coach led him in prayers of surrender in all of these areas, just the way Michael had done as part of the Twelve Step process, in the rehab center. They explored how Michael might become more focused on God and others than on his obsession with himself. Michael brainstormed all sorts of ways in which he could help others as part of giving his life for God.

"Where do you think God is asking you to start?" his coach asked. After some reflection, Michael answered, "I suppose it has to begin with my prayer life. If I'm not spending time with God in prayer, or praying for others, I don't suppose I have much to give." The coach encouraged Michael to experiment with finding regular prayer times, and to ask God specifically whom to pray for and how to pray. He suggested that Michael memorize the key Scriptures they had discussed, so that God's truth would stick in his thinking. Michael and his coach closed their time holding hands in prayer, thanking God for His goodness and asking for His guidance in building a strong relationship with Jesus.

Abigail and Michael have started on the most exciting, profound, and mysterious journey of their lives. But they are still babes in Christ and much of the terrain ahead of them is unknown, hostile, and confusing. There will be many mistakes and many miracles, as God enfolds them in His love and power. But as Abigail and Michael grow in their faith and conquer some of their obstacles, their explorations into the second mansion will bring some surprise challenges.

REFLECTION

- How would you characterize your years in the first mansion?
- Who did God bring into your life to walk alongside?
- Is there someone you might seek out to be a spiritual formation coach for you? Is there someone who might need your coaching?

CHAPTER 5

Between a Rock and a Hard Place: The Second Mansion

*But I say, walk by the Spirit, and you will not carry
out the desire of the flesh. For the flesh sets its desire
against the Spirit, and the Spirit against the flesh;
for these are in opposition to one another, so that you
may not do the things that you please.*

—GALATIANS 5:16–17

WE'RE NOW MOVING INTO A MYSTERIOUS WILDERNESS. The second
mansion of spiritual formation is little understood or seldom
taught in typical discipleship material. Life took a major turn for
the better as we entered the first mansion of new life with Christ,
but the second mansion is a dark valley for which few new believers are prepared. We have all experienced this season, and still
do at times, though it is rarely seen as "spiritual growth." We'll
return to Michael, and then Abigail (in this case a few years
later), to illustrate life in the second mansion. Remember that
although our experience of the mansions is progressive, it is
not linear, one right after another; we journey back and forth.
We may live mainly in one, explore further ahead, and go back.

As we said in the introduction to the first mansion, you will want to ask the Holy Spirit to help you recall a similar season in your life, so that you can not only understand the second mansion but learn from your own experience and deepen your understanding of your spiritual formation. Let's look at Michael's experience of the second mansion.

Michael

A year of walking with Jesus found Michael more convinced than ever that God's way is the only way. He stayed active at his church and support group, but things didn't seem to be going so well for him. Sobriety was more elusive than he had guessed. Fortunately, there were no accidents or arrests this time, but he definitely slipped. He felt like such a failure and so ashamed, he stayed away from his support group for more than a month. His friends at work were also a challenge. It was like living in a totally different world from his church and Christian friends. To be in at the gym, you had to hang out at the bars, be on the hunt for girls, and have some good coarse jokes ready. Michael realized he needed to witness to non-Christians, and he knew that he couldn't hide from alcohol all his life, but these relationships were becoming stressful. He felt he needed to have friends, but began to wonder if this was possible while trying to live as "Saint Michael." However, things were not all bad, he told himself: "I'm a stud and the girls think I'm hot; I have a good rep at the gym and it's not too hard to keep ahead of the other trainers."

Michael's thoughts were another area of discouragement. Although he had managed to stay out of bed with the women who seemed so available, the thoughts in his head were not so pure. Sometimes they actually embarrassed him. Other times, he just let them go and felt guilty and ashamed. He had looked at pornography occasionally on a friend's computer and knew that it could become a real temptation for him. He started journaling. This excerpt further reveals his plight:

> Crap! Where is my relationship with God going? I had no idea that it would be this hard! I feel so ashamed of what's in my head or what I have just been up to that it is almost impossible to pray. After this slip with booze, who knows if I will ever be able to stay sober? God, what is wrong with me? It was cool that my church friends didn't condemn me for drinking and

forgave me, but I am afraid to tell them about the rest. They'd probably just tell me to shape up. Sometimes I come away from our group wondering if I should still be going. I don't really have time, and it just messes me up! The Bible says that God loves me and has a plan for my life. Well, I doubt that this is it! I hate disappointing God this way, but I have to have a life, too! Crap!

The Second Mansion

Like the first mansion, the second mansion, is still the condition of a relatively new Christian, but spiritual growth has taken place. We have come to realize that God's way is right, and we earnestly determine to live according to the God's desires for our lives, with an increasing desire to follow Christ. But the pull of the world, with its false pleasures and gratifications, is still strong. We also experience new levels of spiritual attack as the enemy increases the deceptions that the world, rather than God, is the source of security, significance, and happiness.

Let's look at some biblical examples about life in the second mansion. The Scriptures describe the call to kingdom values and the reality of spiritual warfare:

> But I say, walk by the Spirit, and you will not carry out the desire of the flesh. For the flesh sets its desire against the Spirit, and the Spirit against the flesh; for these are in opposition to one another, so that you may not do the things that you please. But if you are led by the Spirit, you are not under the Law. Now the deeds of the flesh are evident, which are: immorality, impurity, sensuality, idolatry, sorcery, enmities, strife, jealousy, outbursts of anger, disputes, dissensions, factions, envying, drunkenness, carousing, and things like these, of which I forewarn you, just as I have forewarned you, that those who practice such things will not inherit the kingdom of God. But the fruit of the Spirit is love, joy, peace, patience, kindness, goodness, faithfulness, gentleness, self-control; against such things there is no law. Now those who belong to Christ Jesus have crucified the flesh with its passions and desires. If we live by the Spirit, let us also walk by the Spirit.

—GALATIANS 5:16–25

Finally, be strong in the Lord and in His mighty power. Put on
the full armor of God so that you can take your stand against the
devil's schemes. For our struggle is not against flesh and blood, but
against the rulers, against the authorities, against the powers of this
dark world and against the spiritual forces of evil in the heavenly
realms. Therefore put on the full armor of God, so that when the
day of evil comes, you may be able to stand your ground, and after
you have done everything, to stand. . . .

—EPHESIANS 6:10–18

In the Galatians passage, the apostle Paul is writing to Christians
struggling with the mandate to live in a way that reflects commitment to Christ and faithfulness to the Jewish laws of conduct.
His words exemplify our struggle, as second mansion Christians.
Paul also shows our need to grow beyond a bondage to rigid
rules. We are to mature into a life guided by relationship with
God in Christ, and led and empowered by the Holy Spirit. The
Ephesians passage is written to Christians who are under attack
by the devil. It is descriptive of the early mansions because of the
intentionality with which spiritual warfare must be addressed.
Victory in both areas is the result of relationship with God in
Christ through the Holy Spirit. Michael and Abigail are experiencing both dimensions of this struggle.

Abigail

We reconnect with Abigail about four years after she recommitted
her life to Christ. She finished college with a degree in
marketing, moved to Minneapolis, met a man she really liked,
and was enjoying life. Her faith grew over these years, and she now prayed
about most things. Although her new job included a fair amount of travel,
she managed to attend a nearby church a couple times a month.

But life had become more difficult on a number of fronts. Even
though she liked her job, she didn't like being the new kid on the block.
She was frustrated that she often got the "chores" around the office,
and she felt it was hard to really show her boss what she was capable of
doing. To compensate, she worked long hours, often on weekends. To
make matters worse, most of her co-workers weren't Christians, and

language in the office could get a bit off color. It wasn't unusual for her to get kidded, and even ridiculed, for her faith. She wondered if she should just hide it, fit in, and act like everyone else.

Abigail did have one friend at work who was a Christian. It was, in fact, Sally's church that she was attending. Abigail looked forward to opportunities to share lunch and talk. But most of Abigail's friends were co-workers and clients caught up in the rush of getting ahead, playing hard, and looking good. Sometimes it was exciting; other times she wondered what kind of treadmill she was on.

Another stressor for Abigail was her relationship with her boyfriend, Ted. Some time after they started dating seriously, she gave in to sleeping with him. She didn't really feel good about it, but it was what he wanted and what other couples seemed to be doing. Ted wanted to move in together, but Abigail was resisting. She thought she might really love Ted and didn't want to lose him. But neither of them was ready to get married.

The two sides of Abigail's life, her success and her temptations, created a new level of stress. Here is a section from her journal in this season, as she reflected on her relationship with God:

> I haven't made an entry for months! I am so frustrated and worried about my faith. I think I am in trouble; God seems so remote most of the time. I want to do the right thing and live for Him, but it's really hard. Church is great, when I can get there, but Sundays are a premium. I'm either bushed or need to spend time with Ted. I've noticed that the office language is creeping into my vocabulary. I can't believe what I said the other day! What worries me most is that it didn't really bother me at the time. My prayer life is slipping, too—no time! It was easier at school when I could just get up a little earlier or have time between classes. Now, mornings are murder and traffic is enough to kill anyone's faith. Ugh! What am I supposed to do with Ted? I feel trapped. I love the intimacy we have together, but I know it is not what God wants for us. It would be easier if Ted were a Christian. He thinks my concerns are ridiculous. I wish I could talk to Emily, my spiritual formation coach back at school. I don't really have anyone other than Sally to talk to. I feel so alone and discouraged one minute, and then just blow it off the next.

"Your Heart's Desire" in Relationship with God

Let's discuss these same six categories, the rooms in the second mansion that Michael and Abigail are exploring, and see how spiritual growth has taken place, even in the midst of these conflicts and frustrations.

We feel like a schizophrenic in the second mansion. Despite a deepening faith, we find ourselves still engaged in worldly pastimes, as sources of pleasure, security, and significance, half relying on the world and half on God. Yet concerns about "true treasure" are becoming more conscious (cf. Matt. 6:21, 11:44f). The divergence of Christian values and our lifestyles was certainly present in the first mansion, but we didn't recognize it. Improvements in morality and religious activity used to feel like adequate progress, but now this tension is driving us crazy.

The Holy Spirit is enlightening us about the mixed motives present within us. We're becoming more aware of our choices between Kingdom values and those of the world. The "problem" has arisen because we have begun to hear or perceive God to some extent, both in prayer and in the events of life. We've been drawn closer to the Light.

But our soul has become a battleground between darkness and light, the world and the divine (cf. Gal. 5:17). This internal struggle makes the second mansion a difficult stage of Christian growth. Teresa writes about this struggle in the second mansion:

> I say that these rooms involve more effort because those who are in the first dwelling places are like deaf-mutes and thus the difficulty of not speaking is more easily endured by them than it is by those who hear but cannot speak. . . . Thus, as I say, hearing His voice is a greater trial than not hearing it.[1]

Thomas Dubay comments on Teresa's description:

> The man or woman in the second mansions is a battleground where the conflict between the world and the divine call is being waged. There is a tug-of-war going on, and the individual experiences the two opposing pulls. The world's tug is experienced in several ways: earthly pleasures remain attractive, and they appear as though almost eternal. . . . God's tug is likewise felt in diverse manners: reason itself shows the person how mistaken the world's message is and why it is mistaken. Significant growth has taken place and has instilled a conviction that only in God is one's surety.[2]

It's obvious that the second mansion does not feel like spiritual growth!

"Key Activities" in Response to God

We attempt to live the Christian life more intentionally, yet struggle with what this means in the concrete circumstances of life. Teresa says of Christians in the second mansion, "The whole aim for any person who is beginning prayer . . . should be that he work and prepare himself with determination and every possible effort to bring his will into conformity with God's will." The struggles we are experiencing are actually increasing our desire to listen to God. We feel, therefore, a greater attraction to, and need for, people with whom we can discuss our walk with Jesus. We long to hear from God in sermons, Bible study, and Christian books. The difficulty of what it means to love our neighbor is now being worked out in our primary relationships, sometimes with success but oftentimes with failure.

There may also be considerable struggle as the light of Christ helps us discover spiritual and emotional wounding in the past, hurts, and brokenness not easily repaired. Slowly, we are experiencing transformation, seemingly two steps forward and one step back. This spiritual growth is now resulting in a changed life, yet showing us a glimpse of how far there is still to go.

"Changing Patterns of Prayer" in Communication with God

In this relatively early phase of the journey, our prayers are still mainly discursive, telling God what the problem is, and how and when to fix it. But our increasing concern for others has made intercession a greater priority. We've developed more receptiveness to the Holy Spirit's promptings and grace, with the sense that God is communicating with us during our times of prayer, as well as through outward circumstances. Teresa says that in the second mansion we become aware of touches of divine light from God calling us to a deeper level of intimacy:

> I don't mean that these appeals and calls are like the ones
> I shall speak of later on. But they come through words spoken

by other people, or through sermons, or through what is read in good books, or through many things that are heard and by which God calls, or through illnesses and trials, or also through a truth that He teaches during the brief moments we spend in prayer.[3]

But prayer also reflects the battleground that is going on between the world and the call of God and made all the more challenging by the schemes of the enemy. Depending on our level of teaching about spiritual warfare, we may totally misinterpret the situation, blaming the actions of the enemy on God. For example, we have often discerned God's hand through what seemed like a series of "coincidences" that were helpful or related to something we prayed about. However, we can also observe hurtful "coincidences" and wonder what God is trying to teach us. When we understand that "every good thing given and every perfect gift is from above, coming down from the Father of lights" (James 1:17), we realize that God doesn't teach us through negative reinforcement. The situation may simply be actual coincidences, but the enemy is certain to try to make sure God gets the blame. The new insights we gain about past wounding can also be occasions for both misunderstanding and temptation. Our new awareness "feels" painful. It feels as if we are less faithful to God than we were before. Again, Scripture helps us put our experience in proper perspective.

> Consider it all joy, my brethren, when you encounter various trials, knowing that the testing ["testing" here does not imply a pass-fail type of test, but an opportunity to become strengthened] of your faith produces endurance. And let endurance have its perfect result, so that you may be perfect and complete, lacking in nothing. [and] Let no one say when he is tempted, "I am being tempted by God"; for God cannot be tempted by evil, and He Himself does not tempt anyone.
>
> —JAMES 1:2–4, 13

We'll say more about discernment later.

SPIRITUAL WARFARE

Scripture is clear about our spiritual battle. Genesis 3 describes our first encounter with our spiritual enemy as the serpent that tempts Adam and Eve. He turns up again in Job 1:6 as the accuser. Satan tempted Jesus (cf. Matt. 4:1f). Jesus makes it clear, however, that He has overcome the power of the devil (cf. John 12:31, 14:30, 16:11; and Heb. 12:14, 15). The devil, though limited, is still a real danger to us. The apostle Peter describes him as a roaring lion, looking for someone to devour (cf. 1 Pet. 5:8).

We recognize the devil's influence because he a "liar" and speaks contrary to the Word of God (cf. John 8:44). Therefore, even though we should hope in God, the devil tries to convince us to despair. Fear is suggested instead of trusting in God as Perfect Love.

Our defense against the devil, made possible by Jesus' death and resurrection and the Holy Spirit's presence in us, comes in three ways:

1. **Preparation:** In Ephesians 6:10f, the apostle Paul teaches us to grow in our faith similarly to a soldier putting on armor, so that we may stand firm against the schemes of the devil. Our defense is truth; a right relationship with God; the Gospel of peace, faith, and salvation; and our offensive weapon, the word of God.
2. **Discernment:** We are gifted by the Holy Spirit to "discern spirits" (1 Cor. 12:10).
3. **Active resistance:** James 4:7 says that if we resist the devil he will flee from us. Our ability to resist depends on our preparation and our discernment. Our resistance is not passive, but an active and intentional use of the "sword of the Spirit, the word of God." Jesus modeled this, and the disciples followed suit, as they cast out demons by commanding them in the name of Jesus. We can do the same thing through the power of the same Holy Spirit.

But prayer in the second mansion may not bring the same peace it once did in the first mansion. What Brother Boniface said about prayer certainly applies to the second mansion, as well as the rest: "We pray as we live, and we live as we pray." So much of our prayer time reflects the same battles that are going on in daily life. God often waits for us to decide between right and wrong, His way or the alternatives, before He answers. So we learn to wait upon the Lord in new ways.

"Jesus' Initiatives" to Draw Us into Deeper Intimacy with God

As always, God is calling to us ceaselessly through every circumstance of life. He continues to inspire our reading of His Word and conversations with other Christians. Certainly He is measuring the amount of spiritual attack that the enemy is allowed to wield against us (cf. 1 Cor. 10:13). God uses every attack to identify areas of needed growth and healing. But it is often the case that we have not learned discernment well enough to recognize God's light in these attacks.

God continues to woo us. In times of sickness and trial, God prompts us to come to Him in prayer and responds in ways that, we begin to realize, are beyond coincidence. Teresa says, " . . . for the Lord often desires that dryness and bad thoughts afflict and pursue us without our being able to get rid of them. Sometimes He even permits these reptiles to bite us so that afterward we may know how to guard ourselves better and that He may prove whether we are greatly grieved by having offended Him."[4]

Even though we may not realize it, Jesus is continuing to shepherd us with loving tenderness, even if the tenderness feels like a surgeon's scalpel.

"Schemes of the Enemy" to Try to Destroy Our Growth in God

Because of the nature of the second mansion, we have mentioned the devil's influence in the rooms already discussed. But because of its significance in this phase of growth, let's look at it further. Our progress through the second mansion phase of growth makes us a greater threat to the kingdom of darkness. The enemy has intensified the attacks by trying to deceive us about where to find real happiness, security, and significance. He tries to convince us that true discipleship will cost every pleasure. At the same time, Satan enhances exaggerated perceptions of pleasure in recreation, entertainment, and appetites. He highlights issues of material security and success, in opposition to the opportunities to serve Jesus. Temptations to sin increase, in hopes that the struggle with sin will further cloud our relationship with God and allow shame and guilt to block further intimacy. Listen to how Teresa describes the nature of this spiritual warfare in the second mansion.

> But the attacks made by the devils in a thousand ways afflict the soul more in these rooms than in the previous ones. In the previous ones the soul was deaf and dumb—at least it heard a very little and resisted less, as one who has partly lost hope of conquering. Here the intellect is more alive and the faculties are more skilled. The blows from the artillery strike in such a way that the soul cannot fail to hear. It is in this stage that the devils represent these snakes (worldly things) and the temporal pleasures of the present as though almost eternal.[5]

Unfortunately, few churches teach clearly about spiritual warfare. As we said earlier, we often blame God or ourselves, when much of the turmoil in our heads is caused by the devil's harassment. The power of the Holy Spirit is always available, but we fail to recognize what is happening and don't call upon Him. Of course, we remain responsible for the decisions we make, no matter the source of the impetus. We resist some attacks, but some not. Shame, discouragement, and even hopelessness can become dominant themes in our lives in this stage of growth.

The enemy's attacks also increase during prayer. Disguised as our own thoughts, the enemy sends many memories of past sins, shameful thoughts, and messages of condemnation, designed to make us feel unworthy to seek God or ask His help. A flood of distractions about things to do makes it even more difficult to focus on God in prayer. We seldom see these attacks as signs of spiritual growth (if we weren't growing, the devil wouldn't trouble himself), but instead as failures, to be fixed, denied, or hidden. If the enemy can thwart or even stop our conversation with God, spiritual growth may be stopped as well. The second mansion can truly feel like a "valley of the shadow" time in which we have not learned to hold up the shield of faith or wield the sword of the Spirit. For this reason, prayers of intercession by more mature believers are essential. We are not meant to stand in the battle alone, but as part of the Body of Christ.

"Keys for Growth" That Help Us Cooperate with God

The greatest keys to growth in the second mansion are perseverance and prayer. God is faithful in every circumstance, but we must resist the devil and the world to follow God.

We need teaching about spiritual warfare, to enable us to understand what is happening, and to know how to use our relationship with God in Christ to resist the enemy. As I have mentioned, churches seldom teach about spiritual warfare, and then only to "mature" Christians.[6] We all need to discover that we are not alone and that these experiences are normal.

Continued study of Scripture is essential because we are confronted with Kingdom values that conflict with the values of this world. The authoritative nature of the Scriptures is of great value in establishing a new values baseline, consistent with intimacy with our holy God. Eventually experience will validate kingdom values, but for now we need to trust, in His Word and through other believers, that God will honor deeds of the Spirit but not those of the flesh.

Trusted Christian relationships and mentoring are critical through all the mansions. Teresa says, "It is very important to consult persons with experience, for you will be thinking that you are seriously failing to do some necessary thing."[7] Others can often see the line of attack before we can. While journeying in the second mansion, we are apt to interpret the increased level of struggle as failure on our part (and in fact there may be some failure), and we therefore need ongoing encouragement to continue to follow Christ to the best of our ability.

Continued teaching about the love and grace of God is needed to counter the accusations of the enemy, which go so far as to induce us to think that even temptation is itself sin and a sign of failure. Unfortunately, fellow believers—often with good intentions—inflict guilt and pressure on those struggling in the second mansion. This is always counterproductive, and it often drives the struggling Christian away from the family of God. God's love, forgiveness, and grace, as well as truth, must be demonstrated in ways that help to reconcile the lifelong tension of being a sinner in the arms of our loving God. Thomas Dubay comments about Teresa's program for second mansion Christians: "Teresa's first bit of advice concerns companionship: the soul should avoid close association with 'evil' and mediocre people and make it a point to mix with the good, that is, not only with those in the early mansions but also with those who have advanced into the mansions 'nearer the center' where the King is; to be in close touch with these latter is a great help, for they tend to bring others to higher things along with themselves."[8]

This understanding that a bit of sheltering can be helpful during the second mansion produces a tension where missional and evangelistic activity is encouraged for new Christians. It is true that new Christians may have more non-Christian friends than do those who have been Christians longer. However, second mansion believers may just as well get pulled in the other direction. We can guess this was one of the reasons Jesus sent his disciples out two by two.

The second mansion is still a "First Water" condition, using Teresa's analogy. This means that considerable effort is required on our part to persevere in faithfulness and obedience, even though it is always God's grace that makes our effort effective. Teresa speaks of the importance of intentionally conforming one's life to the will of God as a key to growth:

> The whole aim of any person who is beginning prayer . . . should be that he work and prepare himself with determination and every possible effort to bring his will into conformity with God's will. Be certain that, as I shall say later, the greatest perfection attainable along the spiritual path lies in conformity. It is the person who lives

in more perfect conformity, who will receive more from the Lord and be more advanced on this road.[9]

Secure relationships of accountability, within the Body of Christ, can afford ongoing stability and protection from self-delusion and error. But it is essential that this support and accountability come from a position of love, humility, and encouragement. Already steeped in feelings of failure and self-condemnation, we can be very sensitive and easily wounded by the Christian community's good intentions and "shape up" advice. With tremendous gratitude, I remember the phrase, used by Father Patrick at Holy Trinity Abbey, as I complained about my struggles. "Isn't that wonderful? Remember the time when that wouldn't even have bothered you? Don't you see how you have grown?"

We've seen how difficult life can be as we continue to grow spiritually and venture into the second mansion. Unfortunately, there are some who do not make it further but become stalled by the trials that confront them. Without understanding their situation as one of spiritual growth, they may conclude they have given Jesus a "real try" but are simply not up to the unreasonable demands of the Christian life. Here, maybe more than anywhere on the journey into the heart of God, we need mentors and coaches who can reinterpret our experiences and encourage us to persevere. Fortunately, both Abigail and Michael have such a coach available to them. Let's look in as they continue their journey, as part of the Body of Christ.

Abigail

It was Sally who convinced Abigail that she needed to talk to someone. She could sympathize with Abigail's struggles, but she wasn't sure what to say. She had many of the same issues and felt inadequate to point the way. But Sally knew Martha, one of the women's group leaders at church, and suggested that she might be someone who could help.

With some reluctance, Abigail made the appointment. After all, she certainly wasn't in any real crisis, and yet she wasn't proud of her walk with God either. One thing she didn't want was a lecture about what she already knew.

Finally the day came, and Abigail and her new coach met for coffee. Abigail cautiously shared her struggles about trying to live the Christian lifestyle at work and in her relationship with Ted. "I know you don't have these problems," she said as she poured out her story. Martha listened for a long time, asking safe questions for clarification. Finally Martha responded, "Abigail, you sound just like me." She went on to share how tumultuous life had been for her as a new Christian, the mistakes she had made, and how discouraged she had been. She also shared how she still struggled with living like Jesus, and loving Him the way she wanted to. Abigail was surprised by Martha's transparency and vulnerability and felt hope for her faith, for the first time in many months. Then Martha recommended *The Screwtape Letters*, by C. S. Lewis, and showed her passages of Scripture that described the warfare Abigail was experiencing.[10] Her coach helped Abigail see that her dissatisfaction was, in fact, a sign of spiritual growth, and evidence of the loving light of Christ shining in her life. "Don't you know that you wouldn't have been so concerned a few years ago and that most people still aren't?" Martha asked.

They discussed how Jesus dealt with sinners without condemnation, but with encouragement to live life a new way. Martha explained that just trying harder wouldn't help; it was only by the power of the Holy Spirit that she could grow into the person who could love God and live in this world at the same time. They prayed together, thanking God for His faithfulness to Abigail, asking for His power to help her experience the love of Jesus in a new way.

Abigail and her coach met monthly, one-on-one and together weekly with a small group of young women, including Sally, where Abigail discovered that she was not alone. It was a safe place to share her struggles with others who were serious about living for Jesus. Together, they studied the Scriptures and prayed for God's guidance and prayer. In time, she told Ted that sex would have to wait for marriage, where she could truly make it an expression of her love. Life still felt like a roller coaster sometimes, but Abigail began to look for Jesus in the lows as well as the highs. She began to see her life as an adventure; she was excited to see how Jesus would turn hard things into blessings.

Michael

Michael's meeting with his spiritual formation coach
unfortunately came several years later, after he had experienced
two more slips and a return to the recovery program.
His temptation to pornography had metastasized into a full addiction.
The last straw for Michael came when he was fired from the gym because
of a prideful and competitive attitude toward his co-workers, which
caused significant tension.

Michael's friends from his Bible study group set up the "coaching"
meeting, because Michael was too ashamed to ask for help. They
called Jose and suggested that Michael might need some encouragement.
Jose called Michael and, a week or so later, they met for coffee. While
Michael pretended to be excited to meet Jose, inside he was dreading it.
How could he admit how badly he had messed up? The coach wouldn't
understand; nor would God.

Like Abigail's coach, Jose knew how to listen and ask safe questions.
A week later they met privately, and Michael opened up their meeting
with a barrage of accusations against God. "How could a loving God allow
all this to happen to me? Why hadn't Jesus protected me? What good
was it to pray when nothing happened?" Michael's coach listened quietly
for a long time and then asked him, "What hurts the most about all this,
Michael?" Michael thought for a long time and then responded with tears,
"My pride is in the bottom of an outhouse." Jose responded, "Mind if
I give you a hug?"

The ensuing conversations brought forgiveness, insight, and healing
to this prodigal son. Michael never forgot the cross Jose gave him.
"Every time you are tempted, hold on to this cross and call out to Jesus,"
he had told him. Michael discovered many roots of rebellion that lay
below the surface but now were wreaking havoc in his life. Jose referred
Michael to a Christian prayer therapist, who began a process of healing of
memories that was to continue over many years to come. The Holy Spirit
lovingly revealed the spiritual wounds and unforgivenesses in his past,
which had since become festering sores, stealing his peace and serving as
handles for the devil to tempt and accuse him.

Jose helped Michael form a mutual accountability group that would
ask the hard questions and encourage one another to trust and follow
Jesus. They spent time each week in the Gospels, asking the Holy Spirit
to show them Jesus, and to help them experience the spirit-filled life

described in Galatians. The growing friendships with these men, which God brought into his life, helped Michael begin to feel Christ's victory break through, and even flourish. Growth for Michael was slow, and many times discouraging, but he discovered that Jesus was with him in it all. As time went on, Michael's obsession with himself (and pornography) began to fade. But life remained a challenge between God's way and the world's.

REFLECTION

- Where are you experiencing conflicts between God's way and the world's way in your life at the present time?

- What lies is the enemy using to attempt to convince you that these instances of the world's way will best meet your needs, or that there is no real alternative?

- When you talk to God about this battle, do you ask for help doing it His way, or do you make excuses, defending the devil's lies?

- What steps is God asking you to take now?

CHAPTER 6

Following Jesus: The Third Mansion

So then, my beloved, just as you have always obeyed,
not as in my presence only, but now much more in
my absence, work out your salvation with fear and
trembling; for it is God who is at work in you, both
to will and to work for His good pleasure.

—PHILIPPIANS 2:12–13

WE NOW TAKE A HUGE LEAP IN OUR DISCUSSION of spiritual growth, as we move from the second mansion to the third. There is much written about discipleship of relatively new Christians, but the more mature phases of growth seem much more a mystery to us, so we want to spend our time in the later mansions of Christian maturity. We therefore jump to a time in our spiritual growth when the struggles and warfare of the second mansion are largely over, and considerable "discipleship" now exemplifies our life. For most people, this takes a number of years, maybe even decades. We pick up our two spiritual journeyers a bit later in their lives, when they feel they are faithfully following Jesus.

Abigail

We find Abigail ten years later, now thirty-three years old. A lot
has happened since her early career days in Minneapolis, and her
fast pace in the marketplace. Abigail now lives with her husband
and two boys (four and six), in Laguna Beach, California. Bill, raised
a Baptist, is an account executive with a Southern California financial
firm, and doing quite well. They are members of Seaside Community
Church and the local country club, and they have their oldest, Philip, in
a Christian school. Abigail is a stay-at-home mom but hopes to return to
her career in marketing once the boys are both in school.

Abigail's faith has grown significantly. She broke up with Ted, after
some years of dating and even a short engagement. She had realized
that she and Ted were just headed in different directions, both spiritually
and in their personal values. Abigail now felt so fortunate to have
met and fallen in love with a Christian man. Even though Bill was not
quite as "interested in God" as Abigail, he nevertheless was a faithful
husband, father, and church attender.

Abigail, on the other hand, has become quite involved in church life.
She has been active in the women's organization and taught first
grade Sunday school. Her faith grew the most through Seaside's
discipleship retreats, where she discovered a new passion for serving Jesus.
Ministry became an important word in her life as she realized that God
called and gifted her in important ways. She could count on His Holy
Spirit to empower her as she witnessed to her friends at the club, taught
the kids, and led her women's small group.

It was also at this retreat that prayer took on new significance. She
was challenged to ask intentionally for what she needed, and to intercede
for those around her. Abigail felt she had seen a number of miracles as
a result of her prayers. Once, when her parents were in an auto accident
and seriously hurt, she prayed that they would be healed. They did recover
more quickly than expected, and Abigail called them to share that it had
been God's hand.

Scripture was also an important part of Abigail's life, both in her small
group and at home. Her well-worn and marked Bible sat on her bedside
table, and she read a chapter every night. She had, in fact, been through it
several times.

Abigail's only real complaint was her pace of life. Bill spent two hours
a day commuting to and from work and was exhausted by the time he

got home. His job demanded that he work from home some weekends as well. Abigail never thought she would turn out to be one of the notorious "taxi moms" that so many other women complained about being. But here she was: rides to and from school, soccer practice twice a week, midweek Kids Church for Philip, doctors, shopping, her own church activities, and so on. Of course there were all the "mom" and "wife" responsibilities at home, too. Really, she loved it, but sometimes there was just too much.

Abigail did have one Christian friend from church, whom she met with for coffee occasionally, but she complained that she didn't have anyone she could really confide in about personal stuff. She prayed mostly on the run or falling asleep at night. But overall, Abigail felt good about her faith and her life as a Christian. She was both grateful and proud that she knew God loved her and that she would go to heaven when she died. It felt so good to have her life in the secure hands of God.

Abigail came face to face with the impact of her busyness when she had the uncomfortable experience of trying to tell her pastor no. She had headed up the children's Christmas program once before, but when her pastor called this time to ask, she responded: "Pastor, I just can't do it! I am so busy that I don't have a minute to myself, or even with God. I do my devotions most nights and love your sermons, but it feels like I am passing Jesus on the freeway, and He's going the other way!" Her pastor responded, "I understand, Abigail, but we really need you. You have such a gift for working with the other moms and the kids love you. Would you pray about it and call me back?" "Sure," Abigail replied, knowing that she would give in. She recalled the early days of her Christian walk and reminisced about how close Jesus felt. "Will following Jesus always feel like a treadmill?" she wondered.

Abigail is experiencing the growth challenges of the third mansion.

The Third Mansion

By the time we have come to "make our home" in the third mansion, we have developed a relatively balanced life of discipleship. Regular church attendance and ministry, consistent prayer, a concerted effort to live the Christian life, and a genuine desire to please and honor God are evidences of spiritual growth. Teresa says: "I have known some souls and even many—I believe I can say—who have reached this state and have lived many years in this upright and well-ordered way both in body and soul, insofar as can be known."[1]

It is worth observing that the third of the seven mansions is about as far as most churches go in their teaching about the spiritual life. It's an important phase of our growth, and many of us get stuck here. But we will see that there is more, much more.

Some biblical examples of life in the third mansion will help us put this call to a balanced life of following Jesus in context.

> Therefore I, the prisoner of the Lord, implore you to walk in a manner worthy of the calling with which you have been called, with all humility and gentleness, with patience, showing tolerance for one another in love, being diligent to preserve the unity of the Spirit in the bond of peace.
>
> —EPHESIANS 4:1–3

> So then, my beloved, just as you have always obeyed, not as in my presence only, but now much more in my absence, work out your salvation with fear and trembling; for it is God who is at work in you, both to will and to work for His good pleasure.
>
> Do all things without grumbling or disputing; so that you will prove yourselves to be blameless and innocent, children of God above reproach in the midst of a crooked and perverse generation, among whom you appear as lights in the world, holding fast the word of life, so that in the day of Christ I will have reason to glory because I did not run in vain nor toil in vain.
>
> —PHILIPPIANS 2:12–16

In these passages, the apostle Paul explains the importance of living a faithful life of service to Jesus, where Kingdom values must be embraced fully. Let's see how this discipled life is working out for Michael.

Michael

It took a few years for Michael's life to stabilize. As he matured, his pastor suggested that he begin helping out with the singles' group he was attending. It became his job to schedule the meetings at various homes, set up monthly outings, write a monthly newsletter to keep people informed, and meet new people who came to the group and make them feel welcome. Michael liked this last part the most. He enjoyed meeting new people and was able to relate to the loneliness that was common to most singles his age. His new job at the sports equipment outlet was also an excellent opportunity to meet young singles, and he often found ways to extend an invitation to one of the singles' group outings. He also loved setting up the outings. From rock climbing and the ropes courses to quiet picnics at the lake, Michael was able to plan special times for fun, personal relating, and biblical reflections. Over the following three years that Michael worked with the group, many of the singles came to know Christ as Savior and several found spouses.

As a part of his role in Single Ministries, Michael was asked to join a special discipleship group at church. He met weekly with men and women who had responsibility for others in the life of the church. The program included Bible study and Scripture memorization. They practiced sharing their testimonies and the Gospel message. This discipleship training program and the interpersonal accountability it offered helped Michael grow in his faith and develop a balanced lifestyle. He established a regular prayer time in which he took every need to God and prayed for his friends, family, and the young people in the singles' group. These prayer times were very special to Michael, and he felt that God always "showed up" and heard his prayers. He was excited to be able to share specific answers and times of guidance with his discipleship group.

After some time, Michael realized that his life at church and ministry with the singles was far more interesting than his work at the sports outlet. Some of his friends had said, half joking, that he should become a pastor, and now he was actively entertaining the idea. One day he made an appointment for some one-on-one time with his pastor. "Do you think I could become a pastor? What would it take?" Michael asked. The pastor praised Michael for the wonderful progress he had made, both in his ministry and his lifestyle. He was also pleased with Michael's consistency with the discipleship program. The pastor explained the schooling that

(Continued)

would be required and suggested that Michael pray about it. At the next discipleship meeting, Michael asked his friends to pray for guidance and a clear message about God's will.

Ultimately, Michael did hear God's leading toward full-time ministry as a church pastor. It took a long time. First he had to complete his undergraduate degree, and then begin seminary. The studies, as he had guessed, were hard, particularly Greek and Hebrew. But Michael loved it, made friends, and became more certain than ever that he was cut out to be a pastor-evangelist. During his time at Rockwell Seminary, he met Melissa, fell in love, and married.

Premarriage counseling was a significant time of growth for Michael. God used Melissa to show Michael he had never really learned how to share his heart or express love. He began to realize the role that addiction had played in his own needs for self-esteem, approval, and love. Motivated by his desire to love Melissa with his whole heart, he was able to more fully face his past. Michael realized how his childhood needs to succeed had warped the God-image that the Lord had created in him. In a special session with their pastor, both Michael and Melissa confessed and surrendered the wounding of their earlier lives, and they asked God to make them one in love as they committed their lives together.

For the first time, Michael caught a glimpse of what it meant to be loved unconditionally. Melissa knew everything about him and loved him all the more. His relationship with Melissa would prove to be an ongoing gift from God in the journey forward.

Michael's relationship with God also deepened as he had to rely on the Holy Spirit for perseverance, direction, and the ability to really learn. The concept of the "missional" church had caught Michael's attention. He became passionate about the need for the church to reach out to people and engage culture, rather than sit and wait for people to come.

Soon after graduation, God called Michael and Melissa to a small community church in Nebraska. He dived into ministry with the same zeal that had always typified his life. With his background of addiction, Michael was able to relate to hurting people in his town. People came to Christ, and Michael's church grew. Most folks weren't quite ready for Michael's "missional model" of church, but he was patient and tried to demonstrate a life that really engaged the lost and hurting around him. Life was busy. Michael loved ministry and was proud that Mission Hills Church was growing. But life as a pastor, husband, and soon-to-be father would not turn out to be as easy as it looked.

"Your Heart's Desire" in Relationship with God

Let's discuss these same six experiential rooms in the third mansion of our hearts, and see how spiritual growth takes place.

As you and I mature in the third mansion, we become fully convinced that life with Jesus is the only way to live. We've experienced in many specific situations the truth that Jesus will lead us faithfully if we follow biblical teachings. A scriptural worldview and moral values have replaced the worldly ones we may have grown up with, and we try to avoid committing even minor sins. We experience a relatively stable faith, the inner assurance of our salvation, and personal knowledge of God's goodness. Teresa describes this ascent to the third mansion: "What shall we say to those who through perseverance and the mercy of God have won these battles and have entered the rooms of the third stage, if not: *Blessed is the man who fears the Lord?* [Ps. 112:1] . . . Certainly we are right in calling such a man blessed, since if he doesn't turn back he is, from what we can understand, on the secure path to his salvation."[2]

"Key Activities" in Response to God

In the third mansion, our faith has become the center of life and activity. We are typically very active in a local congregation, including regular Bible study and participation in Christian education opportunities. In Michael's case, he has even become its pastor. Our balanced life is reflected by good stewardship of time and money (possibly even tithing) and intentional acts of love and caring. We have begun to discover our spiritual gifts and to manifest the fruit of the Holy Spirit. Teresa describes our life in the third mansion: "I believe that through the goodness of God there are many of these souls in the world. They long not to offend His Majesty, even guarding themselves against venial sins; they are fond of doing Penance and setting aside periods for recollection; they spend their time well, practicing works of charity toward their neighbors and are balanced in their use of speech and dress and in the governing of their households—those who have them."[3]

"Changing Patterns of Prayer" in Communication with God

Our life of prayer has also deepened. We've discovered an ongoing reflection on the presence and activity of God, both in formal prayer times and in daily life. Teresa uses the word *recollection* in the quotation above. This is a technical term meaning a reflective recalling of God's activity in daily events. Our prayers are still mainly discursively talking to God, but times of reflective reading and meditation on Scripture have deepened our quality of prayer and deepened the level of communication and communion with God.

A typical format for prayer in the third mansion might be exemplified in the acronym ACTS. Many of us were taught, in our discipleship programs, that "balanced prayer" includes adoration, confession, thanksgiving, and supplication. We are also told that prayer is usually experienced simply as talking to God.

THIRD MANSION PRAYER THAT LEADS TO THE FOURTH

The ACTS format of prayer can become a wonderful and practical interaction with God that responds to His invitation of love.

Adoration

What does it mean to adore God? When we say we adore another person, it's not because of some character attributes, but because of our love for the person. When we come to this first step in prayer, we need to ask ourselves about the nature of our adoration: What does it feel like? What things have happened that reinforce it? We need to be honest about how we are feeling if we are to have an honest relationship. If we are not having "adoring" sentiments for God, we can say so.

Confession

This one is usually easier for us, but it takes intentionality. The prayer of Examen is a good practice, where we stop to reflect on how our day has gone and how we have responded to our relationship with Jesus. A canned list of imperfections won't bring us closer to Jesus. But an honest assessment, made in the light of God's forgiveness and grace, clears the relationship for the exchange of love.

Thanksgiving

Again, our gratitude to God needs to be genuinely expressed, in the light of what we are really feeling. It helps to begin with the things that we are, in fact, grateful for. But then our prayers of Thanksgiving need to go on to whatever laments there may be. Our gratitude to God is always lived in the context of our longing, and this always expresses what is not yet—hungering and thirsting after righteousness. If we do not express it, we lose vital communication with God.

Supplication

This is probably the easiest part of the third mansion prayer. Jesus tells us to ask and seek. He says that we don't receive because we fail to ask. Sometimes we are taught this is selfish, and we should pray only for others. But unless we are free to express our desires and turn them all to God, we can never be fully His. Jesus is our Provider and Shepherd and wants to us to come to Him alone.

Teresa tells us that, although there is a prayerful communication with God in the third mansion, we have yet to find any real spiritual joys that come purely from intimacy with God. These are to come in later mansions. Teresa says, "But I don't think He gives much spiritual delight unless sometimes in order to invite souls by the sight of what takes place in the remaining dwelling places and so that they will prepare themselves to enter them."[4]

In this increased spiritual growth, we may face a new difficulty. Teresa talks about this difficulty that often comes in the third mansion: "After these years, when it seems they have become lords of the world, at least clearly disillusioned in its regard, His Majesty will try them in some minor matters, and they will go about so disturbed and afflicted that it puzzles me and even makes me fearful. It's useless to give them advice, for since they have engaged so long in the practice of virtue they think they can teach others and that they are more justified in feeling disturbed."[5]

Once we seem to have "mastered" the discipled life, pride and presumption can become a real problem. If God does not respond in a predictable way, we may judge ourselves as faithful and God as unfaithful. We think we are suffering these things from God. Abigail's busyness, for example, is a result of her conformity to the world's belief that one is happiest when doing everything possible to fill the day. Even though her day may be filled with good things, it is not God that is driving her beyond good balance. Yet she believes she is doing everything correctly and that should be doing something more to make her feel better. I think this has happened to all of us and maybe it still does.

A Word About Ministry

Even though we have seen some ministry in each of the preceding mansions, it is in the third mansion where serving God in ministry flourishes. It is primarily here that we fully recognize our calling to follow Christ in His concern for the lost, poor, and marginalized; and the people in our families, neighborhoods, and in our church. We discover our spiritual gifts in the context of the Christian community, and we learn how to use them for the benefit of others. Because the life of faith has "stabilized" to some degree, we can begin to focus more beyond ourselves. Opportunities may range from filling ministry needs at church to short-term mission trips to the inner city or to foreign lands.

For a third mansion Christian, ministry is often focused, however, on the requests of others, as well as attempts to meet our own needs. Despite the emphasis in many churches on discovering our spiritual gifts, we often find ourselves performing ministry tasks that emerge more out of our gender or stage of life such as parenthood, or skills such as music, finance, or organization. But we find joy in knowing that we are serving Jesus and our work has some eternal significance. Working alongside Jesus, to the extent that we recognize it, deepens our relationship with God and continues the process of spiritual formation. In our interaction with others, we learn more about ourselves and look more specifically for the fruit of the Holy Spirit in our lives (cf. Gal. 5:22). Prayer for ministry, particularly when things are going badly, deepens our dependency on God.

A difficulty that we often encounter in third mansion experiences, however, is that work "for" God can too easily be equated with relationship "with" God. We can mistakenly believe that really hard work for God is the same as a really deep relationship with Him. It can be like two co-workers in an office who have developed some sense of friendship around common tasks but know nothing of the other's life outside the office.

It is not uncommon, when we experience dryness in prayer, or discouragement, that "work harder," or "do another job in the church," is the recommended therapy. Joy may come from tasks accomplished and praise received, more than from intimacy and love with God. This work orientation can cause us to focus attention on public ministry, at the expense of quality time with God; "If I'm really busy, I must be important," we may think.

"Jesus' Initiatives" to Draw Us into a Deeper Intimacy with God

While empowering our ministry, and supplying strength to live the Christian life, God is also calling us into deeper personal intimacy with Him. In times of intense prayer, God gives us a few glimpses of Himself and His love, beyond the issue being prayed about in the moment. In stress or recollection, the Lord may give a sense of peace that speaks more of His presence than of the solution to the issue (cf. Phil. 4:7).

God continuously calls us to choose between the opportunities presented by the world and discipleship to Christ, desiring His will alone. Issues of life's wounding and needed healing that have caused us significant relational difficulties, with God and others, may have been dealt with to some extent, but God continues to perform healing surgeries in our hearts, when we realize how we have been distracted away from truly following Jesus.

Teresa writes: "Humility is the ointment for our wounds because if we indeed have humility, even though there may be a time of delay, the surgeon, who is our Lord, will come to heal us."[6]

To draw us closer to Him, God creates within us a "holy dissatisfaction." One of God's significant strategies to prompt our ongoing spiritual growth, one that is often misunderstood, is to create in us a longing for more.

A wonderful illustration of what happens was depicted in our church's recent Christmas program. As the story of Mary, Joseph, innkeepers, and shepherds was acted out, an angel holding a small crown, danced unseen around the characters, inviting them to celebrate the wonderful mystery that was taking place. The characters never really saw the angel, but they would find themselves strangely distracted in its direction, until finally they were compelled to explore the manger and find the baby Jesus.

As His Holy Spirit moves imperceptibly within us, we begin to ask, "Is this all there is? Is working hard for God all there is to life with God? There must be something more." Deep inside, our hearts long for intimacy with Jesus, for the ability to rest in Him and trust in His love. More often than not, we don't recognize this deep longing but feel only its symptoms: frustration and dissatisfaction. Because our feeling is "negative," we often see it as a bad thing. Are we somehow doing the wrong thing, or is it our church that is letting us down? Misunderstanding what is going on within us and then blaming "someone" for it, we may actually become discouraged and back away from God and our Christian community. We desperately need someone to say to us, as Brother Boniface did so often for me, "Isn't that wonderful?"

"Schemes of the Enemy" to Try to Destroy Our Growth in God

As the major temptation and deception in the second mansion have diminished, the line of attack becomes subtler. Now, the primary strategy of the enemy is to keep us out of conscious contact with God, too busy working for God and balancing the demands of daily life. We are also tempted to try to serve God by simply getting "plugged in" to a church program, rather than by following the direct leading of God. Although there is nothing wrong with most church programs, they can become merely religious work. Jesus wants to lead us personally.

Two primary tactics used on us are pride and distractions. The enemy will attempt to convince us that we are really important, mature, and better than most ("After all, look at all the great work you're doing for God"). A superior attitude, the belief that we really know what is right and best, may keep us from readily seeking God for guidance, or listening for the voice of God in others. This prideful blindness ultimately sets us up for major mistakes and alienates us from other Christians, whom we may well blame for the situation. Sound familiar?

Distractions are another tactic in this season of our spiritual growth. This happens both in daily life and in prayer. In daily life, the enemy tempts us to take on too many activities and responsibilities. Too many good things are intended to keep us so busy that we get tired and frustrated. This overload also affects the quality of whatever prayer does occur. It becomes filled with concerns over everything we're not getting done well enough, yet pleading for more and more energy and time. The overcommitment often leads to confusion and frustration about why God doesn't seem to bless all the great work we're trying to do—for Him.

Along the same lines, we're also tempted to build our significance on performance. This focus on doing, of course, will always result in a fear that cripples us: the fear of failure. The devil will use this fear to paralyze us in our service to God. Jesus invites us into an ultimate significance of beloved daughters and sons; the devil tries to make us believe that simply being a worker is enough.

Pride and distractions are specifically designed to keep us from discerning God's call to seek His face and abide in Him. Two things can happen here. First we may well have been taught that faithful service to God is all there really is to the relationship, the goal of spiritual formation. Even though we may long for more, we tell ourselves to just work harder or learn more information. The other danger is that we can get comfortable in a relationship where we appear to be in control. We decide what appropriate service is, what our spiritual gifts are, and how we can protect ourselves from risk and failure. We settle for the status quo in our relationship with God out of fear that if we really abandoned ourselves in following Jesus, life would become out of control. So we get stuck in our spiritual growth. "This little room in the third mansion is good enough, thank you."

"Keys for Growth" That Help Us Cooperate with God

How is it possible for Christians in the third mansion to grow, when they are too busy to do "one more thing?" This is where a spiritual formation roadmap is most useful in showing us that there is still a wonderful adventure with Jesus ahead in the journey. As we discover that there is actually *less* work instead of more work, we can be more courageous about accepting Jesus' invitations to draw closer to Him.

Mentors and teachers are needed, to show us that we must stop relying on own effort in prayer and ministry and become more responsive to God. Teresa makes an important point relative to the need for mentoring, as we progress further: ". . . it would be a great thing for them to have—as do many persons—someone whom they could consult so as not to do their own will in anything. . . . And they shouldn't seek another of their own making, as they say—one who is so circumspect about everything; but seek out someone who is very free from illusion about the things of the world. For in order to know ourselves, it is helpful to speak with someone who already knows the world for what it is."[7]

One of the most important things you and I must learn is to be still in prayer and listen to the heart of God. God invites us to first seek Him, for His own sake and ours. In the context of that growing relationship, we can discern His present and particular direction, rather than following a routine or some proven strategy that works for someone else.

Even though the third mansion is a season of learning to follow Jesus in ministry, God is calling us to a new level of knowing Him in His love. His gentle whispers of love and the mystery of His divine light pique our curiosity and cause a restlessness within us that will eventually lead to the fourth mansion. So, for us to continue our growth, we must focus more toward relationship with God rather than simply work for Him.

FIVE JOURNALING STEPS THAT HELP US BECOME ATTENTIVE TO GOD

1. **Time and date:** In retrospect, we see that rhythms are helpful.

2. **God's recent grace:** Recollection about how we have been experiencing God may set the context for what He will do in the present prayer time.

3. **Present experience with God:** How did our prayer time go? What did God do or not do?

4. **Feelings in prayer:** What was our emotional response to our prayer time? Our subconscious may be revealing more about what was really happening.

5. **God's present grace:** In what ways was God's grace active in our time of prayer?

We need to be encouraged to begin to listen to God, both in Scripture and in prayer, to "take time" to more fully "abide in Christ," where we can learn to hear His voice and respond to the touches of His love. Prayer disciplines, such as the Ignatian Exercises and prayer retreats, that furnish extended times for reflection help us move from discursive prayer to greater degrees of meditation on Scripture and listening with the heart. The journaling discipline in the extended 19th Annotation of the Ignatian Exercises can prove a very helpful practice through the remaining mansions. James Wakefield describes a five-step journaling process for scriptural meditation that can profoundly help us begin to listen to God in prayer.[8]

Ongoing study and meditative reading of the Scriptures provide constant grounding in the truths of orthodox Christianity. Submission to accountability within the Body of Christ can also offer ongoing support and protection from self-delusion and error. Reading the Christian mystics may present insights into the deeper calls of God. *Imitation of Christ*, by Thomas à Kempis, for example, beautifully describes what it means to follow Jesus.[9]

Teresa also says that people in the third mansion need to learn detachment. She compares them to the Rich Young Ruler, who is too attached to his material wealth to follow Jesus.[10] third mansion Christians may be attached not only to their wealth but also to the security of a comfortable church life that protects them from the needs of the world—and from the awesome mystery of God.

One of the things we might admire about our third mansion season is our relatively ordered life. But Teresa says that this, in fact, can be a real danger; the order may be evidence of an attempt to use reason to control one's environment rather than trusting oneself to God.

The tragedy is that most church leaders would be delighted to have their church filled with third mansion Christians. Traditional discipleship models, in most of our churches, give little encouragement to know God more deeply and experience His love more freely, in a manner beyond the third mansion. Leadership's exhortations often have more to do with sharpening one's skills and gifts for ministry than with growing intimacy with the Trinity. But as we shall see, there is much more to life in Christ—much, much more.

Let's return to our stories of Abigail and Michael to see how they're navigating the third mansion, and observe the spiritual coaching that proved to be so helpful for their continued journeys.

Abigail

In time, Abigail became friends with the women's pastor at Seaside Community. Although Mary was some years older, Abigail had always been impressed with her deep faith and ability to listen with her heart. Mary was busy in ministry, but she just didn't seem as harried and hassled as so many others. Over lunch one day, Abigail confided, "I feel sort of stuck in my faith. I'm sorry to have to admit that Jesus seems distant and church feels more like work than worship. I feel so lukewarm." Mary smiled and responded, "If you were lukewarm, Abigail, you wouldn't be here talking to me today."

Mary went on to explain that, even though Abigail's active ministry to her family and at church was a blessing to others, it could be getting in the way of a deeper relationship with God. "God is more interested in you, Abigail, than in all that you do for Him. Maybe you need to take some time to just be with Jesus." "Are you kidding?" Abigail responded in frustration. "I'm lucky to have privacy in the bathroom. Where am I going to get more time to spend hanging out with Jesus?"

Mary helped Abigail explore her daily routine, to assess what was truly needed and what might be just giving in to demands. Abigail was able to recognize some significant spaces in her day that gave her time to pray. One space was while waiting for Philip at school. She had to drive several miles to school and then wait in a long line of cars, as teachers brought the kids out to meet their parents. Abigail decided to listen to praise music while driving, and then turn it off and just be still with God while she waited for Philip. Mary encouraged her not to bring her usual list of prayer requests, but to just talk with Jesus about whatever came to mind, and be sensitive to what Jesus might have to say. It was not long before these school drives became a highlight of the day.

Abigail and Mary met regularly to discuss these prayer times and explored how to listen to God, both in silence and in thoughts that might come. Mary suggested that this same quality of time with Jesus could also be used in her evening reading of the Bible. "Maybe you could do more than read the word—meet the Word," Mary said with a smile. Abigail realized that the real Word of God, of course, was Jesus, and He was the One her heart longed for.

Michael

Michael was not as fortunate as Abigail to find a mentor who could offer some course correction. Melissa was helpful in reining in Michael's compulsive work schedule, by encouraging (sometimes demanding) that he spend quality time with the family. With a newborn girl, Hannah, at home, everyone was tired, and Michael often felt a lose-lose tension between home and ministry.

One of his few times away from church happened at the local ministerial association meeting every month. The group would discuss church life, theology to the extent it wouldn't end in conflict, and issues that faced the town. One day, Michael interrupted. "Do you ever feel like you are on a treadmill? It seems the more I am successful in my work, the more work I have." The group launched into a discussion about delegation and the difficulties of recruiting volunteers into important ministry positions.

(Continued)

On the way home, the pastor Michael was riding with asked him, "So, after our long discussion today, how are you feeling about your ministry?" Michael was silent for several minutes and then groaned, "Tired." Several moments of silence followed, and Michael went on. "Tired describes how I am feeling about my relationship with God, too. What happened to that fire I used to have?" His friend responded, "Oh, we all get that way sometimes. There is a conference coming up on new strategies for missional churches; why don't you sign up. It'll get your fire going again!" Michael was silent the rest of the way home. Somehow, this was not the fire he knew he needed. Had he made the wrong decision about becoming a pastor? Was ministry killing his faith rather than building it? That night, he poured out his heart to Melissa and they prayed that God would show the way.

You can undoubtedly identify many years of your walk with Jesus, in the third mansion. You may feel stuck there now. You may even feel that your church has locked you within its walls, even if you're its pastor. But the truth is that Jesus, in His love for you, has allowed you to taste more and want more. As you conclude this chapter, some reflection may be helpful for you to see the road ahead.

REFLECTION

- In what ways have you learned to follow Jesus, using the gifts of the Spirit?
- Recall the teachers and mentors God has brought into your life, to show you what true discipleship is like, who encouraged you to risk actually following Jesus. Thank God for them and pray for them.
- What "holy dissatisfactions" are you dealing with right now? How do they point to the spiritual growth that God wants for you?
- Among the "keys to growth" listed earlier, which ones appear to be good next steps in your cooperation with God's work of spiritual formation within you?

CHAPTER 7

Discovering the Love of Jesus: The Fourth Mansion

So when they had finished breakfast, Jesus said to Simon Peter, "Simon, son of John, do you love Me more than these?"

—JOHN 21:15

OUR JOURNEY FROM MANSION THREE TO MANSION FOUR is not as great a jump in our spiritual life, as we described from the second to the third mansion, but a subtle transition of huge significance. Over the years, we have made visits and peeked into the mysterious rooms of Jesus' invitation to personal intimacy. Jesus has always been with us, and we have experienced His love to various degrees. Whether we were brought up in the church or became believers later in life, we learned the Gospel message that God loves us. We experienced His love in a variety of ways, mostly through answered prayer, blessings, and deliverance from distress.

But as we enter further into and stay longer in the rooms of the fourth mansion dimension of spiritual growth, God makes Himself and His love known not only in blessings but in inner feelings and awareness of His presence. Even though we have known Christ for many years, this experience of His love and person (touches, Teresa calls them) births a dramatic refocusing of our spiritual walk. Teresa uses the analogy of a developing love affair with Jesus for our spiritual development in the last four mansions. This transition could be compared to a man who attends the college dance as a place to have fun and meet people. One night, he meets a special woman who makes his heart race. He now attends the college dance for only one reason: to meet "her," to get to know her, and maybe share some time with her beyond the monthly dance. That's what happens to us in the fourth mansion. We begin to fall in love with Jesus. Let's see how this transition is happening for Michael, and then Abigail.

Michael

Michael continued to pour his life into Mission Hills Church. It was not too long before they added youth and music staff, and ministry became even more complex. Melissa became involved in children's ministry part-time, and they often kidded that a "parsonage next to the church" would make it easier. The missional nature of Mission Hills, and Michael's history and gifting, meant that many of the membership were people in recovery. Michael bragged that people came for the healing that only Jesus could give, but the needs of the people were sometimes overwhelming. He worked longer and longer hours and put the same demands on his staff. At the same time, Michael's prayer life suffered. Ministry crowded out almost everything else. For a long time, Michael rationalized his sermon preparation was really "time in the word," and his prayer list routine was "time with the Lord." But Michael was dry in his heart—dirt dry.

Returning temptations to drink and look at pornography finally got his attention. He was sober for fifteen years, and hadn't looked at anything inappropriate, even once. But now he felt seriously tempted. As much as he told the devil to take a hike, the temptations persisted and even increased. Michael knew he was in trouble.

One day Michael confided in a pastor friend in the community. Although this brother was not considered "right on" theologically by the Mission Hills denomination, Michael sensed he could trust Paul. The pastor listened for a long time and finally said, "Michael, I have experienced the same frustrations with the demands on my time, almost killing myself and my family. There's more to relationship with Jesus than martyrdom!" Michael smiled and felt understood. Paul had not judged him or told him to shape up. Paul went on: "You know, I discovered that what I needed was to spend more time with God. How do you feel about that?" Michael recalled his prayer time with Melissa and tears welled up. Paul told Michael about a retreat house in the area and suggested that he go for a couple of days with nothing but his Bible.

A few months later Michael went, grateful that Melissa encouraged him to take the time away. At first he didn't know what to do. His extrovert personality certainly wasn't cut out for time alone. Michael read Scripture and prayed a bit, but mostly slept. Then, on the last day, he sat in the chapel and poured his heart out to God. There were tears and sobs, words of anger and doubt, and finally, when Michael was exhausted, just silence. In the quiet evening of that retreat chapel, he felt God's closeness, and these words from Jesus came to his mind: "Why don't you just let me love you? Then follow me."

Michael went home confused. "Let God love me? Follow Jesus?" he mused. Of course he understood that God loved him and Jesus died on the Cross to prove it! He was *already* following Jesus. What else had he been doing all these years? And yet . . . ? Maybe he'd been following a vision or an ideal. Maybe it was approval or success that had been driving him more than the love of Jesus. All he knew now was that it was Jesus he wanted to follow, not just Jesus' principles, but Jesus Himself. But it seemed that Jesus had become distant. Ministry was so much about theology and strategy. Michael recalled the passage in Revelation to the church in Ephesus: "But I have this against you. You have lost your first love."[1] Had that happened to him? As he reflected, he realized that his love for Jesus had not really been lost; it was just underground, covered up by vision, strategy, work, and exhaustion.

Michael returned to the retreat house some weeks later. This time it was different. This time he knew exactly what to do: spend time getting to know Jesus again, learning to love Him again. Maybe he could even feel His love as well.

Michael spent several days just being attentive to his own heart and to the Lord's presence. He put his Bible down and let an inner conversation with Jesus emerge. What seemed like random thoughts would find some pattern, and Michael realized that the Lord was leading him. He noticed a little plaque on the wall of the retreat house. The words on it struck him profoundly:

Be still and know that I am God.
Be still and know.

(Continued)

Be still.
Be.

The days were sweet and Michael knew that this was somehow a turning point. He copied the saying and posted it on his wall at home. It would prove to be a guiding light for years to come.

Michael's life and ministry began to change, probably unnoticed to everyone but Melissa. She noted his new early morning prayer times, and the occasional middle of the nights when she would turn over to find him gone and kneeling silently in the corner of the bedroom. Once, when they were enjoying one of their new "date nights," Melissa asked Michael, "Honey, something special is going on. What is it?" Michael teared up and whispered, "Jesus."

The Fourth Mansion

As we venture into the fourth mansion, God begins to reveal His presence through profound touches of His love and presence. To encourage us to seek Him more fully and singularly, He may take away the affirmation we have been receiving, or the "well done good and faithful servant" we sensed as we saw the fruit of ministry in the third mansion. Although we continue life and ministry characterized by the third mansion, the Holy Spirit gives us the beginnings of new grace to "see" and "feel" God in prayer and in life.

These experiences shift our attention more toward the Giver than the gifts (even the gifts of the experiences themselves). God's love transforms our heart, as we experience a new longing for deeper intimacy with the Lord.

Scriptural foundations for our fourth mansion season of spiritual formation include those that call us to a new depth of intimacy and love with God.

> But whatever things were gain to me, those things I have counted as loss for the sake of Christ. More than that, I count all things to be loss in view of the surpassing value of knowing Christ Jesus my Lord, for whom I have suffered the loss of all things, and count them but rubbish so that I may gain Christ, and may be found in Him, not having a righteousness of my own derived from the Law,

but that which is through faith in Christ, the righteousness which comes from God on the basis of faith, that I may know Him and the power of His resurrection and the fellowship of His sufferings, being conformed to His death; in order that I may attain to the resurrection from the dead.

—Philippians 3:7–11

So when they had finished breakfast, Jesus said to Simon Peter, "Simon, son of John, do you love Me more than these?" He said to Him, "Yes, Lord; You know that I love You." He said to him, "Tend My lambs." He said to him again a second time, "Simon, son of John, do you love Me?" He said to Him, "Yes, Lord; You know that I love You." He said to him, "Shepherd My sheep." He said to him the third time, "Simon, son of John, do you love Me?" Peter was grieved because He said to him the third time, "Do you love Me?" And he said to Him, "Lord, You know all things; You know that I love You." Jesus said to him, "Tend My sheep."

—John 21:15–17

The Philippians passage is chosen because it is exemplary of the kind of passion experienced in the fourth mansion. Paul associates the perfection, which he yearns and strives for, with the *"in Christ"* phrase he uses to describe the indwelling of Christ. He employs the phrase ninety times in his letters. This passage in its context shows that this relationship is both a present reality for all believers and yet a movement of growth and passion in our relationship with God. The passage in John shows Jesus' understanding of love, from a motivational perspective. Jesus is teaching Peter that agape love for Him must be the motivation for service to Him. It is this growing passion of love for Jesus that will lead Peter, eventually, to his own cross (cf. John 21:18, 19).

Abigail

We tune in to Abigail's story about five years later. Life is pretty much the same except her kids are older, with all the adjustments that brings. She is still active in her church, although

(Continued)

her husband, Bill, has strayed somewhat away from church and from God. The pressures of work and travel and his annoyance at Abigail's "always at church" lifestyle have given her an excuse to be too busy or too tired for God. Besides, Abigail was doing just fine in maintaining a "Christian" foundation for the family, and Bill was quite sure he couldn't really keep up, much less do any better. Bill's distance from God bothered Abigail, but she reasoned that she had to just love him the way he was, and she had found that it didn't help to push.

Abigail's practice of daily time with God, on the way to pick up kids and in evening Bible study, expanded to a more focused quiet time in the mornings after Bill and the kids were on their respective ways. Abigail slowly noticed that she was guarding the morning time much more fiercely than before. When a church friend invited her to play tennis early the next morning and Abigail refused, her friend said, "Boy, you'd think that Jesus wouldn't wait until a later time." Abigail realized that she didn't want Jesus to wait for her, but that she was eager to meet with Him. Slowly she learned to put her prayer list down, do less reading, and just sense God's presence.

She also noticed a new reaction to the worship songs in church on Sunday morning. Though the sermon had been the reason she came to church, for better or worse she now found that tears would sometimes come in response to songs of devotion and love for God. Now, she began to look forward most to the worship part of the service.

Abigail had spent some years relatively satisfied, and even proud of her faith, but she now felt restless in her soul. She longed for more, without being sure what the more was. Listen to this entry from Abigail's journal, which sheds more light on what she was experiencing:

> I seem to be on some sort of spiritual roller-coaster. I don't really under-stand it, but I go from tears in worship to anger at my pastor for what seems like shallow sermons. My prayer times have been so good, but now they too are up and down. One day God is so wonderfully there, but on other days, the room seems so empty. I also find myself so frustrated with my Bible study book. I hate those platitudes and the dumb questions at the back. I just want to spend time reading the Gospels, particularly the parts where you can see Jesus in action. What a mysterious man! Why do people call Him by a title like Christ? His name is Jesus! I wonder what it would have been like to be one of His followers, back in biblical times. I don't know what to do with these feelings of frustration. If I tell my pastor, he will just feel criticized. Besides, even though I feel his sermons are light, I am not sure what I think he should say instead. I have been

saying "no" more often, and some folks misunderstand. It is just that all this stuff feels more like organizational machinery than it does loving Jesus. . . . That's it, isn't it? I am hungry for more of Jesus. Great! How does that happen?

"Your Heart's Desire" in Relationship with God

Let's return to the six categories or rooms within the fourth mansion, to enable a more in-depth description and comparison and to understand Abigail's and Michael's experiences more fully. It's possible we'll see ourselves as well.

As we journey further into the fourth mansion, we develop a divinely bestowed passion for knowing, loving, and seeking God. He has now enflamed our heart. Oswald Chambers described it this way: "Once taste God, and nothing but God will ever do again."[2] Our motivations are driven more by love than by obligation, personal gain, blessing others, or even doing the right and Godly thing. As God's beloved, we have heard the call of the Lover and we experience a hunger and thirst and attention to Jesus that we hardly knew before. Thomas Dubay says of the fourth mansion: "Key to St. Teresa's explanation of the fourth mansion is the occupation of the will with God. At the moment when this prayer is given, the soul is captive, she remarks, and I am not free to love anything but God."[3] Teresa explains that this experience begins in prayer but then transcends all of life.

"Key Activities" in Response to God

As we come to "dwell" in the fourth mansion, our relationship with God grows in such a way that the "Mary and Martha" in us begin to work together. There is an integration and balance of our active ministry and our inner life of prayer and reflection.

We actively serve Christ in the fourth mansion, but we become more selective about ministry that is well-suited, not only to our gifts but more important to Christ's calling. We learn to live more on the responsive level, drawn forward by love of God and neighbor.

As our intimacy with Jesus increases, we depend less and less on things we once thought we needed, for safety and security. We learn to depend more on God's love and the gifts of the Holy Spirit working within us. Teresa talks about the effects of our increasing awareness of Jesus in the fourth mansion: "Since its (the soul's) knowledge of God's grandeur grows, it considers itself to be more miserable. Because it has already experienced spiritual delights from God, it sees that worldly delights are like filth. It finds itself withdrawing from them little by little, and it is more master of itself for so doing. In sum, there is an improvement in all the virtues."[4]

Changing Ministry Focus

In the third mansion, ministry was motivated largely by a desire to do the right thing, help out, make a difference, bring people to Christ, and help the poor. Those motivations are still present, but to some degree our desire begins to shift toward loving God through loving others, pleasing and honoring Him. For example, Mother Teresa of Calcutta was being interviewed by a reporter who said he admired her passion for the poor. She replied that she had no passion for the poor. In response to the reporter's puzzled look, she explained that her passion was for Jesus; He has a passion for the poor, and so she served the poor.

As ministry motivation shifts, so does ministry direction. Now that we are learning to discern the heart of God in prayer, we find greater discernment about His call to service. Increasing intimacy with the Trinity also brings greater self-insight, and so we gain better understanding about specific ministry that is consistent with our own passion and calling. As we saw in our case studies, we might observe a fourth mansion believer saying no more often to requests for help at church. This may not be only because we do not feel called to the particular task, but also because we are now trying to carve out sections of time with God. Our first-order calling, discussed in Chapter Two, is taking center stage, and our second-order calling is beginning to emerge out of that center. The new experience of God's love will compel us to respond to that love through loving our neighbor in increasing measure. We experience greater commitment to service, greater compassion for others, and greater willingness to sacrifice for the sake of Jesus' love for others.

"Changing Patterns of Prayer" in Communication with God

As we've mentioned, Teresa believes that our prayer life is most diagnostic of our spiritual growth. It is prayer that changes most dramatically, as we experience these touches of God's love in the fourth mansion. We yearn for greater intimacy with God and therefore seek His presence more in prayer. Although we probably have been quite used to setting the agenda for our times with God, telling Him what to do and how to do it, the fourth mansion marks the wonderful beginning of "infused prayer," a responsive prayer where God sets the agenda.

God's desire to direct my prayer life came to me most vividly while visiting the Monastery for one of my monthly retreats. As I started a time set aside for prayer, God planted this message in my heart: "Tom, for all these years you have told Me when we would talk, what we would talk about, how I was supposed to run the universe, and you asked Me to bless what you had decided to do. Then, you would dismiss Me, when you had decided we were done. Because I love you so much, I have been willing to meet you, in your presumption, and bless your ministry. But now, I would like us to develop a new pattern. I would like to tell *you* when we are to talk, what we are to talk about, what I would like you to do, and when we are done." It was a humbling experience, but I was so grateful to realize His patience with my immaturity, and His persistence in helping me live with Him responsively.

We are called by God to be still and listen, to just "be still and know" (cf. Ps. 46:10). This "prayer of quiet" increases, as we become more interested in the "words" of the One we love than our own. In this phase of spiritual growth, God intends for contemplation to become an important part of our prayer. *Christian contemplation* is the term we use for our attentiveness and focus on God alone. It is much like meditation, where we focus on God through Scripture, the beauty of nature, or other parts of His creation. But in contemplation, we move beyond the starting point of meditation, turn our attention toward God, and simply behold Him. This infused prayer is new to us as we explore the room of prayer in the fourth mansion. Our mind finds it almost impossible to simply be still and focus on God; the mind is like an undisciplined child who can't stop talking or running around. We have to learn to become still and focus on God, letting distractions pass us by.

Our prayers now focus more on our relationship with God than on obtaining specific favors. To be sure, intercession continues, but it is now more responsive to the leading of the Holy Spirit. In *Imago Christi*, we use the term *abiding prayer* to describe this relational dimension of simply being in Christ. In the Gospel of John 15, Jesus gives us a wonderful analogy for prayer. Communication between the Vine and the branches is not about the exchange of information, but a natural, ongoing, and essential communion of life between the two.

Because we have begun to long for closeness to Jesus, we're forced to make lifestyle changes so that our prayer can become more consistent and scheduled. Our desire for extended times of prayer motivates us to plan, structure, and prioritize life more discerningly.

During this phase of my own journey, I struggled to find the right time and place to spend quality time with God. We were up early with our children, worked all day, and fell into bed exhausted after the kids were in bed. Attempts at abiding prayer during the day were abysmal failures. I could think only of the work I had yet to do. Finally, I found that the solution was to get up an hour before the kids—a sacrifice I would never have been willing to make a few years earlier. But now the pain of not being with Jesus, in a quality way, was greater than the pain of less sleep. Different patterns work for different people, but find ours we must, or we will not progress in our journey with God.

"Jesus' Initiatives" to Draw Us into a Deeper Intimacy with God

God encourages us to become more open and available to Him, by providing a gentle awareness of His loving presence, both in formal prayer and in the prayer of daily life. We experience specific "lights" or insights and realizations, both in times of silence and among the activities of work, family, and so on. God increases our subtle awareness of His presence in every aspect of life, deepening our experience of His love and delight for us. Teresa describes this new awareness by using the analogy of God as the Good Shepherd whose whistle was once unheard but is now quietly discerned, causing us to direct our focus on the Shepherd. She calls this attentiveness to God "recollection."[5]

The Desert Fathers teach that the Holy Spirit communes with our spirit in times of prayer, disclosing insights about ourselves, the world around us, and His will for us. This is spiritual communication, not intellectual. But in time, our spirit communicates to our mind what God has said. So, a while after we have been in abiding prayer, a thought or insight pops into our mind; we have this sense that it came from God. But during our prayer time, we may not have been aware that any communication was going on at all.

As we experience God's love more profoundly than before, we gain new insight into how spiritually and emotionally wounded we are and why we have such difficulty loving and being loved freely. In the new experiential safety of His love, we can dare to look more honestly at ourselves and recognize the growth yet to take place. In this growing intimacy, God performs spiritual surgery that will ultimately set us free to life fully in the love of God and love our neighbor. Our heart, the center of our being, has been distorted by sin and wounded by life experiences. In this condition, the light of God only made us turn away with feelings of guilt and shame. For this reason, God has to begin the lifelong process of recreating the heart so that we can have the freedom to receive His love fully and return it unconditionally. This transformation of the heart is both a prerequisite and an outcome of deepening intimacy with God. God foretold what He would do through the prophet Ezekiel: "Moreover, I will give you a new heart and put a new spirit within you; and I will remove the heart of stone from your flesh and give you a heart of flesh. I will put My Spirit within you and cause you to walk in My statutes, and you will be careful to observe My ordinances. You will live in the land that I gave to your forefathers; so you will be My people, and I will be your God" (Ezek. 36:26–29).

As God heals our hearts, remolding us the way we were intended to be (a heart of flesh), we learn to trust His love and forgiveness, to open ourselves freely to Him, and to discern His presence. We begin to gain the ability to see and hear at a heart level. Later in the chapter we will see examples of this surgery in the lives of Michael and Abigail.

Supernatural experiences in prayer become more common, as a result of this increased intimacy with God. As we gain the ability to remain attentive to God during our prayer times, He is able to communicate more to us. These experiences will increase significantly in the next mansions.

"Schemes of the Enemy" to Try to Destroy Our Growth in God

Distraction is a major scheme of the enemy against us, as we fall in love with Jesus. The devil attempts to keep us from recognizing God's touches, through busyness and cluttered thoughts. Specific attacks are directed against our efforts at contemplation and silence. Unsurprisingly, the same tactics are used in daily life. He attempts to keep us overwhelmed with activities and concerns, and our minds so filled with things to do that it becomes very difficult for us to listen. Faithful service in the third mansion is bad enough, but real intimacy with God is dangerous. So our enemy attempts to keep us very busy, and stuck, in the third mansion.

Shame is another line of attack against us. The devil will recall to mind every sin we have ever committed and point out the slightest sinful tendency in our everyday life ("You're not worthy to receive God's love; look at what a mess you are; Jesus may have forgiven you, but He's very disappointed. If you really loved God, you wouldn't keep messing up."). We have all experienced these thoughts, often not even knowing we were being attacked. Unfortunately, it too often works, and we back away from God's loving advances toward us.

Amid these attacks, God develops greater discernment within us, actually using the attacks to teach us. Teresa says of these attacks: "Poisonous creatures rarely enter these dwelling places. If they enter they do no harm; rather they are the occasion of gain."[6] For example, I remember complaining to Brother Boniface about temptations that I was experiencing. I had repeatedly confessed them, repented, and rebuked the devil—all to no avail. Bon asked me, "Tom, why do you think the devil is attacking you along that line?" The question stopped me and caused me to realize the inner needs whose satisfaction the enemy was trying to falsify.

Seeing the scheme, I quickly turned to Jesus to meet those inner needs, and the temptations ceased. In one case, the line of attack had to do with a woman who was upset with a decision I had made. She sent a critical email that I couldn't get out of my mind. I would even wake up at night thinking about it. In truth, the woman had not been unkind; nor was she threatening to cause trouble over it. Finally, I realized I was under attack about the situation and asked the Lord for wisdom. Why was her approval so important to me?

The Lord showed me that I had been feeling unaffirmed and insecure in general. The enemy had diagnosed my situation, but the Lord wanted to meet my need in healthy ways. That night, I spent extra time in prayer, letting His love flow over me. The next day, I sought out a Christian brother, whose affirmation was not contingent on my performance, and asked for prayer. Soon, my agitation at the woman's complaint subsided, and I was able to seek her out to hear more about her concerns. Now I was able to be more concerned about God's love for her than her approval for me. God actually uses the devil against himself, for our good and His glory.

"Keys for Growth" That Help Us Cooperate with God

Spiritual growth in the fourth mansion comes primarily through times of solitude and silence with God. Dallas Willard talks about the importance of a lifestyle that is conducive to spiritual formation: "If we have faith in Christ, we must believe that he knew how to live. We can, through faith and grace, become like Christ by practicing the types of activities he engaged in, by arranging our whole lives around activities he himself practiced in order to remain constantly at home in the fellowship of his Father."[7]

The spiritual disciplines of prayer and contemplation become vital for continued growth in the fourth mansion. Richard Foster says of this need: "The classical Disciplines of the spiritual life call us to move beyond surface living into the depths. They invite us to explore the inner caverns of the spiritual realm."[8] It is important to remember, however, that it is not the practices or disciplines that bring about our transformation; it is the work of the Holy Spirit within us. Spiritual disciplines can only give us an opportunity to be more attentive to our Lord, to love Him more intentionally. But when we come to Him in this way, He never fails to bless us.

CHANGING OUR FOCUS IN PRAYER

I remember when I first met my wife, Charlotte, also a college student at Arizona State. Our initial conversations were all about information exchange (Where do you come from? What is your major?). As the relationship developed, however, I was more interested in being with her than finding out more about her. On a date she caught me staring at her and asked what I was thinking. I responded, "I'm just enjoying looking at you." You could say that I had begun to "contemplate" her, to behold her in a special way.

This is the shift that happens in the fourth mansion, as we begin to fall in love with Jesus. We just want to behold Him; words almost get in the way. Abiding prayer is just that: focusing our attention on God alone. When we focus on God through Scripture or a cross or the beauty of nature, we call it "meditation." When we turn our attention to God alone, to "seek His face," we call this form of prayer contemplation. As we learn to simply "wait upon the Lord," we sometimes enter an inner stillness where there are no words or mental pictures, or even thoughts. We call this dimension of prayer "silence."

When we resided mostly in the third mansion, we were far too busy to waste time like this, Now, we long for the opportunity to rendezvous with God in our hearts, and just be—with Him.

The third mansion was marked by effective discipleship in ministry. Now we are called to build on that foundation and advance in relational intimacy with God. For many of us, our third mansion busy lifestyles have left us with almost no time alone with God. This "being still with God" may be difficult for active people, but the inner call of God challenges us to carve out quality prayer time—times to just *be* with God.

Unfortunately, many of us who are hungry for God have never been taught about meditation and contemplation. To the contrary, many churches have given these concepts over to Eastern religions and New Age religions, and they urge prohibition of these "abiding" forms of prayer. One of two things happens to us when we enter the fourth mansion but have no knowledge of abiding types of prayer. Either we naturally move into a more responsive and listening form of prayer (without knowing anything about contemplation or learning ways that make it easier) or we get stuck, longing for a deeper experience of God but not finding it.

Silent retreats and times away are necessary for us to learn to become more aware of God's presence. Brother Boniface used to call it "getting off the scene." A quiet and restful place to just be with God can become an opportunity to learn how to discern His subtle presence, even in the hustle and bustle of everyday life. Because I am such a driven person, it often takes me two or three days to just relax and put my to-do list away. Then I am able to begin to be attentive to God.

Journaling is another important discipline that helps us reflect on our transitions in prayer and as we record spiritual experiences, both pleasant and difficult. Because spiritual growth happens so slowly, we may not be aware that growth is happening at all. But as we review our journals, we can be amazed at what God is doing in us.

Mentors, who can help us interpret God's movements of love, are very important. The fourth mansion is a significant transition season in which we often need someone who has already been there, to help us realize what is happening.

Reading and teaching about contemplative prayer and spiritual warfare in prayer are essential. Although sermons and books and mentors can be very helpful, we must not look to others for what only God can give. If we expect the church to "bring us to Jesus," we will ultimately become frustrated and critical of church and of ourselves, for not satisfying our new spiritual hunger. The whole movement of the fourth mansion is God's desire to "infuse" us directly with His life and love. He wants to "feed" us Himself.

Ongoing reflective study of the Scriptures can offer continuous grounding in the boundaries of orthodox Christianity. Visions or insights in prayer may encourage and even excite us, but they must always be subjected to the clear teaching of Scripture. In the times of the Spanish Inquisition, in which Teresa wrote, it was particularly important that one's spiritual experiences not become the basis for theology or doctrine. The same is true of us today. The physical penalty is not so extreme, but it is equally important today for Christians to assess our subjective spiritual experience in light of the clear teaching of Scripture.

Continued reading of the Christian mystics will help to bring sources of inspiration, teaching, and encouragement. Bernard of Clairvaux, for example, opened up a whole new world for me about living fully in the love of God.[9]

Teresa is consistent in her insistence that it is not spiritual experiences that are the important indicators of growth, but love in action: "For perfection as well as its reward does not consist in spiritual delights but in greater love and in deeds done with greater justice and truth."[10]

We still need accountability within the Body of Christ, because it can supply ongoing support and protection from self-delusion and error. Spiritual direction and mentoring help us understand our new focus on Jesus, and the shift we are experiencing in prayer.

Ongoing intentionality in all these endeavors is vitally important. It may seem surprising that Teresa considers the fourth mansion as only a Second Water relationship between personal effort and divine grace. We may not be carrying buckets of water, but we are still working hard at cranking the waterwheel of grace. Now we are being called beyond the "doing" aspect of discipleship into the "being" of relationship. But the shift in focus and identity is in its early stages, and there is still considerable attention and effort required on our part. It is true that we are learning responsiveness in prayer and life, but we are only beginning.

Now that we have gained some insight into the fourth mansion, let's return to Abigail and Michael. How is this phase of their spiritual experience affecting their lives? How does God lead them on into a deeper experience of His love? Again, we find our pilgrims in a spiritual formation coaching session. We may make this sound "normal," but it is sadly true that there are few churches where we can find such resources, particularly as we enter the fourth mansion and beyond.

Abigail

Abigail's frustrations increased until she was on the verge of leaving the church. During her prayer time, her friend Mary came to mind. Abigail called her for coffee and they met the next day in the corner chairs at a cafe. Abigail poured out her heart about all that had been happening, about her disappointing prayer times, and her frustrations with her life and experience with church. Mary listened quietly, asking a few clarifying questions that led Abigail deeper into her negative spiritual assessment.

Finally, Mary looked at Abigail with a smile. "Looks like Jesus is doing some wonderful things in your life." Abigail responded immediately, "Wonderfully confusing!" Mary went on: "Don't you see what Jesus is doing? He is drawing you into His love, in a new way, and you aren't satisfied with the old fare; you want to find *Him* in what you do."

They went on to discuss many specific instances where Abigail had experienced God's amazing presence and love, as well as the times when He seemed totally absent. They discussed the areas where Abigail felt closest to God, and areas where she just couldn't relate to Him. Mary explained that Jesus comes to us in the ways that are natural to us; all we have to do is make ourselves available there. They closed their time together with this prayer, which Abigail later recorded in her journal: "Jesus, thank you so much for showing me your love. I have to admit that I don't really understand it. I mean, I do intellectually, but I haven't learned how to live in it yet. I surrender myself to you anew and ask you to help me live my life in your heart of love."

Abigail began to watch for Jesus in her daily circumstances, with new interest and excitement. To her amazement, the Lord seemed to give her hints of His presence, in all sorts of situations. One example was a ride home from school with the kids. Phillip unexpectedly looked up and said, "Mom, guess what Jesus said to me today?" "What was that?" his mother

(Continued)

replied. "I think He said that we need to love each other more at home."
"Did they teach you that in Sunday School?" Abigail asked. "No," Phillip
replied, "I thought of it on the playground."

The next morning Abigail was on her knees in her prayer closet at
home. This had become a regular custom, but today she went to God
in all earnestness about Phillip's comment the day before. "Jesus?" She
knelt in silence, attentive to her own heart and to impressions that might
come. Soon a picture emerged. She saw Bill's look as she hauled the kids
off to church, a look of loneliness and hurt she had never noticed before.
The next Sunday morning she asked Bill at breakfast, "What should we
do together today, Honey?" Bill almost choked on his eggs, and it took
Abigail some convincing that she really wanted them to spend the day as
a family, even if it meant skipping church. It took many similar "touches
of love," where Abigail surrendered her religious activities to express her
love, and God's love, to her husband. Bill knew how much these things
meant to her and ultimately was deeply touched.

It was not too many months before they were in church together as
a family. Strangely, the "shallow" sermon no longer bugged Abigail, and
she earnestly prayed that Bill would hear its message. Later the same day,
Abigail wrote in her journal:

> Oh Jesus! You are so amazing, so wonderful, so wise, so tender with me! You
> could have condemned me for my religious pride and insensitivity to Bill, but
> you showed me how to love him, by loving me. Bill and I have a long way to
> go as a couple, to really live together in your love, but I want to learn how
> to do my part, Lord. Help me to hear your tender thoughts in my heart, in
> my kids, and in every aspect of my life. I love you Jesus, my Master, my King!

In ongoing coffees with Mary, Abigail learned about abiding prayer,
where being with God is all we're after. She realized that so much of her
prayer had been trying to get something out of God, rather than loving Him.

Abigail went with a group of women to a silent retreat at a nearby
retreat house. Bill offered to stay home from work and watch the kids and
run them around. Abigail was so touched that the retreat was a success
before she ever got there. But God met her profoundly. She described the
experience to another retreatant:

> I had been sitting in silence for some time, just letting the thoughts flow
> though, but keeping my focus on God. After a while, it was if the room

became warm and bright, in an amazing way. Nothing really changed in the room really, but in me. I could "feel" the Lord's presence and His love. It was as though He was looking at me with tenderness, forgiveness, and affection. There were no words, no impressions, no instructions, just tenderness, forgiveness, and love. I will never forget that time. Why have I spent so many years not recognizing that He has been here for me in such a wonderful way? I want to learn how to make myself available to Him, to live in His love, and to share that love with my family and others the Lord brings to me.

Michael

After Michael's experience with God at the retreat house, it seemed as though he had been given a new set of eyes. Over time, he began to know himself more realistically. He saw his sinful thoughts and mixed motives, yet strangely without condemnation. Repentance changed from a gut-wrenching ordeal to a natural response to God's love.

Michael also began to see his staff differently. Instead of workers to be driven on to excellence, he saw their giftedness and how they struggle to please him. He started regular lunch times with each of them, where he intentionally opened his own heart, revealed weakness, and invited their ministry to him. "How can I pray for you?" was his constant question. Soon a mutual trust developed, as the staff saw just how serious Michael was about loving them.

The most amazing change, at least to Michael, was the even greater heart God gave him for the poor and the addicted. Michael had always said he understood these people because he had "been there." But now he really saw. He saw their hearts, their uniqueness, their aspirations, their hopes and dreams. "How can I pray for you?" was the question everyone expected. And it was no idle question.

Michael spent hours each day in prayer for every aspect of his life. Unlike his previous intercessions, there were no more long lists and detailed instructions for God. Michael simply brought each person to mind silently before the Lord, and saw the person in His light, love, and power, trusting them to Him.

It was not too long before Michael realized he was in over his head. How could he spend all this time in prayer and still do his ministry, preach, and be a good husband and father? He and Paul began to meet

(Continued)

weekly. "I need some coaching!" Michael said as he sat down at the table. Paul shared his own story of his fourth mansion journey. He recommended several books on prayer and spiritual disciplines that might help Michael learn to loosen his control and just "be" with God. Paul and Michael started a weekly spiritual formation group with a few other pastors, who were amazingly open to discovering a new way to relate to God and follow Him in ministry.

Michael returned often to the retreat house for times of silence, listening for God's heart, in Scripture, nature, and in his own heart. Because Michael was so active, sitting for long periods was really hard. Soon he discovered that some of his best abiding time came when he was running. There was something about giving his whole body to God in the run that enabled him to give his whole mind and heart as well. After one such stay at the retreat house, Michael wrote this note to Paul, his spiritual friend and mentor:

> Dear Paul:
> Today I ran with Jesus. I felt the sun and wind in my face and the dirt He created, pounding against my feet. Suddenly, I realized that I was not alone. Although I couldn't see anything or anyone, there was Someone else in the run. He was not racing me, but setting a pace that allowed me to feel as though I could run forever. I know it was Jesus! As we ran together, I could feel what it might be like to live my life in His stride, His pace, His rest, and His sprints. Paul, is such a life really possible? Is ministry or marriage like that really possible? I know your answer, Paul. Thanks. Jesus, please make it so.

REFLECTIONS

The fact that you're reading this book indicates that you're experiencing, to some degree, the fourth mansion.

- Reflect a bit on your experiences of falling in love with Jesus.
- What has God used to call you deeper? What tends to keep you from responding as you really want to?
- What do you find frightening about intimacy with God?
- How can you cooperate with what God is doing in you?

CHAPTER 8

Longing for Oneness with God: The Fifth Mansion

*. . . so that Christ may dwell in your hearts through
faith; and that you, being rooted and grounded in
love, may be able to comprehend with all the saints
what is the breadth and length and height and
depth, and to know the love of Christ which sur-
passes knowledge, that you may be filled up to all the
fullness of God.*

—EPHESIANS 3:17–19

AS YOU AND I JOURNEY IN THIS SEASON OF OUR SPIRITUAL growth,
we have stumbled headlong into the mystery and wonder of a
Love beyond expectations, a relationship with the Creator of the
Universe that seems presumptuous to even think about.

All through this transformation process, God has been revealing a greater Truth, a greater Reality, a greater Work, a greater
Life. Through the Holy Spirit's gentle "touches of love," God has
been revealing *Himself.* As our gaze is distracted from our work
and service toward these glimpses of His love and grandeur and
glory, our heart's attention begins to shift.

We are smitten by love and it is to Love we are drawn. Instead
of the urge to exert our own power to learn, understand, and

serve, we now find ourselves weak, hungry, thirsty, yearning, in love and desiring only to respond to the Love that has possessed us.

The roadmap, from here on, will use the biblical images of Bride and Bridegroom, of Lover and Beloved, to describe the overpowering desire that emerges in us to experience the fulfillment of the prayer of Jesus in John 17: union.

Abigail

Abigail sat in her living room one morning and stared out the window, reflecting. So much had happened in the last ten years. Phillip, now twenty-one, and Jason, almost nineteen, were in college. Bill had now started his own business and traveled a great deal. Ministry at church continued, but in less traditional roles. Abigail found that "listening" to other women seemed to be her primary gifting and calling.

The relationship with Mary, her spiritual formation coach, continued to deepen. After a few years, Mary began to invite Abigail to join her during coaching times with other women. Mary explained that this group was a covenant group: "We agree to pray for one another daily and keep what is said in the group to ourselves." Abigail was amazed how Mary could listen "with both ears." One day, Abigail asked Mary, "How do you do that?" "Do what?" Mary responded. "Listen to every word, said and unsaid, and at the same time hear what God wants you to say in response." "I listen with both ears," Mary replied, "one ear to the person, and the ear of my heart to Jesus. I listen to His love for that person." Abigail was silent for a long time and then asked, "Where did you learn to do that?" "In my prayer closet," Mary smiled. "As I've learned to let God love me, and give myself totally to that Love, I find I can recognize the longing for Him in others and sense Jesus heart of love for the person."

Abigail had for some years learned to spend quality time in her own prayer closet. In the busy years when her boys were younger she actually had to establish a prayer closet in her home. She converted a corner of the attic; Bill constructed walls and a door with a sign on it: "Knock Only for Emergencies." There was a window overlooking the yard, a comfortable chair, a kneeler, a small table and lamp, and an old bookshelf with a candle and a cross. It had become a holy place for Abigail to meet with God. Sometimes she would go up, only to find Bill had beat her there!

Her earlier conversation with Mary was a milestone, of sorts. The words, "As I've learned to let God love me, and give myself totally to that Love . . ." seemed to stick, creating an ever-deepening longing for intimacy in her relationship with God. It was if her heart were praying, "Holy Father, Blessed Son, Spirit of Love, I want to know and live in the fullness of your love for me in such a way that all my being loves you back. I want You to be my all-in-all."

During the ensuing years, the quality of Abigail's prayer time changed. For many years she entered prayer with some pretty definite things she wanted to say to God and hear from Him about. Now she entered her prayer closet, whether in the little attic cloister or the mobile one she carried in her heart, with a delighted expectancy. "What will my Lord want to talk to me about?" she would think. Often she would find that it was the very things she had on her heart; at other times, there were more important matters. It was also not unusual for there to be extended times of silence. Abigail found this silence had a quality of communion to it that words could only interrupt. Although it had once frustrated her, she now longed for silence. It was more than just not saying anything or thinking anything. This abiding silence was filled with His unfelt presence. Glory, Majesty, Wonder, Power, Love were the quality of the air she breathed, of the chair she sat on, of the light that streamed through the window. Just being . . . there . . . with Him . . . was more than enough. Abigail's love for God matured into a quiet adoration. Even when God seemed absent from her, she was content to wait.

Abigail was surprised that the quality of her time in the prayer closet became more and more the quality of her daily life. The same atmosphere was present when she cleaned house, shared with Bill or the boys, listened to a friend, or served meals in the Rescue Mission downtown. It was as though she could just invite others into that sacred space and be there with them and Jesus. Others felt it too, and would seek her out for talk and prayer.

Not everything about Abigail's spiritual life was easy, though. She discovered that experiencing more of God's holiness brought with it a greater realization of her own sin. Some days, it was as though God were holding up a mirror in which she could see every imperfection, every blemish, and every potential in her to betray her Lord. Even with the best of intentions toward others, she could see the presence of selfish motives. "Will they think I am Christ-like? Will they tell others how much I helped them?" Those realizations were like torture. It's one thing

(Continued)

to know you are a sinner; it's another to see it all the time. Something else that really bothered Abigail was how trivial her ministry seemed, in light of the magnificence of Jesus. He had done everything for her, loved her eternally, and she felt she was only dabbling at serving Him. There were times she fantasized about becoming a nun and spending every waking hour serving others in Jesus' name. But of course she had a family, a home to manage. She knew she served Jesus in these ways, but the word *trivial* kept coming to mind.

What nagged at her the most was the growing awareness of a subtle resistance in her heart to letting God get closer. There were times in her prayer closet when she felt God's presence and love in a way that was almost frightening. After such times, she realized, she would avoid the prayer closet and make herself busier. She knew there was some wall, some barrier that still lay between her and the One she wanted to give herself to fully. It was more than discouraging; it hurt her deeply and she wondered if it hurt Jesus deeply as well.

The Fifth Mansion

The fifth mansion is a time of transition where our focus moves even further from doing to being, from serving to loving. God is calling us to begin to live according to the High Priestly Prayer of Jesus in John 17, the call to union with God. Our one desire is for God, Himself. We want more than anything else in the world to know Him, to love Him, and to experience His love. We desire to serve Jesus by somehow sharing His suffering in the lives of others. Teresa believes that most Christians enter the fifth mansion to some extent: "And although I have said 'some,' there are indeed only a few who fail to enter this dwelling place of which I shall now speak. There are various degrees, and for that reason I say that most enter these places. But I believe that only a few will experience some of the things that I say are in this room."[1]

This statement is exemplary of Teresa's understanding that the journey is not linear. Progressing generally from the first toward the seventh mansion, we travel around within a given mansion as well as traveling back and forth between mansions. We may experience a sense of the call to unity with God in the fifth mansion, but we may not dwell there long enough to experience all the spiritual experiences God would like to give us.

It is important to note that the call to union happens in the fifth mansion while union itself does not take place fully until the seventh. Like engagement in the relationship between a woman and a man, we have totally fallen in love with Jesus and feel called to a commitment to God alone. This singly focused love and commitment are intensified in the following mansions, but it is introduced by the Holy Spirit here.

Not everything in this phase of our spiritual growth is bliss. St. John of the Cross makes a significant contribution to our understanding of the fifth, sixth, and seventh mansions by his description of difficult and "dark" times that are experienced here. He calls these times Dark Nights. These experiences may begin to some extent in the fifth mansion, but we'll save our exploration of the Dark Nights as part of the introduction to the sixth mansion.

These two biblical passages are examples of the call to union and deepening intimacy described in the fifth mansion.

> For I am convinced that neither death, nor life, nor angels, nor principalities, nor things present, nor things to come, nor powers, nor height, nor depth, nor any other created thing, will be able to separate us from the love of God, which is in Christ Jesus our Lord.
>
> —Romans 8:38–39

> I do not ask on behalf of these alone, but for those also who believe in Me through their word; that they may all be one; even as You, Father, are in Me and I in You, that they also may be in Us, . . . I in them and You in Me, that they may be perfected in unity, so that the world may know that You sent Me, and loved them, even as You have loved Me. Father, I desire that they also, whom You have given Me, be with Me where I am, so that they may see My glory which You have given Me, . . . so that the love with which You loved Me may be in them, and I in them.
>
> —John 17:20–26

The Romans passage, taken in the light of the experiences described in the fifth mansion, is reflective of both the call to the intimacy of love and the confidence in its stability. In what has been called the High Priestly Prayer, Jesus expressed His desire for this same intimacy and unity with us. It is clear that Jesus is praying to the Father for a reality that is not yet fully realized.

Michael

Running continued to be the primary way Michael experienced intimacy with God, even though he was approaching fifty and his friends kidded him that his knees would go now that he was "old." Each morning's run was a rendezvous that he looked forward to with eager anticipation. Sometimes Jesus "was there," and sometimes Michael had no sense of His presence but knew they were together. Like Abigail, Michael had once started every prayer time with his agenda, but soon he learned that the times when he ran out of things to say were the most precious. Sometimes he would get insights during the run time, but often a thought, realization, or insight could bubble to the surface later in the day with what Michael would characterize as having "the smell of sweat on it."

Ministry at church had its ups and downs. It was a hard time to be a pastor. Everyone had his own idea about what church should be like, and some were willing to fight for it. Strangely enough, these conflicts turned out to be a significant way in which God drew Michael closer. Sometimes he just couldn't wait until tomorrow's run to get recentered with Jesus. After some angry phone call, Michael would be boiling. "Who the hell do they think I am: God?" he would yell inside his head. "I can't please everybody!" After such an encounter, he would just hole up in his office or go for coffee, afraid that he would bark at a staff member.

One day, after one of these irritating encounters, Michael slipped away to the small wedding chapel at the far end of the building. He sat in silence, at first pouting, then pleading, then despairing, then just quietly looking at the cross over the altar. A workman was making repairs to a classroom near the chapel. The slow pounding of his hammer filled the room. As Michael's attention focused more and more on the cross, he could sense, almost see, the person of Jesus hanging on the cross, the nails being driven deeper and deeper through His flesh. "For you, for this, for love." There were no audible words, but there were words nevertheless, piercing words, powerful words, personal words! Almost imperceptibly Michael's anger melted away. In his mind, Jesus' eyes seemed to be pleading with him from the cross: "Don't you love Me? Can't you share this cross with Me?" Michael cried back, "I want to love you more; help me love you more!" That day, in the wedding chapel, Michael learned to sit still. Runs in the morning; stillness in the wedding chapel in the late afternoon. Both slowly took on the fragrance of adoration, worship, and love. Michael journaled some months later: "Jesus, I am willing to give up this church, my ministry, everything, if it gets in the way of loving You. I have to admit that's a scary thing to say, but loving you in and around everything else is not enough for me anymore. I've always said you are Number One; now I want to live it fully. I don't know how to do that, Jesus; please change my heart."

Michael's consistent time with Jesus began to focus his ministry. "Jesus?" was the word on his heart and mind before every encounter, every sermon preparation, every meeting. One day an elder came to report his dissatisfaction with the "modern" music that was being introduced into the worship service. Michael listened for some time and then responded, "Fred, would you come with me to a special place of mine?" Fred followed him to the other end of the church building, to the wedding chapel. "What are we doing here?" Fred questioned, annoyed. "Let's just sit here for a few minutes with Jesus," Michael responded, "and then we can talk about it again in a few days. That would really help me consider seriously what you have said." It was not too many months before every elder meeting began with a time of silence and prayer in the wedding chapel.

But there were struggles in this season of spiritual growth. The most significant struggle had to do with life at home. Even though he felt more and more in love with God, he was horrified at his uncontrolled outbursts of anger at Melissa and Hannah. Sure, he was tired and stressed sometimes, but where was this coming from, he asked himself. Although the outbursts didn't happen often, sometimes his words were cutting and harsh and the next days were spent in tearful apologies and repentance.

Their relationship was suffering, and he knew he needed counseling and some deeper level of healing. Michael felt like such a hypocrite that it was hard for him to preach on Sundays. The silence of his runs and chapel times was now replaced with cries to God for help. How could he say he loved God and act in such an ungodly way?

"Your Heart's Desire" in Relationship with God

Let's discuss the same six experiential rooms, as they apply to our journey in the fifth mansion. Our deep desire to serve Christ and a hunger for greater intimacy with God continue to intensify and have become the sole motive for our service. Because of this heightened desire to serve Christ in love, we often feel that our ability to follow Jesus is never enough; it can never fully express the depth of love that is forming. Teresa says, "Yet at the same time this person feels acutely that he cannot serve God well enough, and he is pained that there are so few men and women in the world who care much about the Lord and so many who offend Him freely and often."[2]

The fifth mansion can be a time filled with frustrations, actually caused by our spiritual growth. We begin to long for seventh mansion union, in the same way that a man and woman who have fallen in love now long to become married. This longing is difficult to put into words. At the same time we feel a deep gratitude for the gift of God and His abundant love, and a deep dissatisfaction with the depth or quality of our love for Jesus and our experience of intimacy with Him. Like all love relationships, the more we love, the more we want to show it meaningfully. It is this heightened "hunger and thirst" that pulls us forward in making ourselves available to Jesus, no matter what the cost.

"Key Activities" in Response to God

The fire of love for God drives a new effectiveness in ministry. People may tell us that they see increased zeal. Teresa says that our desire to do totally and only the will of God is the key to the experience of growing union with God. The touches of the flames of God's love (as John of the Cross would describe the experience) ignited a response of flaming love in the fourth mansion, but those flames are now powering our life of devotion and ministry.

Work has become prayer and prayer has become work, all loving God. With this deepened communication and intimacy, our responsive nature of prayer is reproduced in our life and ministry.

Rather than doing what we think Jesus might like (What would Jesus do?), we transition toward doing what Jesus is doing. We become so intuitive about the will of God that our actions can't help but continue the work Jesus is already doing in people's lives. Our "intuition" has been enlightened by the Holy Spirit's indwelling; our will is being conformed to God's. Co-orientation has developed where we have begun to be able to predict and know the thoughts and actions of God, much as a husband and wife can know what the other will do and say, after having been married many years.

The fifth mansion is a Third Water experience. God's grace is a far greater power than any effort we could exert. Using the garden analogy, we now only have to direct the flow of water from the stream to the garden through a duct. Recall that the first, second, and third mansions were like drawing water from a well and carrying it to the garden. In the fourth mansion the effort was compared to the use of a water wheel. Now, we are able to simply cooperate with the thought and movement of God. The perpetual yielding in response to God's movements within us draws us toward the experience of our own cross, "death to self." Living only to Christ invites the experience of union with God. Although the prayer experiences of the fifth mansion make death to all but God's will easier, nevertheless considerable effort is still required in crucifying the flesh.[3]

Ministry

Our ministry continues to shift in both motivation and focus. No longer do roles or giftedness determine our ministry direction, but the personal leading of the Lord. As we come to a better understanding and knowledge of ourselves, we experience a greater congruence of our true self and its expression of the love of Jesus to others.

This new congruence may appear to be a subtle change, yet it is profound. For example, you might have taught Sunday school primarily because you have patience with children or have a child that age. Now the same ministry would be undertaken only because it expresses your own deep compassion for children and God's love for them.

Because quality time with our Lover has become so important, we will continue to make lifestyle changes to make it possible. Regardless of the changes in balanced time and focus, as we experience life in this mansion we find ourselves more committed than ever to sacrificial living and investment in the Kingdom of God. Teresa says of the goal of life: "Here in our religious life the Lord asks of us only two things: love of His Majesty and love of our neighbor. The most certain sign, in my opinion, as to whether or not we are observing these two laws is whether we observe well the love of neighbor."[4]

"Changing Patterns of Prayer" in Communication with God

The responsive nature of prayer increases in the fifth mansion. Contemplation becomes the focus of prayer, and there are times of absorption and silence where distractions cease and we are able to rest in the presence of God without words, thoughts, or mental images. This absorption can last up to ten or fifteen minutes, and sometimes longer.

Teresa says of these times of union:

> There is no need here to use any technique to suspend the mind since all the faculties are asleep in this state—and truly asleep—to the things of the world and to ourselves. As a matter of fact, during this time that the union lasts the soul is left as though without its senses, for it has no power to think even if it wants to. In loving, if it does love, it doesn't understand how or what it is it loves or what it would want. In sum, it is like one who in every respect has died to the world so as to live more completely to God.[5]

Prayer has become the activity of love where the Lover sets the agenda and the Beloved responds. Not only is the will taken up in God in prayer, but also the imagination. All our attention is on God during these times of true silence. This does not mean that we no longer experience times of desert dryness in prayer, or that we don't struggle with distractions. To the contrary, there is a new level of hunger and thirst for the quality of prayer that is not satisfied much of the time.

Our prayers of intercession also shift. Instead of making long petitions, we are more apt to hold the person before the Lord, trusting Him to know our heart's desire and His best for the person.

Scripture offers insight into this level of prayer in a number of places. For example:

There will be silence before You, and praise in Zion, O God,
And to You the vow will be performed.
O You who hear prayer,
To You all men come.

—Psalm 65:1–2

Be still, and know that I am God.

—Psalm 6:10 (NKJV)

In the same way the Spirit also helps our weakness; for we do not know how to pray as we should, but the Spirit Himself intercedes for us with groanings too deep for words; and He who searches the hearts knows what the mind of the Spirit is, because He intercedes for the saints according to the will of God.

—Romans 8:26–27

We can now pray for ourselves and others in this way because we have learned that we do not have to try to control God with our words.

"Jesus' Initiatives" to Draw Us into a Deeper Intimacy with God

We've all heard the expression, "Absence makes the heart grow fonder." This truth also describes a surprising and terribly frustrating dimension of our life in the fifth mansion. We have felt times when God seemed closer than others, but now our Lover seems to just disappear on occasion. God continues to kindle the flames of love in us, but He doesn't fully show us the depth of the growing intensity of our relationship with Him. Although our heart cries out for the experience of God, He often hides Himself from clear view, causing us to have to trust Him more deeply.

An increasing awareness of our own sinfulness makes the fifth mansion a difficult time of life. God's revelation of Himself is often hidden, but He continues to shine His light on us, revealing our fallen humanity. The Dark Night of the Senses can begin during this time of growth. We become intensely aware of the temptations and impurity of all our sense experiences and perceptions. We want, more than anything, to demonstrate our love for God and please Him. But we also become aware of how impossible it seems to do it, by action or thought.

It is not uncommon for us, as we journey in the fifth mansion, to have old wounds resurface with disturbing ferocity. Part of this resurfacing may well have to do with the developmental stage of many believers whose age and life transition invite it. But God is also at work to bring new levels of healing that were not possible at earlier stages of self-awareness and faith. As we long for and experience a new level of intimacy with our Lord our old intimacy issues are touched. Our own healing increases our humility and compassion for others. Despite the times of desert and pain brought on by having to face our old wounds amidst God's apparent absence, our Lord gives us enough relief and grace to enable us to continue seeking His face.

It is easy to see, then, that the fifth mansion is a time of great paradox. Even though our intimacy with God is growing profoundly, the growth is largely hidden to us. Our very growth in love for God and passion to love Him by loving our neighbor makes us impatient with our inability to do so fully. This season of our journey is often typified, therefore, by a deep dissatisfaction with our spiritual progress. Like the second mansion, the fifth does not always feel like spiritual growth at all.

Teresa reminds us that the experience of union with God is totally the work of God. She uses the analogy of wax and seal to describe it: "For indeed the soul does no more in this union than does the wax when another impresses the seal on it."[6]

"Schemes of the Enemy" to Try to Destroy Our Growth in God

John and Teresa both teach that God allows increased attacks against us as "diagnostics" of needed healing and growth.

Teresa says that self-love is a real danger. The tactic of the enemy is that "little by little he darkens the intellect, cools the will's ardor, and makes self-love grow until in one way or another he withdraws the soul from the will of God and brings it to his own."[7]

Discouragement can be one of the greatest strategies of the enemy during the fifth mansion, with attempts to convince the believer that there is no real progress and that any Dark Night experience is, in fact, regression. The enemy can also evoke ridicule from other believers who are not aflame with love for God and do not understand either the passion or the pain associated with the fifth mansion.

The devil even attempts to use our deepening compassion for others against us. During prayer, the enemy will still attempt to distract us with thoughts of tasks to be done and the needs of others, trying to prevent times of true stillness with God. Teresa says, "Great are the wiles of the devil; to make us think we have one virtue—when we don't—he would circle hell a thousand times . . . it is in the imagination that the devil produces his wiles and deceits."[8]

But about the times of true union with God in prayer, Teresa says, "And I would dare say that if the prayer is truly that of union with God the devil cannot even enter or do any damage. His Majesty is so joined and united with the essence of the soul that the devil will not dare approach nor will even know about this secret."[9]

"Keys for Growth" That Help Us Cooperate with God

In the fifth mansion, God is touching the believer with His love and kindling a desire to live only for Him. Teresa calls this deeply committed relationship "betrothal," which will be experienced more fully in the sixth mansion. However, we must still exert intentional effort to grow, to cooperate with the work of God in us: "It must always be understood that one has to strive to go forward in the service of our Lord and in self-knowledge."[10]

Continued cooperation with God in service to others and extended times of silent communion with God are the most important practices for growth. Greater intimacy is developed as we work alongside Jesus, as He cares for His sheep and calls out to the lost. Times with God in the prayer of silence, where Spirit communicates with spirit, are just as important. We learn to intuit the heart of God in the prayer closet, without the distractions of daily life. This does not mean we must become cloistered or withdraw from society. But we desperately need intentional, consistent, and extended times of solitude and silence, where God can both minister and heal our heart, times when we can become aware of the infinite Love surrounding us.

As I have said in the prior mansions, mentors and spiritual directors can play an extremely important role in our growth process, lending a listening ear, encouragement, and help with interpretation of our experience. For example, Teresa discusses the doubt the fifth mansion believer can have in beginning to experience union in prayer: ". . . the soul remains doubtful that it was union. It doubts whether it imagined the experience; whether it was asleep; whether the experience was given by God; or whether the devil transformed himself into an angel of light."[11] We often need assistance to interpret our experiences of intense love, pain, self-insight, and the sense of God's absence when it happens. Journaling continues to be important and is particularly helpful in facilitating a mentoring relationship. As the believer gains self-knowledge in the greater intensity of God's light closer to the center of the castle, areas of woundedness and need for healing will become better known. Benjamin Groeschel, a psychologist who has written about the spiritual phases of purgation, illumination, and union, discusses this need for healing as one enters the "illuminative way," which is equivalent to the fourth through seventh mansions:

> The journey through the purgative way usually leaves an
> individual with a badly battered self-image. Often a spiritual
> traveler has a poor self-image to begin with, and although it
> is not worsened by purgation, at the end of purgation one
> appears like an infected person who has been shaved and
> deloused. The result is an antiseptic but not attractive image. . . .
> The illuminative way is usually an experience of the late
> middle life which is also the period during which an indi-
> vidual normally encountered the psychological resolution of
> opposites.[12]

READINGS FOR THE FIFTH MANSION

Augustine. *The Confessions*, Trans. Hal M. Helms, Orleans, Mass.: Paraclete Press, 1986. A classical look at the spiritual formation of one of history's greatest fathers.

Bernard of Clairvaux. *On the Song of Songs*. Cistercian Fathers Series, Kilian J. Walsh, and Irene M. Edmonds, eds. vol. 40. Spencer, Mass.: Cistercian, 1971–1980. An important work on understanding life in the love of God and responding to that love.

———. *The Love of God*. Portland, Ore.: Multnomah Press, 1983. Another great work for one who is being called into a life of love in God.

Englebert, Omer. *St. Francis of Assisi*. Ann Arbor, Mich.: Servant Books, 1965. A good introduction to the life of St. Francis as a model of one attempting to live a live totally devoted to Christ.

Guyon, Jeanne. *Experiencing the Depths of Jesus Christ*. Auburn, Maine: The Seed Sowers, 1975. This readable version of Madame Guyon's classic sparked a spiritual revival in eighteenth-century France. Those familiar with contemplative prayer will find Guyon's descriptions of the inward journey helpful as well.

Eckhart, Johannes. *Meister Eckhart: Selected Writings*. (Penguin Classics.) London: Penguin Books, 1994. Great insights into Christian mysticism.

Nouwen, Henri J. M. *Life of the Beloved*. New York: Crossroads, 1996. A devotional work focusing on a love relationship with God.

Pennington, Basil. *Centering Prayer*. New York: Image Books, 1982. A classic work on the method of contemplation. The reader may need to dismiss some references that do not fit evangelical language so as not to miss the historic and important insights.

Palmer, G.E.H., Phillip Sherrard, and Kallistos Ware, eds. *The Philokalia— The Complete Text. Translated by St. Nikodimos of the Holy Mountain & St. Makarios of Corinth*. Vol. 1–4, London/Boston: Faber and Faber, 1979–1984. The entire work is foundational for understanding the roots of the mystical life and the prayer of the heart and silence. Evagrios, in Volume 1, is particularly important in understanding infused contemplation and spiritual warfare in

(Continued)

prayer. Peter of Damascus, in Volume 2, is also very helpful in understanding personal holiness and struggles in prayer.

Russell, Norman. *The Lives of the Desert Fathers: The Historia Monachorum in Aegypto*. Kalamazoo, Mich.: Cistercian, 1980. A classic work detailing accounts of the early Desert Fathers in Northern Africa.

Seamands, David A. *Healing for Damaged Emotions*. Wheaton, Ill.: Victor Books, 1981. A helpful perspective for spiritual healing that underlies emotional issues.

Wigglesworth, Smith. *Ever Increasing Faith*. Springfield, Mo.: Gospel, 1924. The story of one of our greatest evangelists, who struggles to live the intimate life amidst the passion of bringing others to Christ.

Willard, Dallas. *Renovation of the Heart: Putting on the Character of Christ*. Colorado Springs, Colo.: NavPress, 2002. This is important for understanding the most influential writings for evangelicals in spiritual formation. Like many others, love relationship with God comes very close to becoming a by-product of a greater purpose.

Although it is possible for believers to pray for healing themselves, it is of great help to have a fellow traveler who knows how to minister healing. Groeschel says, "Spiritual direction becomes a *sine qua non* if we are to avoid dangers while attempting to advance spiritually."[13]

Spiritually forming community, although important for us along our whole journey, is essential for followers of Jesus in these responsive mansions. As fifth mansion believers, we often have few people available who can truly understand the dynamics that are being experienced in our prayer and in our life, people who have traveled ahead and can give guidance and encouragement. Communities of believers who are aware of the seven mansions and who recognize their own relative place in the journey can lend essential support. Rightly, church fellowships, both on Sunday and in small groups, must necessarily focus on pre-Christians and new Christians and those in the early mansions.

Ongoing spiritual reading of the Scriptures and the Christian mystics will offer sources of inspiration, teaching, and encouragement. "Spiritual" reading is done as an opportunity to hear from God personally rather than to learn information. After listing books by a number of classical and contemporary mystics, Richard Foster states: "These writings have been listed to help you see the excellent amount of literature at our disposal to guide us in the spiritual walk. Many others have traveled the same path and have left markers."[14]

As is true of the prior mansions, relationships within the Body of Christ bring ongoing accountability and protection from self-delusion and error. In Teresa's time, an abbot, priest, or confessor supplied the accountability relationship. In our own time, this spiritual accountability is often arranged through mutual relationships or small groups.

Teresa and John of the Cross both discuss various spiritual attitudes and practices appropriate for all the mansions, but particularly for the latter ones. Thomas Dubay summarizes these experiences as he comments on their absence in contemporary writing:

> Humility, detachment, solitude, suffering, obedience and generosity are not only often bypassed but also sometimes looked upon with a degree of disdain. These virtues are considered "negative" and hardly worthy of serious consideration by people who have "come of age." The chronological snobbery implicit in this attitude of supposed superiority over our ancestors does not merit attention, but it may be useful to point out that men and women who lack these virtues are never known for their depth of prayer.[15]

Now that we have gained some insight into the fifth mansion, let's return to Abigail and Michael to see how this phase of their spiritual experience is affecting their lives and how God leads them on into a deeper experience of His love, toward the unity for which Jesus prayed and gave His life. As before, we find our pilgrims in a spiritual formation coaching session.

Abigail

One night, Abigail had a dream. She was walking down a long winding road in the country. Far ahead she saw a church, maybe a cathedral. She was curious and walked faster as she approached.

(Continued)

The cathedral was made of huge ornate stones and had a bell tower that seemed to disappear into the bright sunlight. The wide doors on the front and beautiful gardens that surrounded the cathedral impressed Abigail, and she wondered what it was like inside and who might be there. As she approached, she spotted an old man on the front steps, just standing and looking at her.

As she started to turn from the road toward the mysterious cathedral, the old man shouted at her, "Stop! You are not welcome here!" "Please," Abigail responded, "I want to meet the pastor of this church." "You are not welcome here; you do not please the Lord of this church." Abigail woke up crying. She felt so rejected, so abandoned. The dream seemed to permeate her life for the following days and troubled her deeply. The memory of the dream continually surfaced in her prayer times; she became convinced that God was mysteriously speaking. She resolved to discuss it with Mary.

In their brief telephone conversation, Mary asked if Abigail might be willing to share her dream with the whole group and ask them to partici-pate in a time of discernment. The covenant group met at Mary's house. Abigail felt more than nervous, with some second thoughts, as the group turned to her and waited for her to share. She began, "This is probably nothing, but this dream has been troubling me for the last several weeks. I don't know what it means or what God might be saying to me in it. Maybe I just need to forget it, but I would appreciate your insights and prayers." Abigail went on to recall the dream, which, somewhat to her surprise, still existed in her mind with vivid detail.

The women listened attentively until Abigail finally said, "Well, there it is! What do you make of that?" Mary suggested the group take ten minutes for listening silence, followed by any clarifying questions. Various questions emerged about the scenes in the dream and about what was going on in Abigail's life. One person asked, "What do you think would have happened if you had been invited in?" Abigail was prayerfully quiet for some time and then responded, "As I imagined myself running up the stairs, I began to get fearful as I approached the door. I think I would have been afraid to actually go in!" Someone else observed, "Maybe the old man at the door was really you."

Abigail later sought out a Christian therapist with whom to dis-cuss her dream and explore why she might be afraid of God when He seems to get too close. The ongoing therapy sessions finally focused on a time of sexual abuse that Abigail had experienced as a youth. Even though her parents had taken her to counseling after the incident, there were still wounds that surfaced fears of intimacy and feelings of unworthiness.

Prayers of forgiveness and deep healing brought a new release for Abigail, both in her marriage and in her relationship with God. She would have said she loved God with her whole heart, but she now realized there was much more of her heart to give to God. Some months later, Abigail and Bill attended a wedding of some close friends. Abigail found herself imagining the church as the cathedral in her dream. There was a radiance flowing from the chancel that obscured everything except the groom and the cross on the altar behind him. She was the bride walking up the aisle, and Jesus was the waiting Groom. She could hear the words coming from Jesus: "I love you, Abigail. Please trust my love." A wonderful anticipation and joy filled her heart as she looked forward to the coming years when she could fully stand with her Lord before the Father, in the fullness of that love.

Michael

After several prayer times with Melissa, Michael texted Paul: "Need to talk—extra time. Can we meet—retreat center—an afternoon?" The next week Michael and Paul sat in one of the little meeting rooms as Michael poured out his heart: "I feel more screwed up than ever, Paul. I keep blowing up at home. It's like, before I know it, my thermometer shoots up and goes over the top. Before I can really feel the rage, I've already made a cutting remark or some criticism. I don't think it's just stress; things aren't all that terrible. I think I love God more than I can put into words, but my behavior sure says different! Where is this anger coming from? It's not my family's fault."

Paul asked a lot of personal questions, but Michael let him probe and trusted the Holy Spirit in him. Together, they looked at the history of Michael's anger, tracing it back into his early childhood. Michael had been the middle kid and remembered that the unwritten and even unspoken family rule for him was to "fit in and get along." There was no safe place to deal with the ordinary frustrations of growing up, of being compared to his older sister and younger brother. He realized that his early experiments with chemicals were in some way a

(Continued)

reaction to the pent-up frustration within him and the need to be his own person. There was no God to turn to in those days and no friends that were safe.

Paul suggested, "Michael, why don't we sit for a bit in silent prayer and let Jesus tell us what He wants us to do with all this?" Ten or fifteen minutes later, Michael broke the silence. "I think God is showing me that I never really dealt with my anger at my folks. I'm not sure that I realized it was there. I've held it all these years! Worst of all, Paul, I think I have projected my old family system onto my relationship with God. I know He loves me, but I've just assumed that He wants me to fit in and get along. I've never been able to express my anger toward Him, either; I just blamed myself or somebody else."

Michael later wrote in his journal:

I feel like God is somehow rewiring me. It started after my prayer time with Paul. The "light" of my unforgiveness toward my parents was soon followed by the "darkness" of my remorse. I had lived with this hidden crap all these years, and now it was clear how its stench had permeated my relationships and limited my ability to love Melissa, Hannah, anyone for that matter, and worst of all, Jesus. In my efforts to avoid conflict, I had been living as a liar, pretending to be OK with things. I couldn't even be honest with God!

That prayer with Paul felt as though a cross-shaped knife cut deep into my heart, lancing the wounds of unforgiveness that I had held for my parents. The blood that gushed out brought my forgiveness to them for not being perfect parents. Then the knife turned and brought repentance for the ways I had dishonored my parents in my heart as well as in my rebellious life. I had asked forgiveness from God and my parents during the twelve-step program years ago, but now my repentance was for the attitude of my heart more than the things I did or didn't do. As the imagery of the cross-shaped knife, doing surgery in my heart, developed, I realized that the blood that was gushing was not my own, but it was Jesus' blood! My heart prayed for forgiveness and healing and a release to live and love in truth. I asked for the courage to really be myself with God and others.

The passage from Ezekiel came to mind: "And I will take the heart of stone out of their flesh and give them a heart of flesh, that they may walk in My statutes and keep My ordinances and do them. Then they will be My people, and I shall be their God."[16] "Sweet tears. Oh, I love you Jesus! I love you with all my heart! Create within me a clean heart."[17]

REFLECTION

Can you find elements of the fifth mansion of spiritual growth that correlate with your life? Remember we said that, in any of the mansions, none of us experiences all of what is described. But as you reflect on how God is calling you on, ask yourself these questions:

- What seems to motivate your service to others?
- When you pray, do you spend more time talking or listening?
- What do you long for in your relationship with God?
- What strategy does the enemy seem to be using to cause you discouragement?

CHAPTER 9

The Long Dark Corridor: The Dark Nights of the Soul

On my bed night after night I sought him
Whom my soul loves;
I sought him but did not find him.
"I must arise now and go about the city;
In the streets and in the squares
I must seek him whom my soul loves."
I sought him but did not find him.

—SONG OF SOLOMON 3:1–2

AT THIS POINT LET'S TAKE TIME OUT IN OUR EXPLORATION of the Teresian Mansions to discuss one of the great mysteries of the Christian life: long dark corridors of our spiritual growth called the Dark Nights of the Soul. Although we all know there are times of discouragement in our spiritual journeys, it is often assumed that, as we grow spiritually, the terrain becomes more and more level and easier. Yet the lives of committed and mature women and men described in the Bible and in history—people "after God's own heart"—often experience extended times where God seemed absent and life seemed dark. These times of feeling abandoned are not just related to physical or emotional difficulty, when our prayers don't seem to be answered. They are created by God as an essential part of our pilgrimage, occurring in the more mature years of our Christian journey toward a union of love with Him. The Dark Nights, wrongly interpreted, have derailed many a maturing follower of Jesus. It's therefore important for us to understand them for our own sake and to be able to encourage our fellow travelers.

Both Teresa and John of the Cross teach about these particularly dark and difficult experiences in our relationship with God. The Dark Nights can be experienced as early as the fifth mansion, but are more typical of the sixth and the beginning of the seventh. Though the Dark Nights are significant experiences within our journey in these mansions, they are not descriptive of their essence, and trying to discuss them within the mansions themselves can be confusing. So, we'll explore them in some detail here and simply refer to them in the following sixth and seventh mansion chapters, and see examples of the way they are experienced in the lives of Michael and Abigail.

Over the years I have listened to many people who tearfully shared that things changed for the worse in their spiritual lives. They felt stuck, or even that they were backsliding. Some were relatively new or immature Christians who became focused on life's issues or snagged into sinful behavior. But others were faithful followers of Jesus who spent years in dedicated service and were known for their deep spirituality. Time after time, I would hear people say something like, "My prayer life seems to have just dried up. God just doesn't show up anymore. Where have I gone wrong?" It is possible that many of these brothers and sisters were unknowingly experiencing a Dark Night.

Why the Dark Nights?

Let's set the stage for our discussion of this difficult time in our spiritual journey by using an analogy that illustrates this long dark corridor in our spiritual journey. As with any analogy there are limits in the comparison, but let's try "boot camp" and "vision quest" and see if they will give us a feel for what God is doing in us in the Dark Nights.

Most of us are familiar with the idea of a military boot camp. It is special training that builds strength of mind and body so that the soldier-to-be is equipped to "begin" military service. Such training is necessary because these men and women have various mental and physical weaknesses that would put them at great risk in battle. To identify these weaknesses, the boot camp experience is designed first to deprive its participants of things that support their weaknesses. The recruit walks onto the boot camp base and suddenly everything changes, seemingly for the worse. Physical comforts, affirmations, access to friends and family, familiar surroundings, rest, and days off are removed. Even worse, these supports are replaced by severe challenges such as rigorous exercise, strenuous trials, unexpected dangers, fatigue, harassment, and fierce competition that seem to go on forever, with little opportunity to rest and recover. If the process is successful, weaknesses are identified and strengthened, and skills are developed for surviving and navigating the dangerous battles that lie ahead in real combat. Boot camp, then, might be compared to the first Dark Night: the Dark Night of the Senses.

The vision quest might be compared in modern military terms to Special Forces training. But it is even more than that. We find—in the histories of almost every culture—stories, legends, and rituals that represent the rite of passage for a boy to become a man, or for a man to become a warrior. The typical vision quest involves a long, dangerous journey where the would-be warrior must face physical and emotional enemies, extreme dangers, and situations that require skill and proficiency. Each culture's version of such a quest contains real and mythical deadly creatures, rivers, jungles, or deserts that must be traversed, as well as cunning enemies to be faced and overcome in accomplishing whatever feat is at the heart of the quest. Boot camp develops strength of mind and body; In a vision quest the attributes of will, patience, fortitude, and courage are tested and strengthened, and character and humility are developed.

Let's take a step further and adapt our analogies to picture "warriors of love"—followers of Jesus who have given their lives to love God with their whole heart, mind, and strength, and then love their neighbor as themselves. To know and serve Jesus in this fully committed way, they must face and overcome the enemies of sin and evil, and learn how to follow their King exactly. In the same way that a warrior must be strengthened and equipped for battle, we who would pursue the union of love with God must be stripped of the weaknesses that cannot tolerate God's holiness, and be given a transformed heart that will love and trust God fully. For those of us willing to journey onward to the heart of the Trinity, the Holy Spirit leads us into the boot camp and vision quest of these Dark Nights.

So what are these "weaknesses" that God purges in the Dark Nights? Maybe you're already saying, "Stop right there, I already know my weaknesses; I'm working on them." But the ones God addresses in the Dark Nights are subtler ones that we can entirely overlook, or that can easily be hidden in our Christian niceties. For example, spiritual pride can lurk within our hearts as we conde-scendingly compliment the pastor on his nice (but not quite fully developed, we may think) sermon. Or, we may not be aware of how good it feels to receive compliments, or how something seems missing when they don't come. These secret sins and attachments can go unnoticed because no one else sees what is in our hearts.

Yes, we've made progress. In becoming Christians, we discov-ered that only God can truly satisfy us, and over the years we've come to experience wonderful joy and fulfillment from our com-munion with God. But it is the nature of our fallen sinfulness to rely on ourselves and the pleasures of this world for meaning and fulfillment. We underestimate the depth of our dependence on this world, our distrust of God's goodness, and the brokenness our human nature. God sees it all but loves us too much to let us remain there.

God calls us to go further than simply enjoying His love: to love and depend on Him alone, abandoning our dependencies on the counterfeits of the world. Ultimately, He will not share our affections and reliance with anything else; He wants us exclusively for Himself. We see His desire for this single focused relationship in the first Commandment: "You shall have no other gods before Me. You shall not make for yourself an idol, or any likeness of what is in heaven above or on the earth beneath or in the water under the earth. You shall not worship them or serve them; for I, the LORD your God, am a jealous God" (Exod. 20:3–5).

You and I might quickly say that we don't even believe in other gods, much less worship them, but we know that our sin dynamic runs deep. We find that our fundamental needs for love, affirmation, identity, and security are connected to people, places, possessions, and accomplishments. This connection has become so much a part of us that we may not realize the attachments are even there. However, when one of them lets us down, we're hurt and angry. We quickly run to God for comfort but then return to our "dependencies" without even realizing it. If we are ever to fully experience oneness with God, He has to reveal our other gods to us so that we can let them go. We must also learn to live with Him in the single-mindedness of faith, rather than the pleasures even of spiritual experiences. This is what God does for us in the Dark Nights.

Thomas Dubay introduces his discussion of the Dark Nights, which he calls "fire in the nights," with these words: "But this assumption (that the practice of prayer and virtues discussed above are adequate for growth) could only arise from an inadequate grasp of the boundless perfection of God on the one hand and the extent of our woundedness on the other. Until the Lord beams inwardly the searching light of advancing prayer and discloses this to us, we have little or no idea of the vast number of unredeemed clingings that still need to be burned away in us."[1]

To understand these "dark" boot camp and vision quest experiences, we'll turn to John of the Cross, the writer who has been most explicit about the Dark Nights.[2] He describes two distinct nights: Dark Night of the Senses and Dark Night of the Spirit. Let's discuss each one in turn. John introduces the Dark Nights through a commentary on his poem, "One Dark Night."[3] St. John of the Cross was considered the poet laureate of his time. Though people loved his poetry as lyrics of love, John was really describing deep spiritual truths about our journey with God. The first two stanzas represent the two Dark Nights of the Soul. We'll introduce the poem here, with the first two stanzas, and then explore its meaning in our discussion of the Dark Nights.

1. One dark night,
   Fired with love's urgent longings
   —Ah, the sheer grace!—
   I went out unseen,
   My house being all stilled;

2. In darkness, and secure,
   By the secret ladder, disguised,
   —Ah, the sheer grace!—
   In darkness and concealment,
   My house being all stilled;

Dark Night of the Senses

Imagine a mother holding her soon-to-be toddler. For more than a year she has held her baby, nursed her, and cared for her every need. Mommy's closeness has brought security and safety. But as Mother senses that her child is ready, she puts her down on the floor, maybe holding on to a table, and then walks away. The baby feels abandoned and starts to cry, but the mother knows better than to come running. She waits and calls her little one to step out and dare to walk, to grow into her next phase of life.

It is this analogy that John of the Cross uses to describe a similar time in our journey with God. For some years, we enjoyed meeting with God in prayer and meditation. As we studied Scripture, the Holy Spirit brought new insights into the nature of God and His love. As we poured out our hearts in prayer, we received glimpses of God in our minds, and our feelings were warmed with joy, peace, and love. Good Christian friends, inspiring sermons, and enthralling worship seemed to bring us into the very presence of God.

But suddenly, to our dismay, all these experiences of God, received through our senses of thought, emotion, touch, sight, and sound, simply stopped. Our meditation on Scripture became dull and insights disappeared. Prayers seemed to bounce off the ceiling. In fact, God just seemed to have gone; none of our "senses" now experienced Him. It was as though one minute we were walking comfortably with God and then someone suddenly turned off our spiritual headlights and we found ourselves totally in the dark. All the metaphors we once used to describe our experience with God seemed to reverse. Rivers, wells, and oases dried up. Lights and fires went out. Whispers were silenced. That inner presence was gone. We felt abandoned and, despite our cries for help God did not return. The boot camp has begun.

With our senses stumbling in the darkness, we frantically look around for what went wrong. Intellectually, we know that God has not left us, but there must be something causing this distance from God. We return with renewed energy to the spiritual disciplines that used to make us feel close to God, but to no avail. We may repent of some unconfessed sin or associate the darkness with some aspect of our lives that is not going the way we want it to go. But something has definitely changed, apparently for the worse.

We might think that this lack of experience of God should makes us apathetic or turn us to things that would make us feel better, but in fact our hunger and thirst for God only increase. Instead of losing interest, we seek God all the more intensely. But all our desires and longings cannot control this long dark corridor through which we are journeying. God alone controls the duration of His apparent hiddenness and will "return" only when we can take no more or we have grown as He desired.

Even though we have all had experiences of feeling distant from God, the Dark Night of the Senses is *a particular experience with identifiable symptoms*, described by John of the Cross. Although not every person necessarily experiences all these symptoms, we can get a good feel for this painful time by looking at the characteristics he describes:[4]

- The Dark Night of the Senses usually comes after a season of consistent and satisfying meditative prayer, and we have been experiencing some detachment from old dependencies on worldly things.
- In the darkness, we no longer derive real satisfaction or consolation from spiritual practices or from other people.
- The darkness does not have any apparent causes; it is not the result of depression or newly committed sins or imperfections.[5]
- We feel as though we are not serving God well, but backsliding in our faith, and we become concerned about failing God.
- We experience a powerlessness to meditate on God's Word and to make use of our imagination to relate to the truths of

Scripture. God doesn't seem to speak to us through our analysis and synthesis of the ideas in the text. Prayer may well feel like a waste of time.

- In the midst of our spiritual dryness and the absence of God's consolations, a "dark light" shines that brings us even greater pain. As this dark light shines on us, we gain a greater awareness of our own sinful nature and the extent to which every thought and action is tainted with self.
- We find ourselves deeply grieved over our sinful nature and the sins of others.
- In the light of our greater self-knowledge, we find ourselves humbler and more patient with the struggles of others.
- The Dark Night season often feels even emptier by the absence of qualified spiritual direction to help interpret what is happening, or worse, by bad advice from others.
- Whether the Dark Night time is relatively short or extends for years, it is terribly painful, like that endured by a lover separated from her beloved.

Each person experiences the Dark Night of the Senses in unique ways. My own taste may serve as an illustration. I had probably experienced "touches" of this night here and there over the years following my initial visits to Holy Trinity Abbey, this boot camp experience hit me full-on about fifteen years later. I had left the Lutheran pastorate to join Church Resource Ministries (CRM) and to found *Imago Christi*.[6] It was a particularly busy season of raising financial support for this new missionary role, working on a doctor of ministry degree in spiritual formation at George Fox Evangelical Seminary, and traveling around the world meeting with CRM missionaries.

At first, I attributed the change in my prayer life to the busy schedule and to fatigue. I continued to get up most mornings for my hour with God, but it now felt like just a long hour of sitting there, rather than spending time with God. In earlier days, the hour would seem to almost fly by; now I found myself looking at my watch every ten minutes, wondering when it would be over. I was teaching others about centering prayer; my own prayer experiences seemed empty.

As this dryness persisted, I became more and more aware of my own thoughts and actions. There was no "light" in prayer; now every thought and action seemed to light up, exposing my sin. I was horrified to actually see that everything I did or even thought was, in some way, associated with my sinful nature. It was like having someone next to me all the time, constantly pointing out my faults and mistakes, objectively, without condemnation. It didn't feel as though God was doing it; my sins were simply apparent. They were apparent not only to me but, it seemed, to all of heaven. It was like being naked on a downtown street.

I remember a very vivid example. I told Charlotte that I loved her. But as the words came out of my mouth, I could almost see the P.S. that was attached in my heart: "I need you to show me how much you love me, too. I need to be really important to you so I can feel important to myself." There are too many more examples I could share.

At first I assumed that it was the devil trying to load me with guilt and shame, but when my resisting and "putting on the full armor of God" did not turn the awful light off, I realized that it wasn't the enemy. Then I tried repenting for what I thought might be a narcissistic self-preoccupation. But the dark light continued to shine with searing intensity. It is one thing to know that you are a sinner, and to have it show up now and then, but to live 24/7 in this awareness is torturous. At one point, I compared it to being at a nice party and continually smelling dog poop that turned out to be on my shoes. No one else commented, but I knew that I reeked.

Some months later, I visited the monastery and talked with Brother Boniface about my wretched condition. "Isn't that wonderful!" he responded. "Don't you see how God has blessed you by letting you see the truth?" "You mean I'm not being punished?" I asked. "Oh no, it's God's love illuminating your heart. He loves the real you, Tom, not the person you wish you were. If you look for His love there, you will miss it. We can't really know God's love for us until we know the one He loves." He paused, and then smiled. "The Dark Night is a good thing, you know."

Well, it sure didn't feel like a good thing, but I was so relieved to know that it was something that God was doing rather than my backsliding. Even so, the dark light did not let up for many more months. Finally, I came to accept it as God's grace to me. Rather than cringing from the revealing light that left me feeling naked and smelly, I leaned into it.

> For I know my transgressions,
> And my sin is ever before me.
> Against You, You only, I have sinned
> And done what is evil in Your sight,
> So that You are justified when You speak
> And blameless when You judge.
> Let the bones which You have broken rejoice.
> Create in me a clean heart, O God,
> And renew a steadfast spirit within me.
>
> —Psalm 51:3, 8–10

I embraced anew the truth that Jesus died for me. My sin is no trivial thing. Jesus needed to die for me. His cross is still the central place of our relationship. This new heightened awareness of my sin eventually brought an increased awareness of God's grace. Instead of fussing and complaining about God's experiential absence in my daily life, I became grateful that He was just there—unseen, unfelt, but there.

Now with these descriptions of some of the symptoms of the Dark Night of the Senses, let's look at what John of the Cross says is actually happening in our hearts and how this results in spiritual growth. For a more detailed discussion, review the pages noted in *The Collected Works of John of the Cross*. But for our understanding of this phase of our spiritual journey, I'll just compile a summary.

John says that God begins to actually shift how He feeds our hearts. Even though He once nourished us (by His word, love, and presence) through our human senses, He begins now to give us that same food, instead, in our spirit. Jesus speaks many times of this "food" by which God nourishes us. One instance was recorded while Jesus traveled in Samaria. After He visited with a woman at a well in Jericho, the disciples came up and asked Him if He was hungry. His response was surprising: "But He [Jesus] said to them, 'I have food to eat that you do not know about.' So the disciples were saying to one another, 'No one brought Him anything to eat, did he?' Jesus said to them, 'My food is to do the will of Him who sent Me and to accomplish His work' " (John 4:32–35).

In a number of other passages, Jesus teaches about the food that nourishes our souls.

> Do not work for the food which perishes, but for the food which endures to eternal life, which the Son of Man will give to you, for on Him the Father, God, has set His seal.
>
> —JOHN 6:27

> Jesus then said to them, "Truly, truly, I say to you, it is not Moses who has given you the bread out of heaven, but it is My Father who gives you the true bread out of heaven. For the bread of God is that which comes down out of heaven, and gives life to the world." Then they said to Him, "Lord, always give us this bread." Jesus said to them, "I am the bread of life; he who comes to Me will not hunger, and he who believes in Me will never thirst."
>
> —JOHN 6:32–36

> For My flesh is true food, and My blood is true drink. He who eats My flesh and drinks My blood abides in Me, and I in him. As the living Father sent Me, and I live because of the Father, so he who eats Me, he also will live because of Me. This is the bread which came down out of heaven; not as the fathers ate and died; he who eats this bread will live forever.
>
> —JOHN 6:55–58

> I am the vine; you are the branches. If a man remains in Me and I in him, he will bear much fruit; apart from Me you can do nothing.
>
> —JOHN 15:5

Apostles Paul and Peter use this analogy of food to describe stages in our spiritual growth and the way the Lord works with us.

> And I, brethren, could not speak to you as to spiritual men, but as to men of flesh, as to infants in Christ. I gave you milk to drink, not solid food; for you were not yet able to receive it.
>
> —1 CORINTHIANS 3:1–2

> For everyone who partakes only of milk is not accustomed to the
> word of righteousness, for he is an infant. But solid food is for
> the mature, who because of practice have their senses trained to
> discern good and evil.
>
> —HEBREWS 5:12–14

> Like newborn babies, crave pure spiritual milk, so that by it you
> may grow up in your salvation, now that you have tasted that the
> Lord is good.
>
> —1 PETER 2:2–3 (NIV)

John of the Cross tells us that this change in the way the Lord
feeds us is so difficult for us because we don't understand what's
happening. It feels as though we are not being fed at all. John
says: "At the time of the aridities of this sensory night, God makes
the exchange we mentioned by withdrawing the soul from the
life of the senses and placing it in that of the spirit—that is, He
brings it from meditation to contemplation—where the soul no
longer has the power to work or meditate with its faculties on the
things of God."[7]

John is talking about more than our experience of prayer
here. In meditation, we use our own faculties to relate to God,
but in contemplation God relates to us in the spirit, beyond
thoughts, words, and pictures. So, like the baby who needs to
learn to walk by letting go of what she can control, or the soldier
who must depend solely on every instruction of his superior, we
must learn to trust God's word in our hearts in ways that we cannot discern or understand.

Scripture makes reference to the pain we feel during this
purifying time as well as the need for perseverance of raw faith.
David says, for example: "When my heart was embittered and
I was pierced within, then I was senseless and ignorant; I was like
a beast before You. Nevertheless I am continually with You; You
have taken hold of my right hand. With Your counsel You will
guide me, and afterward receive me to glory" (Ps. 73:21–24).

As we persevere, we learn not to rely on our "sensual" experience of God, but to look for Him in new and hidden ways—in
our hearts. How can God be found when all we experience is our

own sinfulness? We look deep into our own hearts and ask ourselves, "Do you believe that Jesus is here and that He loves you?"
Everything seems to say otherwise, but you realize you can answer
the question in only one way: "I believe; help my unbelief"
(Mark 9:24). Our hearts have been captivated by His love, and
we are helpless to deny it. At the same time, we learn not to rely
on the emotional satisfactions that come from the world, because
they obviously can't fulfill the void we feel within us. In a new
way, we are gaining detachment from the "cares of the world"
and relying more and more on God alone—unfelt and unseen.
Though we may long for the emotional experience of His love,
we must finally say to Him, "You, Lord, are enough."

But one of the greatest benefits of this Dark Night of the
Senses, says John, is "the knowledge of self and of one's own misery."[8] In the apparent absence of God's light, we see with vivid
awareness the reality of our own nature. Because we cannot "look
at God," we look at ourselves. We become more aware than ever
of our need and our proclivity to look to others and to things
to fill our basic desires. With the power of God's secret spiritual
feeding that is going on in the heart, we see how far our lives are
from the majestic holiness of our God. In this awful knowledge,
we become even more deeply aware of our desperate condition
apart from the Cross of Christ and the forgiveness and grace that
is ours in Him alone. We long even more for that warm sense of
His love and presence. But a great work is going on in us. True
humility is birthed in ways we have never experienced before,
and the dangers of spiritual pride are reduced. John says: "Aware
of his own dryness and wretchedness, the thought of his being
more advanced than others does not even occur in its first movements, as it did before; on the contrary, he realizes that others
are better."[9]

In the Dark Night of the Senses, our growing love for God,
and for those God loves, can prompt deep grief over the condition of the lives of others and the world. Maybe worst of all is the
pain caused because we have been so touched by the love of God
and so enflamed with love for Him that it is almost intolerable to
live in this body of sin and in this world of corruption. We become
intensely aware of duality, mixed motives, and inability to live
a truly holy life as an expression of love for God. This may well

be the experience of the apostle Paul, described in Romans 7, which concludes: "Who will deliver me from the body of this death?" (Rom. 7:24).

In the Dark Night of the Senses, our hearts long to experience the new fruit described in Galatians 5:16–22, renouncing the deeds of the flesh and embracing, even clinging to, the fruits of the Spirit. Though we may not have been outwardly practicing the fleshly deeds listed there, we are aware that they have been hidden in our heart. It becomes our deepest prayer that the Lord will "create a new heart within me."[10]

So what do we do if we find ourselves in the Dark Night of the Senses? John encourages us not to try to regain our experience of God by harder effort at what used to work. We are to wait on the Lord in faith, trusting His goodness and tenderness. He encourages us to deepen our practice of silence in prayer, simply allowing God to be with us, for His sake, not for what we can receive from Him. Oswald Chambers shares the same insight: " 'Be still and know that I am God' (Ps. 46:10). Are you in the dark just now in your circumstances, or in your life with God? Then remain quiet. If you open your mouth in the dark, you will talk in the wrong mood: darkness is the time to listen."[11]

In due time, the Lord will lift the darkness and allow us to see what He has been doing. Although this purifying night may return, we can receive it with gratitude and confidence, if we understand what is happening. Some of the worst pain of the Dark Nights is the fear that can accompany them. We are afraid we will not experience our Beloved again. Now we can wait, knowing that this trial is truly an expression of His love. John says that most dedicated believers experience this night to some extent, but few pass beyond it. He blames the lack of perseverance and poor spiritual direction.[12] But John tells us that the suffering of the Dark Night of the Senses is light compared to the one that is to come.

Before we proceed to discuss the second Dark Night, we want to point out the blessed "intermission" that occurs. John of the Cross says the Dark Nights do not come back-to-back. Once we have completed the Dark Night of the Senses, we usually enjoy a long period of consolation in which we are able to commune with God in contemplation. No longer dependent on the experiences of the senses to affirm God's presence or to know His love, we are freer to abandon ourselves to experience Him spiritually and to rejoice in deepening intimacy with Him. John says, "This was great happiness and a sheer grace for me, because through the annihilation and calming of my faculties, passions, appetites, and affections, by which my experience and satisfaction in God was base, I went out from my human operation and way of acting to God's operation way of acting."[13]

John goes on to say that we are now able to relate to God more from our newly created divine nature than from our "old self," the way we had before.[14] We no longer need meditation as a doorway to contemplation and silence; we can go more directly to a relationship of spiritual delight.

However, there still remain many weaknesses and hindrances in our soul that inhibit our ability to experience full union with God. There is still, within our spirit, a natural dullness that we all contract through sin. Our hearts are easily distracted and inattentive to God's presence with us. Taking advantage of this spiritual dullness, the devil may even attempt to trick us into believing in false visions and prophecies, in an attempt to fill us with presumption and pride. Therefore, even though the delights of deepening relationship with God in the sixth mansion continue, we may also experience brief times of dryness in prayer and inner conflicts, as a foreshadowing of the more intense Dark Night of the Spirit that is to come. Our "spiritual senses" have been strengthened and purified; the spirit must also be released from all its propensities to trust in anything but God alone. The vision quest aspect of our spiritual journey to union with God in love lies ahead, if we are willing and able.

The Dark Night of the Spirit

The Dark Night of the Spirit is aimed at the very roots of our sin. In this Dark Night, God seems to withdraw in an even more profound way. Dubay explains that "the person is further divested of merely human ways in memory, imagination, intellect and will. Cozy feelings in prayer are gone, and one feels left high and dry, suspended between heaven and earth."[15] Even though we may have experienced tastes of the "third heaven" in our sixth mansion experiences, and we know, with assurance, that we truly live and move in God and His Kingdom, all spiritual (much less sensual) awareness of God is taken away.[16] Our soul is darkened.

All the while, the light of God is flooding us, yet unperceived. All we feel is dislocation and discomfort. John says that the Dark Night of the Spirit can feel like divine rejection, so vivid that the soul feels as though it is in hell. He also likens what God does to a mother who has breastfed her child but then puts bitter herbs on her breasts to enable the child to grow up. We no longer feel delight in God. Again there are no other explanations or apparent causes for this darkness apart from God's action. We are forced to live in the darkness and rely totally on faith. Although God is present and active, we have no perception of His guidance and no experience of delight in prayer. Despite this darkness, our hearts and minds remain set on nothing but God, in knowing and serving Him in love.

Teresa does not use the term "dark night," but she describes it: "The Lord, it seems, gives the devil license so that the soul might be tried and even be made to think it is rejected by God. Many are the things that war against it with an interior oppression so keen and unbearable that I don't know what to compare this experience to if not to the oppression of those that suffer hell, for no consolation is allowed in the midst of this tempest."[17]

John of the Cross is much more descriptive of the difficulties of this second Dark Night: "In this night both the sensory and spiritual parts are despoiled of all its apprehensions and delights, and the soul is made to walk in dark and pure faith, which is proper and adequate means to divine union. . . . He leaves the intellect in darkness, the will in aridity, the memory in emptiness, and the affections in supreme affliction, bitterness, and anguish, by depriving the soul of the feeling and satisfaction it previously obtained from spiritual blessings."[18]

John says that the gold of the soul is purified so that it may eventually experience union with God in the purity of love.

We have learned that we cannot return to the old ways of experiencing God through Scripture meditation, techniques of centering prayer, and the like. We must continue to simply be with God in silence—and now darkness—unfelt, unseen, unperceived. Because we have come to love God so profoundly,

His perceived absence is also profoundly painful. We had once experienced satisfactions to our hunger and thirst, comfort for our afflictions, and visions for our spiritual poverty; now we feel left in the misery of our human condition. Now as lost sheep, we feel left to wander the barren rocks and flee from the lurking wolf, unaware of the strength that is being given to us by the powerful light of His love.

But the very fire that purges us also gives new life in our deepest soul. Dubay explains the experience as "a cutting away, a removal of the roots of spiritual maladies, and a separation from the egocentrism that wounds us."[19] John of the Cross says of it: "The very fire of love which afterwards is united with the soul, glorifying it, is that which previously assails it by purging it."[20] In the fire of this darkness, spiritual pride and presumption are stripped away. Any illusions that we can find God, meet, or connect with Him are suffocated by our useless attempts. There remain only two alternatives: give up or persevere. Long since, the first has ceased to be an option.

We may not give up, but we can wander in frustration and anguish if we don't know what is happening to us. In the midst of this confusion, we can become like a ship lost in the foggy doldrums of a sea that has no direction or means of escape. We may blame God for the lack of wind or blame ourselves for being rudderless, but either way we feel abandoned. It is so critical that we make ourselves available for one another, to listen to the other with our hearts as well as our ears, sensitive to give the word of encouragement that our brothers and sisters long to hear. But God will not leave us in the Dark Night longer than we can persevere or learn.

John believes that if the Dark Night is to truly have its effect, it must last for some years, no matter how intense it may be. He says, however, that for brief intervals we may be allowed to perceive some of the light that is being poured out on us, so that we may experience the new freedom and spaciousness to love and be loved by God. But then the darkness returns and perseverance in love becomes our single focus. Our quest, to return to that analogy, changes from our own spiritual growth to oneness with God Himself. He alone is our destiny, our goal.

John of the Cross insists that these Dark Nights are not optional; nor may they be avoided if we are to grow in relationship to God, beyond a certain point. Modern writers such as Gerald May, a prominent Christian psychologist; and Thomas Dubay, a noted writer about John and Teresa, agree.[21] Neither can they be induced by us; the Dark Nights are produced only by God when He knows we are ready: "Until a soul is placed by God in the passive purgation of the dark night, which we shall soon explain, it cannot purify itself completely from these imperfections nor from the others. . . . No matter how much an individual does through his own efforts, he cannot actively purify himself enough to be disposed in the least degree for the divine union of the perfection of love. God must take over and purge him in that fire that is dark for him."[22]

Kavanaugh and Rodriguez, in their introduction to the *Collected Works of John of the Cross*, explain why it is so important for John to write about the Dark Nights:

> But his deepest concern was for those who in their spiritual life were suffering. The needs of souls undergoing interior trials prompted him to write *The Ascent of Mount Carmel* and *The Dark Night*. If his vehement portrayal of the afflictions of the dark night proves frightening to some, it is only because he wished to describe these sufferings in their most intense form and thereby exclude no one. Everyone could then take comfort in the thought that no matter how severe the purifications, it is still the work of God's gentle hand, clearing away the debris of inordinate affection and making room for the divine light.[23]

The Dark Nights may be an intense experience of Jesus' teaching: "Blessed are those who hunger and thirst for righteousness, for they will be satisfied" and "Blessed are those who have been persecuted for the sake of righteousness, for theirs is the kingdom of heaven" (Matt. 5:6, 10). Many Christians are unaware that these times of deep hunger, thirst, suffering, and persecution for the sake of righteousness are great gifts; they interpret them as backsliding and failure. But in fact, when God sees that we have the desire and potential to join with Him in Trinitarian love, He designs for us both the boot camp and then the vision quest that will transform us into warriors of love. Remember, however, that no two of us will experience the Dark Nights in exactly the same way. Our Lord's work of purification is uniquely tailored to produce within each of us the beautiful person we were created to be.

Now, with some greater understanding of these Dark Night experiences, let's return again to the poem of John of the Cross, *The Dark Night*, and see if we can discern his deeper meaning.[24]

1. One dark night,
   Fired with love's urgent longings
   —Ah, the sheer grace!—
   I went out unseen,
   My house being now all stilled;

2. In darkness and secure,
   By the secret ladder, disguised,
   —Ah, the sheer grace!—
   The darkness and concealment,
   My house being now all stilled;

3. On that glad night,
   In secret, for no one saw me,
   Nor did I look at anything,
   With no other light or guide
   Than the one that burned in my heart;

4. This guided me
   More surely than the light of noon
   To where He waited for me
   —Him I knew so well—
   In a place where no else appeared.

5. O guiding night!
   O night more lovely than the dawn!
   O night that has united
   The Lover with His beloved,
   Transforming the beloved in her Lover,

6. Upon my flowering breast
   Which I kept wholly for Him alone,

There He lay sleeping,
And I caressing Him
There in a breeze from the fanning cedars.

7. When the breeze blew from the turret
Parting His hair,
He wounded my neck
With His gentle hand,
Suspending all my senses.

8. I abandoned and forgot myself,
Laying my face on my Beloved;
All things ceased; I went out from myself,
Leaving my cares
Forgotten among the lilies.

Blessed are those who are chosen for this journey of purification, for in tribulation they will find infinite Love. Watch for Dark Night experiences in the lives of Michael and Abigail in the chapters to come.

REFLECTION

Remember that the Dark Nights come in the midst of significant maturity. We have experienced times of desolation all along, but this heart surgery is a distinct work of God. Consider these questions:

- In what ways might you have you experienced tastes of the Dark Nights?
- How do you feel about the possibility that they may be lying in wait, to bless you in the years to come?
- Do you want union with God enough to wish for the Dark Nights?
- Have you come to desire purity of heart as an expression of your love for God rather than as a condition of His acceptance?
- How might you let God strengthen you today so that you can persevere if, someday, He hides Himself from you?

CHAPTER 10

The Passion of God's Love: The Sixth Mansion

One thing I have asked from the LORD, that I shall seek: That I may dwell in the house of the LORD all the days of my life, to behold the beauty of the LORD and to meditate in His temple.

—PSALM 27:4–6

IT'S BEEN A LONG JOURNEY. YEARS AGO, WE WERE DRAWN by the light of Christ into the castle of His love, as we first received Him as Lord and Savior, and the freedom that only His forgiveness and grace can bring dawned within our souls. It was the first mansion.

We survived the battle of the kingdoms in our hearts, clinging with outstretched hands to God's firm grasp, as we said *yes*, again and again, amidst the flood of choices that opposed our commitment to follow Jesus. This was the second mansion.

Finding our place in the family of God, we learned of His Spirit's gifting and discovered the joy of serving Jesus in our daily lives. All the while, God used our circumstances to invite us into the heart transformation that would allow us to know and love Him more deeply. We were confronted, time and again, with the realization that we could follow Him no further with the crippling handicaps of sin and the enemy's constant manipulations. Time and time again, we surrendered in repentance to His pruning and love. In the family of God's love, the church, we found our new identity and destiny: a child of the Most High. We were in the third mansion.

As the years passed, we continued to follow Jesus. In mountaintop worship and on the plains of service, our focus strangely shifted. Like flickers of light or fire, His glance, His smile, His compassion, His love, began to capture our attention. The familiar Jesus/Leader became more and more the beckoning, mysterious Captivator of our hearts. The old chorus "There's something about that Name" expressed the inner pull on our hearts that half excited and half frightened us. Jesus. Who is He, really? Information about Him had once sufficed, but now it was Jesus Himself that we craved. Once, a sight or two of His miracles would leave us spellbound for months; now, we wanted only Him. In fact, the miracles, when they happened, made us only hungrier and thirstier to sit at His feet, listen to His heart, and know His love. Jesus, and His love, became the treasure for which we longed. And so, we explored the fourth mansion.

Subtly, we realized that our hearts would no longer settle for occasional rendezvous with God and the "first place" we had so magnanimously given Him on the throne of our activates. Somehow the tables had to be turned. Instead of having Jesus live as part of *our* lives, we had to discover how to live as part of His. We were grateful for the gentle place He took within us, but we now sought the King of Kings and the Lord of Lords in *His* throne room.

We developed the audacity to see ourselves as His beloved. Lamb, child, follower, apprentice, son, daughter, all had been at one time adequate self-understandings. Now our hearts longed to know Him as His bride. We saw that when we visited the fifth mansion this longing increased. His light and love both drew us closer and purified us to be able to behold His beauty more completely. The thoughts of oneness with God once whispered to us from the silences of our prayer times; now they consumed us and we longed to be fully His. We were ready to let go of all that the world offers, shed the significances we had accumulated, and live for Him alone. We wanted to be able to join the apostle

John in his relationship as the "disciple who Jesus loves," and we explored the rooms of the fifth mansion.

Now, our exploration into the sixth mansion will bring us face to face with the grandeur of our King, but it will also show us how far we have to go to fully become the beautiful beings He created us to be. We will taste what it is like to behold His glory and yet know, more vividly than ever, the darkness left within us. His love will become a radical call to love others unconditionally, in the truth of His holiness. We shall long to be formed into the image of Christ, into His likeness, and become caught up in the whirlwind of the Trinity's love. In the sixth mansion, we will become like a bride, fully betrothed, yet not knowing the day of her wedding.

Let's look again into the lives of Michael, and Abigail, to catch a glimpse of how they are experiencing this mysterious venture toward the Union that their hearts have come to crave.

Michael

Now in his late fifties, Michael is still pastoring Mission Hills Church. The congregation has continued to grow as the "recovery church" in the community, and many have come to know the Lord and His healing power there. Michael's sermons and preaching style have changed significantly, in the years following the healing prayer with Paul about suppressed childhood anger. A new joy and openness to live in the love of Jesus set him free to powerfully proclaim the absolute love of God and to expect in others the kind of total response that Love invited. Freedom in God's love allowed Michael to be himself, both in the pulpit and in personal relationships. The combination of his transparency and vulnerability to his own brokenness, and his gregarious fun-filled nature, enabled God to use him powerfully.

Although running had now become "power walking," Michael continued his twofold rhythm of daily prayer. Whether walking or sitting in the wedding chapel, prayer became filled with the presence of Jesus. Times of reflection on the Word, followed by silence and attentiveness, brought a new dimension to Michael's relationship with His Lord. Even though he enjoyed many years of knowing Jesus as friend, guide, and savior, his attention slowly began to change to the Father part of God. When Michael

(Continued)

tried to focus on Jesus, he would find himself following the Lord's loving gaze toward the Father. He was amazed that his old "father" stereotypes of judgment and sternness were not at all like the loving grace-filled Person he sensed in and around him. Contemplation of God's holiness, majesty, beauty, and power began to permeate his times of prayer. On one occasion, he was on a power prayer walk and was so overcome with the wonder of God that he knelt down and then fell on his face in worship. A passerby almost called 911!

Michael continued to return regularly to extended solitude. In addition to trips to the monastery, he would go camping alone, to those secret places where the Lord had met him. This excerpt from a letter to Paul, his old spiritual coach, illustrates the profound nature of some of these experiences alone with God.

> I was hiking at about seven thousand feet and came upon a high mountain meadow, rimmed with trees. A small dazzling blue lake formed the headwaters of the roaring river below. I sat for an hour or so in the warm sunshine, taking in the beauty and praising the Lord who created it all—today just for me. As I stooped over to drink from the lake, the flickering sunlight on the water brightened and seemed to fill the air as well. Soon, the whole meadow was filled with moving, swirling living light. I fell to my knees and stared into the light. There seemed to be people in the light. I couldn't really see them, only a hint of their shape and movement. Finally only one shape seemed present in the light and it approached me. I knew who it was because of the way my heart responded. I loved that Person in the light! I profoundly loved and adored that Person! I would have gladly died to reach out and touch Him! I knew it was the Lord. No words were spoken, no thoughts came—only a great peace and joy! There were earlier days when I would have been sure I was experiencing the altitude or dehydration, but that day, I knew He had shown Himself to me in a special way, maybe to strengthen my faith for times to come. I lay still upon the rocks for another hour before my knees had the strength for the hike down.

Michael's faith was strengthened and prayer now permeated his life in a new way. He had always been confused by the passage, "Pray without ceasing," but now he understood its meaning.[1] He told his spiritual formation group, "I am discovering that prayer is not something you do; it is how you live in communion with the Father."

Michael's vision did turn out to be a preparation for very difficult and confusing times to come. Some months later, without warning, his spiritual life seemed to just dry up. Once, he couldn't wait to get time to walk or sit alone in prayer. Now he would plan it and later realize he had become distracted until there was no more time. The prayer times he did have seemed empty and fruitless—no more visions, no more sweet presence, no more silence. Instead, his mind was always racing and his prayers just seemed to disappear into nothingness. Michael talked to Melissa about his frustration, wondering what he was doing wrong or why God might be punishing him. Melissa suggested that maybe he was overstressed and needed to seek out a counselor. He didn't think a counselor would understand, but he shared his struggle with his formation group, who prayed for him. Nothing helped. He wrote in his journal the extent of his pain.

> Jesus, Father, Holy Spirit, where are you? I have looked for you in all our secret places only to find myself alone. I wait for the sense of your presence in my prayers and in my preaching, but it feels like I am just on my own. Why can't I receive the inspirations that you so freely gave? Father, I know that I am a sinner, but I am not aware that I have rebelled against you in some new way. This desert is almost more than I can bear!

Michael's greatest fear was that he would never experience God again. He knew that he just had to "wait upon the Lord," but how long? Could he survive? Would his ministry survive?

The Sixth Mansion

Remember that the divisions between the last three mansions are less distinct than for the earlier mansions, and this is particularly true of the fifth and sixth. The sixth mansion is marked by deeper experiences of God's transforming love. We fully enter a "fallen in love" phase in our relationship with God that produces both great joy (when we are experiencing it) and great pain (when it is suddenly gone again). In the sixth mansion, God shows what it means to live fully "in Christ."[2] Through spiritual experiences, Jesus heals our hearts so we can live more fully in the mystery of God, in the unseen as well as the seen.

Although in the fifth mansion we were largely unaware of significant spiritual growth, we now realize a wonderful change has taken place. In the sixth mansion, we intensely long to live with God alone, sense His presence constantly, and serve Him in utter responsiveness and obedience. This desire was created in the fifth mansion, but it is more fully experienced here. Therefore the differences between the fifth and sixth mansions are a matter of degree. Teresa speaks of this increasing love and commitment in her introduction to the sixth mansion: ". . . where the soul is now wounded with love for its Spouse and strives for more opportunities to be alone and, in conformity with its state, to rid itself of everything that can be an obstacle to this solitude. That . . . meeting left such an impression that the soul's whole desire is to enjoy it again. . . . Now it is fully determined to take no other spouse."[3]

Prayer becomes an intense experience of the fire and passion of God's love for us and our love for Him. In contrast, however, the dark nights are also experienced where there is virtually no sensation of God's presence. But even with the presence of the dark nights, the sixth mansion is characterized by a deep longing for God and a "counting as loss" those things that don't facilitate greater intimacy and devotion (cf. Phil. 3:8). Betrothal, in biblical times, was much more than engagement. It was a complete commitment to marriage that provided time for love to mature and develop. Yet complete union, consummated sexually, did not happen until marriage. This is the analogy that Teresa used to describe the sixth mansion, in which the passion and depth of love for God is ablaze and we long to be fully consumed by the fire of His love.

Scriptures that best describe the sixth mansion are ones that speak of total commitment and love for God. Here are two examples.

> One thing I have asked from the LORD, that I shall seek: That I may dwell in the house of the LORD all the days of my life, to behold the beauty of the LORD and to meditate in His temple. For in the day of trouble He will conceal me in His tabernacle; In the secret place of His tent He will hide me; He will lift me up on a rock. And now my head will be lifted up above my enemies around me, And I will offer in His tent sacrifices with shouts of joy; I will sing, yes, I will sing praises to the LORD.
>
> —PSALM 27:4–6

> But whatever things were gain to me, those things I have counted as loss for the sake of Christ. More than that, I count all things to be loss in view of the surpassing value of knowing Christ Jesus my Lord, for whom I have suffered the loss of all things, and count

them but rubbish so that I may gain Christ, and may be found in Him, not having a righteousness of my own derived from the Law, but that which is through faith in Christ, the righteousness which comes from God on the basis of faith, that I may know Him and the power of His resurrection and the fellowship of His sufferings, being conformed to His death; in order that I may attain to the resurrection from the dead.

—PHILIPPIANS 3:7–11

The passage in the Psalms puts words to the kind of longing and passion that Teresa describes for the sixth mansion. David expresses this longing not only in terms of the physical Temple or Tabernacle but in terms of the intimacy of being hidden in God, gazing upon the Beloved, not to analyze or even praise Him but to exult in and be fed by the glory and greatness of His beauty. The apostle Paul, in the Philippians passage, describes the radical devotion to Christ and rejection of physical or social security that is typical in the sixth mansion. These passages are also reflective of the fourth mansion because they reflect the same zeal for intimacy with God. In the fourth mansion the fire is lit, and in the sixth mansion it is in full flame.

Abigail

We join Abigail fourteen years later, at sixty-two. Her sons, Phillip and Jason, are married, and Abigail is delighted to be a grandmother. Abigail and Bill have moved from Laguna Beach to the Chicago area because of a job change for Bill, now contemplating retirement and time for them to travel together. They have found a new church, a small one this time, where they feel more a part of community life. Abigail returned to work for several years, to help with college expenses for the boys, but is now "retired." She continues to coach and disciple women she meets from her church.

Three changes have been important to Abigail's spiritual growth during this season. One is a new compassion for the poor. It was birthed in her annual trip to Haiti to minister with a team from her church. St. James had a sister-church relationship with a small Baptist church in southern Haiti, and Abigail became a regular part of the team that went

(Continued)

annually. She was profoundly struck by the shining faith of the members of the little Haitian church, despite their dark poverty. Her journal speaks about her first visit and the impact it made on her life.

> We drove into the village by overland jeep, fording several rivers to get there. As we finally pulled up to the church, it seemed the whole church came out to meet us with singing and warm greetings. To my surprise, most of the people were dressed nicely. Later, I saw the shacks they lived in and realized they only had one good set of clothes, and that was secondhand. The first night we were there, I sat up all night in prayer. My heart was so burdened by the Voodoo that permeated the whole culture, the governmental corruption that kept these people locked in poverty, and the amazing courage of this little church to boldly proclaim Jesus. Early in the morning, I heard Jesus say to me, "There is more need here than you can fill, Abigail. You are to watch for three women that I will point out to you. Love them with My love and I will produce great fruit." The next day, three women came up to me, and with a translator, shared a dream they'd all had the night before. A Light told them to find me at the church and that I would help them. My first inclination was to see how I could tend to their poverty, hygiene, or child rearing, but I remembered the dream and told them that I wanted to get to know them. Within a few days, they began to teach me Creole and I taught them English. It was amazing how we could communicate, even before we learned to understand bits of each other's language. Those relationships began my journey into the world of all kinds of poverty, and I'm realizing why Jesus called the physically and spiritually poor "blessed." Jesus, may I come to you always in the humility of my own poverty and may I bring with me those you have laid upon my heart?

The three women began to teach the Bible to other women in the Haitian church, and a new wave of love for Jesus began to flow.

Back home, Abigail learned to simplify her life so she could relate more to the people whose lives were simple, out of necessity. Many of her collectables went to the kids or the church thrift store. Social events were minimized so she and Bill could spend at least one evening a week at the local Rescue Mission, where they served hot meals and listened to sad stories. It was not long before a group of women would regularly gather at a table with Abigail for a coffee party, to listen to a short Scripture, discuss its meaning for them, and then pray together. The homeless ladies were amazed at Abigail's prayers. It felt as though Jesus was sitting right at the table and she was simply relaying His thoughts about their conversation. Each prayer was accompanied by a warm touch and a blessing.

Abigail often commented that she felt closer to her Lord with those women or with her threesome in Haiti than almost anywhere else.

Another shift in Abigail's spiritual life had to do with her personal spiritual community, and it was a really hard transition at first. She had left Mary, her spiritual formation coach, behind in Laguna Beach and had not found anyone in Chicago. So, she decided to form a spiritual formation community, a small group of women who were maturing in their faith and wanted mutual support in a deepening relationship with Jesus. At first it was difficult to share things with the group that she once shared only with Mary. But her courage and vulnerability drew out the other women, and soon it was a safe place for all of them. They met together every month and shared a portion of their journal that represented a significant encounter with God or a special need for prayer. What distinguished this group from many small support groups was their use of silence. After one of the group members would share, they would be silent for about five minutes, to listen to their own hearts and to Jesus, before they responded. When it was time to pray, they would lay hands on the person who had shared and pray silently. Abigail taught them that the prayer of the Holy Spirit within them was often all that was needed.[4] The truth of the admonition was obvious from the deep blessings that were experienced following those times of prayer. There were many answers to prayers never verbalized but later apparent. It was not unusual for a member to report the next week that she had become particularly sensitive to a person or situation around them for no seeming reason, only to find out later that there was a real need for prayer. The Holy Spirit was praying in them for the right thing, even though their minds at first didn't realize it.

The third shift for Abigail was her personal prayer life. Silent adoration of God filled most of her time in her prayer closet. Often a half hour or more would pass without her realizing it. Even her intercessions were usually wordless. She would simply hold the person in her mind before the Lord, trusting His love, wisdom, mercy, and power. She genuinely believed that the same Love enfolding her also enfolded the person she prayed for, even if the person couldn't feel it. It was not uncommon for her friends to come up to her later, tell her of some blessing, and say she must have prayed for it. Abigail would respond, "No, I didn't ask God for that; it must just be His love for you."

Abigail's relationship with Jesus could well be called a "love affair." She knew God had always loved her and she had learned to love Him

(Continued)

many years ago, but now there was a mutuality to it that was new and exciting. It was as though the King of Glory would step down from His throne, take her by the hand, and lead her for a walk through the garden of her soul. There were times when she could almost see or feel a heavenly garden where she knew she would wander with the Lord fully only after death. Sometimes these "walks" were absolute ecstasy and the radiant love she felt from the Lord would fill her consciousness for days. At other times, and sometimes for days or even months, she would sit in her prayer closet seemingly alone; it felt as if God were totally absent. Of course, she knew God never really left her, but the feeling of His "absence" left her lonely, sometimes to the point of agony. She had thought it hard when Bill was gone for weeks on business, but it was nothing to this. Abigail learned that God sometimes uses "Dark Nights" to teach us not to depend on our feelings but to trust in Him absolutely. So she would wait and trust that one day soon she would sense His face close to hers and become lost in His love again. Bill could sense these painful times for Abigail and would occasionally say, "Honey, He won't seem gone for long, you know." She would smile, sometimes with a tear, and nod. "Someday, we will be able to enjoy Him forever!"

Let's take a deeper look at our experience of the sixth mansion, from the perspective of the same six aspects of our life with God that we have used before. This more objective look will permit greater clarity about this amazing season of our journey and enable us to compare it with the other mansions.

"Your Heart's Desire" in Relationship with God

As we experience deep union with God, our will becomes fully occupied with God. We want to understand His intention and follow Him in every circumstance. We have become so completely dependent on God that we are no longer attached to created things. This doesn't mean we don't care about things or people, but we value them only when they are part of our love and obedience to God. We no longer need people or things in the same way we once did. God alone gives us our identity, significance, security, and approval. Our souls are on fire with love for God.

In this season, we also can experience the extreme depths of the Dark Night of the Senses mentioned earlier. By this time, our will is continuously absorbed in God, but our imagination and memory are not. They can still roam and have yet to be brought into full unity with God. In the light of our new knowledge of the holiness of God, these wandering thoughts can give us real consternation.

"Key Activities" in Response to God

In the sixth mansion, we continue to advance in God-enteredness and devotion to living the specifics of the Gospel message in everyday circumstances. We have come to realize that every aspect of life contains the presence and will of God, and therefore the opportunity to experience Him. Issues of personal significance dim in the increasing light of the ultimate significance of our Lover and His grand design for all creation. We feel joy in serving Him in the simplest of tasks, in humility and obedience. Greater ability to know the mind of the Lord enables us to live more responsively to His movements.

Like the other characteristics of these latter mansions, the change here is in degree. In the fifth mansion, we might have had a vague sense of God's will, but now we see it more clearly and respond more naturally. Because of the intensity of love for God and the awareness of His love for us, we develop a constant inner joy in all we do, a joy that transcends our emotions.

THE GROWING DIMENSIONS OF SILENCE

Spiritual silence is one of the great mysteries of prayer, as we grow in deepening intimacy with God.

In the fourth mansion, silence is a surprising relief from the need for words or thoughts, a chance to just be with God.

In the fifth mansion, silence takes on a whole new dimension of communication. Silence becomes much more than the absence of words or thoughts—the "presence" of God communicating directly in

(Continued)

our heart. In this silence, God is re-creating our heart in such a way that we become comfortable with His abiding presence within us.

In the sixth mansion, silence includes an even more profound experience of God. Not only can we remain still and commune with the Trinity within our heart, but we are sometimes drawn "outside" ourselves into the heavenly presence of God, in His transcendent (everywhere present) nature. In this unseen silence that is beyond us, God continues the heart re-creation process so that we become able to abide with Him beyond ourselves and the fixed time-space reality that we have always known.

In the seventh mansion, we experience full union with God the Father, God the Son, and God the Holy Spirit.

Difficulties also come in this season of our journey; not everyone understands what is happening in us. Teresa mentions that people may begin to gossip, saying we are trying to be holier than others. We may also get criticism from pastors and teachers who don't really understand why we no longer jump to every request at church. She says that praise can also be a trial because it can focus us on ourselves rather than on God. But even these difficulties are used by God to bless us. As we grow, "blame does not intimidate the soul but strengthens it . . . it acquires a special and very tender love for its persecutors."[5] Difficulties can also come from the distractions of various physical ailments (both Teresa and John suffered significantly from illness), but instead of complaining the way we used to we now see them as a way to "share the sufferings of Christ" (cf.1 Pet. 4:13).

"Changing Patterns of Prayer" in Communication with God

Even though we still experience an ebb and flow in the intensity of communion with God, prayer has definitely become an experiential time. Contemplation has deepened to the point that God is able to communicate beyond the limits of the senses and of language. In the fourth mansion, we learned that to know God we needed to "listen" to Him in prayer, more than talk to Him.

In the fifth mansion, we learned to focus our attention on God alone in a way that allowed prayer to become a simple abiding in Christ. Now, this silent abiding—the contemplation of God alone—has become the very nature of our prayer life. In this wonderful "silence," we may experience ecstasy, rapture, locutions, transport, and flight of the spirit.

These terms were certainly new to me as I began reading about spiritual experiences in prayer. Maybe they are new to you as well. Let me explain briefly what they mean. *Ecstasy* is an experience of intense joy. The term *rapture* has been used historically for the experience of being so absorbed in the wonder of God that we are unaware of our surroundings. *Locutions* are experiences of hearing audible words from God. *Transport* refers to the sense of being somewhere else and experiencing that reality; it can be either a visionary experience or a physical one (cf. Acts 8:39–40). *Flight of the spirit* refers to experiences of heavenly places, as the apostles Paul and John describe (cf. Col. 2:12; Rev. 4:1). These experiences can be unnerving and even frightening. Teresa warns us to be constantly vigilant against the schemes of the enemy and the tricks of the mind. She gives three tests to ensure that the experiences are from God, explaining them in great depth. Here's a summary statement: "[Concerning words from God] The first and truest is the power and authority they bear, for locutions from God effect what they say. . . . The second sign is the great quiet left in the soul, the devout and peaceful recollection, the readiness to engage in the praises of God. . . . The third sign is that these words remain in the memory for a very long time, and some are never forgotten, as are those we listen to here on earth—I mean those we hear from men."[6]

Her extended discussions are very helpful for a person touching the sixth mansion or the spiritual director who is coaching such a person.[7]

"Jesus' Initiatives" to Draw Us into a Deeper Intimacy with God

Teresa and John of the Cross describe occasions where the communication of God's love is so powerful but fleeting that it feels like "wounds of love." Teresa describes the experience: "I was thinking now that it is as though, from this fire enkindled in the brazier that is my God, a spark leapt forth and so struck the soul that the flaming fire was felt by it. And since the spark was not enough to set the soul on fire, and the fire is so delightful, the soul is left with pain . . . but just as the fire is about to start, the spark goes out and the soul is left with the desire to suffer again that loving pain the spark causes."[8]

John describes it this way: "The touch of this divine love and fire so dries up the spirit and so enkindles the soul's longings to slake its thirst for this love that a person will go over these longings in his mind a thousand times and pine for God in a thousand ways. David expresses this state very well in a psalm: *My soul thirsts for You; in how many ways does my flesh long for You* [Ps. 62:2], that is in its desires."[9]

As we are enveloped in the radiant light of God's love, there is unimaginable joy, wonder, fulfillment, and life. However, when these times subside, there is a corresponding feeling of emptiness and awareness of the darkness of this life, and how truly dark is the mirror in which we see God. Through these deep impressions of His love, God continues to call us to live as His beloved. But this hunger and thirst is painful in its yearning.

In the light of His amazing holiness and love, we see even more clearly our own sinful nature. We realize that beyond the particular "sins" of commission or omission there resides within us the sinful tendency toward selfishness that taints all our thoughts and actions. Our brokenness and woundedness is ever before us, and at times it feels almost unbearable: "Our great God wants us to know our own misery and that He is king; and this is very important for what lies ahead. . . . This suffering comes so that the one may enter the seventh dwelling place."[10] This statement can apply to the Dark Nights, but it is also descriptive of these wounds of love where Jesus at once fills us with His presence and then is gone again, as quickly as He came.

"Schemes of the Enemy" to Try to Destroy Our Growth in God

Like the fifth mansion, spiritual warfare in the sixth mansion is encountered primarily in the Dark Nights. Here the enemy attempts to accuse and prick us into thinking that it is through some error that this awareness of sin or absence of God is happening. Conversely, the enemy may try to induce us to think that God is unjust and unloving to allow such an experience. It is also clear from Teresa's discussion of the tests for legitimate mystical experiences that the devil attempts to counterfeit these experiences and lead us astray. Even apart from the dark nights, discouragement is always a line of attack. We must discern, resist, and persevere.

"Keys for Growth" That Help Us Cooperate with God

Spiritual growth takes place in the sixth mansion as we increasingly respond to God's initiatives. We now live with God in a Fourth Water time, when our transformation happens almost entirely through the initiative and grace of God. Using Teresa's analogy of watering the garden of our soul, we no longer work at our spiritual growth, as we once did as though carrying buckets of water, turning the crank of a water wheel, or moving a duct to direct the water of God's grace. Now our growth is watered entirely by God's initiative and power, like a bubbling spring or gentle rain. The Holy Spirit moves the process along according to His will and timing. We continue to cooperate with God through obedience in service and in prayer, to discern the movement of God in the surrounding situations, and to participate as He leads. Therefore, ministry becomes more focused and sometimes less structured so that we are free to move "with the wind of the Holy Spirit."[11]

Similarly, we recognize the need for life to become less cluttered with busyness and be more balanced. Times for extended prayer and reflection are essential for this discerning process, because the intellect (thought life and will) and memories have not become completely absorbed in God.

Mentors are still helpful, maybe more so than ever before. But because there are fewer Christians at these depths of spiritual formation, capable mentors are harder to find. Nevertheless, the right spiritual director can be very helpful. After discussing the tests for locutions, Teresa says, "But the certainty shouldn't be so strong . . . without the opinion of a learned and prudent confessor and servant of God. . . . His Majesty wants the soul to consult in this way."[12] Because prophecy must be submitted to the other prophets of the church (cf. 1 Cor. 4:32), the believer's experiences in prayer need the solid and objective assessments of mature believers who can help us interpret those experiences. We need encouragement to persevere and maintain balance against the constant threat of discouragement. Journaling continues to be a helpful discipline, particularly as we attempt to remember spiritual experiences and look to God for confirmation and insight. Spiritual reading of the Scriptures is an ongoing opportunity to hear from God personally. Continued reading of the Christian mystics, particularly Teresa of Avila, John of the Cross, and Bernard of Clairvaux, will help to furnish sources of inspiration, teaching, and encouragement. Supportive community, where we are understood and affirmed, helps us navigate these unfamiliar waters and keeps us centered and grounded in the Body of Christ. Close spiritual friendships, with one or more who understand what we are experiencing, can be a wonderful blessing. Though it may seem as if there is no one out there, God always provides. More often than not, we must look.

Spiritual experiences in prayer and in daily life launch us into a deeper reality of being "in" the world, but not "of" it. This becomes clearer to us as we experience being in the Kingdom for brief times. Someday, this duality will become comfortable, but for now it is exhilarating, frightening, and confusing. Michael and Abigail are navigating these amazing waters. Let's eavesdrop again on experiences that will prove significant in their ongoing journey into the heart of God.

Michael

Michael continued to be frustrated by the dryness of his prayer life and the seeming absence of God. It was particularly frustrating in light of his earlier amazing experiences with God. His daily prayer routine continued, but nothing seemed to happen. He heard about a monastery in the mountains not too far from their home and decided that he had to get away, really seek the heart of God, and find out what he was doing wrong. He made his reservations, and right after service on Sunday he headed into the mountains to find St. Stephen's Abbey. The drive up was beautiful and soothing. Michael was somehow expectant that he would meet God in a new way, but he was cautious not to try to make things happen. He had learned years ago that God wouldn't let Himself be manipulated into doing what Michael wanted.

He checked into his room, unpacked his clothes for the week's stay, and asked to speak to the Guest Master. Father Patrick was a warm, easygoing monk with a twinkle in his blue eyes. He had entered the monastery after the Second World War and hadn't left St. Stephen's since. Years of the rhythm of prayer, worship, and work, combined with visits with hundreds of men like Michael, birthed a wisdom that permeated everything about him. As they talked, Father Pat too seemed expectant about Michael's visit and what God would do during the times of worship, Scripture meditation, and silence. They made an appointment for the next day to meet in the garden.

He met Father Pat in the manicured garden in the center of the monastery at the appointed time. The bright flowers cast a sweet fragrance and the old fountain's trickles sounded like a distant melody. The garden seemed like a perfect place to quench the terrible thirst Michael had been feeling. They sat on a stone bench in the warm sunlight, bathed by the fresh mountain air. After the old monk prayed for their time together, Michael shared about his journey with Jesus and his current frustration with the sudden disappearance of the dreams and visions that had once made His love affair with God so very real. Father Pat looked into Michael's eyes and asked, "What do you want God to do?" Michael thought for a long time. Finally, with tears streaming down His face, he said to his new friend, "I want God to hold me, to touch me, to tell me that He loves me. I know this sounds crazy, but I want to actually feel God touch me; I want to know His love in the depths of my heart."

Father Pat sat silently for a long time. Finally he responded, "What you want, Michael, is what God wants for you too. But you've described what you long for in human terms, physically, like what might happen between you and your wife or best friend. God is Spirit, Michael, and He wants you to experience Him as He really is, not just through your human senses." "But I don't know how to do that," Michael moaned, shaking his head. "Precisely!" Father Pat was now on his feet pacing back and forth in their corner of the garden. "You have to let the Holy Spirit teach you how to live in the Trinity, to relate to the Father the way Jesus does and to

(*Continued*)

Jesus the way the Father does. It's about living in faith and hope. God's love is present, but you don't yet know how to fully live in its reality. You've felt it, touched it, longed for it, but now God wants to teach you how to live in Him, in the fullness of His love for you and for the world." Abruptly Father Pat smiled and turned to walk out of the garden. He whispered in a voice soft from years of silence, "Just let Him do it."

The rest of the week was really quite amazing. The more Michael "just let," the more God's presence seemed evident. There were no words, no emotions, no new insights, but here and there Michael sensed God's love envelop him. When it happened, he would just stand or sit still and simply let it be. Before, he would have asked for an explanation, or stopped to ponder its greater meaning. But now Michael was learning to just let it be . . . to just let Him be. In the following days, every moment and every thing became pregnant with the presence of God, and the presence of God became pregnant within Michael. He felt he was on holy ground; no, he realized that he *was* holy ground. One night he awoke and went immediately to his journal and began to write.

> "Michael, it's always been like this. I've always been this close to you. But only now are you ready to 'see it' without trying to control Me or without becoming prideful. As daily life pushes in on you, My presence will seem to dim, but don't worry, it is just as real. Just let Me do it."

Michael smiled and went back to bed. "Oh Lord . . . ," he said as he dozed off.

Abigail

One winter evening, Abigail was sitting before a warm fire in her family room. The doorbell rang. There stood a shabbily dressed woman from the shelter downtown. "May I come in?" she asked. Abigail had always set pretty clear boundaries between her home life and her ministry, but tonight she sensed that God was at work in some unexpected way.

Jane joined Abigail in front of the fire. "I am sorry to bother you at home. I found your address in the phone book. I need to talk and be with someone, and I just took a chance," Jane confessed. "It's OK," Abigail responded. "How can I help?" Jane went on to explain how discouraged she was about trying to stay off the street. The system seemed to be stacked against her. She couldn't get a job because she didn't have an address and phone number, except the shelter's. She couldn't get a home and telephone because she couldn't get work. All she wanted was a chance.

Abigail held Jane's hand, and they sat together for some time in silence looking at the fire. Abigail knew the system well and the trap it could be for people like Jane. She also knew that Jane had made her share of mistakes in years past. But Abigail's heart broke, not only for this Jane but for all the Janes of the world. "I am so sorry." After a few more minutes of silence, Jane rose and headed for the door. "Thanks for caring," she said, as Abigail showed her out.

Abigail returned to the fire, wondering what had just happened. Jane had not asked for money or a place to stay. She didn't keep talking and talking, draining her listener, as so many from the shelter did. On the way up the stairs to bed, Abigail heard a quiet voice, "Thank you for loving my Son in His pain." Her eyes filled with tears and love, and gratitude that she had made herself available. What an amazing privilege to share her Lord's suffering. She never saw Jane again at the shelter, but she really didn't expect to. As Abigail reflected on that special night, she regretted not really looking more deeply into this shabbily dressed woman's eyes or holding her hands more tightly. She looked forward to the day when she would be able to show her love more fully to both the Father and the Son. But for now, she would keep the eyes of her heart more open and love with less reservation.

REFLECTION

Can you find elements of the sixth mansion of spiritual growth that correlate with your life? Remember that none of us will experience all of what is described in any of the mansions. But as you reflect on how God is calling you on, ask yourself these questions:

- How does your love for God express itself?

- How is silence invading your prayer time? Are you cooperating with it or fighting it?

(*Continued*)

- What do you long for in your relationship with God?
- What helps you persevere when you become very conscious of your sinfulness or feel that God is hiding Himself from you?
- How is God calling you to experience Him in the "least of these"?

CHAPTER II

A Life of Love in the Trinity: The Seventh Mansion

I am my beloved's,
And his desire is for me.
Come, my beloved, let us go out into the country,
Let us spend the night in the villages.
Let us rise early and go to the vineyards;
Let us see whether the vine has budded
And its blossoms have opened,
And whether the pomegranates have bloomed.
There I will give you my love.

—SONG OF SOLOMON 7:10–12

CAN YOU IMAGINE THE KIND OF EXPERIENCE WITH Jesus described in this passage? Think what our lives would be like if we could say of any given day, "I experienced God today, as my beloved. We spent the whole day together caring for people in the countryside and then the whole night in the radiance of our love for one another. The next day, in the intimacy of our night together, we went into the lives of people very special to Him, those God has given to me as a vineyard, to see how His love was blooming in them. It is here, in sharing His love with others, that I give myself most fully in love to Jesus." How incredible it would be to truly live in the reality of which our longings had only given glimpses. Let's continue, to get a glimpse.

We've finally entered the final mansion of spiritual growth, described by Teresa, after many years of pilgrimage. Like me, she had misgivings about even trying to describe the mystery and wonder of Union with the King of Kings and Lords of Lords.

> O great God! It seems that a creature as miserable as I should tremble to deal with a thing so foreign to what I deserve to understand. And, indeed, I have been covered with confusion wondering if it might not be better to conclude my discussion of this dwelling place with just a few words. For it seems to me that others will think I know about it through experience. This makes me extremely ashamed; for, knowing what I am, such a thought is a terrible thing. On the other hand, the thought of neglecting to explain this dwelling place seemed to me to be a temptation and weakness on my part, no matter how many of the above judgments you make about me. May God be praised and understood a little more.[1]

But despite the possible presumption, there are people, like you and me, who need to know what spiritual maturity can finally look like this side of heaven, and who, tasting it, need to be encouraged that it is more wonderful than we ever guessed. And some, who may have entered the seventh mansion, need to realize that there is great variety and wide expanses here yet to be explored. So, I hope you'll agree that we should proceed.

The seventh mansion represents the ultimate degree of intimacy with God that one can experience in this life: spiritual union with the Trinity. As is true with each of the prior mansions, this is still a season of our journey, not a milestone or destination. But in this season, we come to experience a complete integration of mind, body, and spirit in the life of Christ. At its fullest, it is the realization of the apostle Paul's statement, "It is no longer I who live, but Christ lives in me" (cf. Gal. 2:20). Our relationship with God becomes a fulfillment of Jesus' High Priestly Prayer, recorded in the Gospel of John:

> . . . that they may all be one; even as You, Father, are in Me and I in You, that they also may be in Us, so that the world may believe that You sent Me. The glory which You have given Me I have given to them, that they may be one, just as We are one; I in them and

You in Me, that they may be perfected in unity, so that the world may know that You sent Me, and loved them, even as You have loved Me. Father, I desire that they also, whom You have given Me, be with Me where I am, so that they may see My glory which You have given Me, for You loved Me before the foundation of the world.

—JOHN 17:21–24

Some of us have visited the seventh mansion and tasted this unity, but not many fully live here. It's hard for most of us to even imagine a life in which we live fully "in Christ" and Christ lives fully in us, where our character, our very being, is perfected in His image. What might it be like to no longer combat daily struggles with sinful tendencies? What might it mean to live fully and freely in the life of the Trinity, knowing and loving God the Father, Son, and Holy Spirit as they know and love each other? Impossible? Absolutely not. We will see that Scripture promises it, God wants it for us, and many followers of Jesus have experienced it. Maybe a final look at Michael and Abigail will help us grasp what lies ahead.

Michael

Michael continued to experience long Dark Night seasons, interspersed with months of relief when he could feel God's love rekindle his own heart. In the ten ensuing years, he learned to stop complaining about the darkness, and to trust God's presence in it. His ministry continued to flourish as Mission Hills Church planted two other churches. Growth in the congregation enabled Mission Hills to call a Shepherding Pastor, who guided the staff and oversaw the ministries of the church. Michael now had time to work closely with the church plant teams and provide spiritual direction for other pastors in the area. Michael was always surprised at how others felt Jesus in him, even when he personally was not feeling God at all. "God, you are so good to this blind and deaf follower of Yours," Michael would often whisper to himself. Yet he knew there was so much more to this love affair with the Creator of the Universe, and he wondered if it would take his death to discover it.

(Continued)

One Sunday, Michael plopped down in a church pew after everyone left. It was Communion Sunday, and he felt a special presence of the Lord as people came forward for the bread and wine. He could sense that God was actually touching them in some unseen way. As he sat and rested before cleaning up, the bread and cup seemed to capture his attention. He stared in wonder and amazement at how the Lord could be present in such a simple way. All that Jesus had done in His life, death, and resurrection is available for everyone, simply by receiving it, like receiving the bread and wine. Yet it seemed that this mystery is hidden and misunderstood by most.

If you had been watching Michael, you might have thought he'd dozed off, exhausted from preaching two services. But inside something wonderful was happening; he was more awake than he had ever been in his life. His lips seemed to mumble over and over, "In the name of the Father and the Son and the Holy Spirit." He sat and stared for almost an hour.

Michael was never the same again. The dryness in prayer disappeared and the Dark Nights never returned. Some days later, he wrote in his journal.

> Oh, Lord, how beautiful you are. I am so humbled to be shown what lies within me! All this time I thought that your wonder and power and eternal nature were mainly revealed in the universe around me. But now I see that there is a universe, Your Kingdom within me, where you also reside. I saw—no, I experienced—space and stars and galaxies, a universe within my heart. In the midst of this vast and endless place, I saw You, Father, loving your Son Jesus. I saw You, Jesus, loving our Father. I saw You, Holy Spirit, loving Them Both and wrapping me, like a cloud of light, in the love of Your Trinity. I know that heaven will be the full revelation of your glory, but I know that you invited me into it for this moment. Although I no longer sense you now in the same way, I know that You, Holy Trinity, are still here, in the same way that I saw you. May Your presence always be the greatest reality that I know. And please, O Lord, may You flow through me, even to the world that hates you.

This experience would have been enough for Michael to savor for a lifetime, but God had more in store. Some months later, he was praying in the Wedding Chapel, sitting and gazing at the large cross that hung in the front. Suddenly, Jesus stood physically before him, in an almost blinding light. He smiled lovingly and said, "Michael, will you give yourself to me completely?" Jesus held out His hand in invitation. As Michael responded, Jesus pulled Michael toward Him until they seemed to occupy the very same space. Michael could feel the blood of Jesus rush through his own veins. He could sense the Lord's thoughts, maybe millions of them all at the same time. He could feel the infinite love Jesus has for him and for all the world. Michael could have stood there, on that spot, for all eternity. But soon he heard a whisper from within him: "Come on, my friend, we have things to do."

The Seventh Mansion

By the seventh mansion, the Dark Night of the Spirit is finally over. We can't place the Dark Nights precisely in our roadmap because John of the Cross doesn't tie the Dark Night experiences directly to Teresa's mansion description, and Teresa does not mention the Dark Nights by name. But we do know that sometime before the fullness of the seventh mansion they have purged us of everything that might stand between us and complete union with the holy fire of God.

Teresa describes three experiences or movements in this mansion that carry us onward to the end of our lives on this earth. Although these three experiences are unique for each of us, we can see examples in the lives of Michael and Abigail. Let's list them first and then look at each one individually at a summary level, and then more in-depth as we explore the six rooms of the seventh mansion. (1) We are given a unique vision of the Trinity, which transforms our "understanding" of God in Three Persons into an experiential knowledge. (2) Jesus reveals Himself to us in His humanity, similar to the way He revealed Himself to the disciples after His resurrection, and draws us into oneness likened to spiritual marriage. (3) Then, for the rest of our lives, we live in an ongoing and deepening relationship of unique union with God. They are distinct experiences, but they overlap and are related. Let's wade in a little deeper.

Sometime following our "survival" of the Dark Night of the Spirit that birthed blind trust in God's presence, God further strengthens our faith by giving us a unique experience of the reality of the Trinity within us. Here is Teresa's description of the essence of this vision:

> In this seventh dwelling place the union comes about in a different way: our good God now desires to remove the scales from the soul's eyes and let it see and understand. . . . When the soul is brought into that dwelling place, the Most Blessed Trinity, all three Persons, through an intellectual vision, is revealed to it through a certain representation of the truth. First there comes an enkindling in the spirit in the manner of a cloud of magnificent splendor; and these Persons are distinct, and through an admirable knowledge the soul understands a most profound truth that all three Persons are one substance and one power and one knowledge and one God alone. . . . Here all three Persons com-municate themselves to it, speak to it, and explain those words of the Lord in the Gospel: that He and the Father and the Holy Spirit will come to dwell with the soul that loves Him and keeps His commandments.[2]

This Trinitarian vision is unique, different from anything we may have experienced before. Teresa calls it an "intellectual vision." It is different because we don't experience the Trinity, imaginatively or visually with our eyes, but we "see" in our heart in a way that actually communicates and accomplishes the truth of what we experience. Unlike past visions that have come and gone, this "communication" remains present within our heart, although not always discernible or felt as clearly as the first time it happened. But we know, from this time forward, that the three Persons of the Trinity are there, within us. An example of an intellectual vision might be Paul's implied visit to the third heaven, where he experienced wonders too great for human words (cf. 2 Cor. 12:2–4).

Next Teresa describes the revelation of Jesus in His humanity and the reality of divine and spiritual marriage, which she says does not come to its fullness until after death.[3] Teresa describes the experience, which, she says, comes in many forms, depending on the individual: "The first time the favor is granted, His Majesty desires to show Himself to the soul through an imaginative vision of His most sacred humanity so that the soul will understand and not be ignorant of receiving this sovereign gift."[4]

Teresa says this first happened to her just after she received Holy Communion. Jesus came in the form of a shining splendor, in the same way the Bible described Jesus after His resurrection. She "saw" Jesus and heard Him speak to her. This experience of the humanity of Jesus allows us to understand, in a totally new way, His invitation to be His bride, to become one with Him, to know His life within us in the secret place of our heart. Teresa attempts to describe what is really beyond description: "What God communicates here to the soul in an instant is a secret so great and a favor so sublime—and the delight the soul experiences so extreme—that I don't know what to compare it to. . . . One can say no more—insofar as can be understood—than that soul, I mean the spirit, is made one with God."[5]

This experience, like the first one, is not transitory in the way touches of union have been experienced in past years; it remains a living reality. We abide with our God in the center of our heart, in a very conscious way, as fully as can happen without being transported into heaven itself.

Finally, these two experiences form a union that is new. Teresa describes the difference using several analogies. She likens earlier experiences to two candles that burn together so closely that their flames become one. Yet the candles can be separated, as can the wicks. But this spiritual marriage is more like the union that happens when rain water falls into a river or lake, when a little stream enters the sea, or when two beams of sunlight shine into a room through two windows but become one light within. There is no way to separate one from the other; they become one. This union is, at some level, a conscious experience of what the apostle Paul was talking about when he said, "But he who joins himself to the Lord is one spirit with Him." (1 Cor. 6:17) and "For to me, to live is Christ and to die is gain" (Phil. 1:21). The Lord puts our soul in this most interior dwelling place (of the interior castle of our heart) that is His and keeps us safe there. It is from this place of union with the Trinity that we now see life fully from God's perspective, and from it His love pours through us into all our circumstances. Every day brings increasing fullness of this wonderful reality.

These Scripture passages describe the seventh mansion's unity with God and the complete emergence of the life of Christ in us.

> For this reason I bow my knees before the Father, from whom every family in heaven and on earth derives its name, that He would grant you, according to the riches of His glory, to be strengthened with power through His Spirit in the inner man, so that Christ may dwell in your hearts through faith; and that you, being rooted and grounded in love, may be able to comprehend with all the saints what is the breadth and length and height and depth, *and to know the love of Christ which surpasses knowledge, that you may be filled up to all the fullness of God.*
>
> —EPHESIANS 3:14–19

> I have been crucified with Christ; and it is no longer I who live, but Christ lives in me; and the life which I now live in the flesh I live by faith in the Son of God, who loved me and gave Himself up for me.
>
> —GALATIANS 2:20

Paul's prayer for the Ephesian Christians expounds the goal of the Christian life. It is progressive throughout the Christian experience, but this aspect of its "fullness" is experienced in the seventh mansion. Death to self and new life in Christ happens to us "transactionally" on the cross of Christ; it is completed through the process of sanctification, culminating in the transformation represented by the seventh mansion.

Life in this mansion, though still containing times of significant mystical experience, has fewer highs and lows than we experienced in the fourth, fifth, and particularly the sixth. We live continuously and transcendently in the present moment, in the fullness of Christ's love. Teresa says we experience "relative perfection" in the Christian life. We'll discuss this relative perfection further when we discuss the Key Activities characteristic later.

Finally, the seventh mansion is a time when we are totally free to follow Jesus into the lives of others. At one time we may have wished we could even die so that we could experience the fullness of God, but now we desire to live a long life so that we might touch the world with our Lord's love and invite others to become His.

The seventh mansion is fully a Fourth Water time, using Teresa's analogy of watering the garden. Continued growth requires virtually no effort on our part; the Holy Spirit leads us completely, and is in full control, as He waters our soul with the love of God.

I remember reflecting on this lack of effort as I watched Brother Boniface in his later years. I was struggling to develop stillness in my prayer life and experimenting with various forms of silent retreats; Bon's journey seemed effortless. Although he struggled with faltering physical health, his relationship with God had a peace and gentleness to it that encouraged me onward. It was not that he acted as though he had arrived at any destination. To the contrary, the mystery of God's infinite love and grace expanded his horizons even further. After choir, he would invite me to follow him into the tiny bell tower room, where the steam pipes could keep him warm. We would sit on upside-down buckets, in silence and prayer. Then, in our discussions, we wandered into the depths of transcendent theology and reflected on the reality of the day's gospel text for us. Bon didn't have to look for the water of God's depths; it was simply there.

We'll look further into this life of union from the perspective of the six markers for the seventh mansion, but first let's see how this union is experienced in Abigail's life.

Abigail

We find Abigail still living in the Chicago area. With Bill retired, they are both deeply involved in their church, the Rescue Mission, and the church's ministry in Haiti. The last several years have been a real trial for Abigail, as the Dark Night of the Spirit has been severe. Day after day, month after month, she returned to her prayer chair each morning—seemingly alone. There were no lights or insights or visions. Although she tried to return to Scripture meditation as a way to hear from God, all she experienced were words on pages. Her small-group members and her Mission coffee group ladies were all blessed by Abigail's love and wisdom, but during this Dark Night of the Spirit time she didn't sense God with her at all.

(Continued)

Fortunately, Abigail had heard about the writings of the late Mother Teresa of Calcutta's suffering with her own Dark Night experiences.[6] Mother Teresa's steadfast faith and fortitude encouraged Abigail to remain constant in her prayer and ministry, knowing that God was only hidden, not absent. It was useless to try to share her pain with her small group. They didn't really understand what was happening and tried to give advice. Abigail knew they meant well, but she also knew that nothing she could do, or anything they could say, would change what God was doing. Her heart was being strengthened to trust God, her humility deepened, and her hunger and longing for God had increased immensely. But at the time, she couldn't see it or even take solace from realizing the wonderful transformation that was happening within her.

The real beginning of Abigail's seventh mansion relationship with God began in a small art gallery a few blocks from the Rescue Mission. Some months earlier, a street lady had invited Abigail to her "secret place." "It's truly beautiful; I feel safe there," she whispered as she led Abigail down a back alley. They stopped in front of an old rustic stone building and went in through a door marked "Art for Your Heart." Inside they found a spacious room with paintings on the walls and sculptures placed on crate boxes here and there. One wall had a beautiful stained glass window. The adjacent art store kept this area open to give patrons an opportunity simply to sit and reflect in silence on various works of art. Abigail was surprised that the proprietor had not chased the homeless lady away.

One painting captivated Abigail as soon as she went to it. On the large oil canvas, a rough wood crucifix outlined the figure of Jesus, almost in relief. The Jesus figure appeared to be looking right at her. The artist had managed to capture an expression for Jesus that communicated love, compassion, and forgiveness, amidst His suffering. Abigail could see why this homeless lady felt safe here.

In the following weeks, Abigail would occasionally stop by the art gallery on her way home, after meeting with her ladies' coffee group. She would sit on a bench, on the sunny side of the room. On clear days, the sunlight would cast a warm pink and blue hue across the room from the stained glass window. Abigail would sit in silence, inviting every painting and sculpture to communicate God's love to her in some unique way. In her favorite painting, the Jesus of the crucifix became so well known to her that she could easily recall the face when she was not there.

One day Abigail settled herself into her accustomed spot and noticed that a new painting had been added to the collection. The fine brush oil depicted a bride in her white gown, standing under a rose-covered arch. The bride looked wistfully through the arch into a beautiful garden beyond, as if looking for her groom to appear. Abigail could almost feel the bride's longing, one much like what she felt for God.

After some time in silence, Abigail thought she heard a voice near her. Assuming that it was probably the curator, she opened her eyes. There, before her in a blue haze, stood a Man dressed in a white wedding tuxedo, with a garland wreath about His head. The sunlight streamed through the stained glass window, covering Him with dazzling light. The pinks and blues bathed the room, but only pure white light seemed to touch the Man. As she stared in amazement, she realized that the light was actually coming from this Groom; even more startlingly, His face looked just like the painting of the crucifix, but now smiling. "Jesus!" she exclaimed in her heart.

Jesus extended His arm toward her as though bidding her come. Without thinking, she rose from her seat and started forward. Now another realization struck her. She was clothed in the beautiful wedding dress from the other picture, her hand held a vibrant white bouquet, and she was standing in the scene of the bridal garden painting. Moving up the steps toward the rose arch, Abigail took His hand. He looked deep within her eyes with a love so intense that she thought she might swoon. She felt Him saying, "I have loved you before you ever knew me. I have led you step by step over these many years, in darkness and in light. You have been faithful in your love, and I want us to live together in an even more personal way . . ." His voice seemed to fill the room like the fragrance of roses, flowing together with the light, and seemed to be the longing she had dreamed of for as long as she could remember. "I do, I am," she heard herself respond. The scene seemed frozen in time. She felt embraced and loved with a love that flooded every cell in her body. A peace and joy welled up within her as she had never felt before. After what seemed forever, she opened her eyes. Only the Light remained; He was gone.

Then she heard the distinct words, "We love you, Abigail." She looked up and there near her were now three distinct figures, in the middle of the room. Jesus reached out put her hand in the Father's, and the Spirit wrapped around them like a shawl of living Light. The stone gallery filled with laughter and singing and music and applause. Abigail knew in an instant the mystery of the Trinity. They were three and yet one. "We have made our home in you, Abigail," they said in unison, "Make your home in us."

(Continued)

The next thing Abigail experienced was her hands on the steering wheel as she turned her car into the driveway of her home. Bill met her at the door. "You're late, Honey," he said at first. Then he saw her tears and radiant smile and responded, "Come in, Abby, and tell me about it." Some months later, Bill told a close friend about that evening: "I have never seen her so radiant, even on our wedding day. That radiance has never left her; it warms the people around her, and I feel more loved by her every day."

With this overview, and the examples of Michael and Abigail, let's look at the experiential rooms we visit in the seventh mansion. The spiritual experiences of Michael and Abigail may seem random, but they exemplify specific actions that God takes to deepen our relationship with Him in a profound way.

"Your Heart's Desire" in Relationship with God

By the time we are drawn by Jesus into the seventh mansion, our one desire is to know, love, and serve Him. Through the experiences of the Dark Nights, our hearts have been purified. We have abandoned our attachments and earthly needs so that we may devote our undivided hearts to God. Every fiber of our being has been united with Jesus in a way that enables us to fully participate with Him, in the situations where He has placed us. We work with and care for others, together with God, in a conscious reality that we have known only in brief moments before. Now, there is a "we" in daily life.

The longings and fears that have been so much a part of our spiritual experience have passed. We are no longer afraid of displeasing Him, but confident that He leads us according to His will. No longer searching for Him or longing to experience Him, we enjoy the full awareness of His presence in our hearts. The struggle between worship and work, contemplation and serving, has gone. Now, every effort, no matter how painful or distasteful, is a participation with our Lover and a contemplation of His holiness. We are now one person, fully ourselves, fully alive, fully available to Him. It is in the seventh mansion that the spiritual formation goal of a love relationship with God, resulting in wholeness, holiness, and service, is fully realized.

"Key Activities" in Response to God

Seventh mansion life can be described in two categories, which have become, ultimately, the same thing: loving and serving our Lord. Now we see and understand, more fully than ever, our Lord's passion for the world; we understand the extent of His suffering to reconcile all things to Himself; and we desire to live out our love, for Jesus and the world, by sharing those sufferings in the lives of others.

Teresa says that the Mary and Martha parts of us are now joined together. We experience a complete integration of worship and work, of adoration and service, of being and doing. In response to the call of God, we are fully engaged in a life of service. For some, this may be a life of solitude and contemplation, but for most, like Teresa and John, it meant a life of service to Jesus in others. Loving God expresses itself in loving our neighbor. Teresa's position on love of neighbor, as quoted in her discussion of the fifth mansion, is still the same in the seventh: "Here in our religious life the Lord asks of us only two things: love of His Majesty and love of neighbor. . . . The most certain sign, in my opinion, as to whether or not we are observing these two laws is whether we observe well the love of neighbor."[7]

We love and serve from the sure foundation of that dwelling place in our hearts where the Trinity resides, and we experience an inner stability and security, even though on the sense or emotional levels there may be little or no peace. We still live in a fallen world with its struggles and rebellion. In fact, we see them more clearly and are grieved by them much more deeply. This new union with God does not protect us from the pain of this world but launches us into it.

Yet, at the center of our heart there is a peace, knowing that our Lord is in control, working His plan for all creation. This is the "peace that passes all understanding" Paul describes in Philippians 4:7, a peace not conditioned by the surrounding circumstances or our own health or sickness.

I remember walking with Brother Boniface along the winding road that led to Holy Trinity Abbey. In response to some grumbling about something that was not going my way, Bon said, "Tom, you have to rest in the 'unfelt peace and unfelt joy' within you." It was a concept that at first seemed contradictory to me, but as I looked within myself it was there; despite my frustration and confusion, deep inside my heart there was joy in His love and peace in the safety of His shepherding. The recognition brought a bit of peace, if not joy, to surface in my feelings. Think about it: these "fruits of the Holy Spirit," described by the apostle Paul, are really spiritual in nature, not primarily emotional. "But the fruit of the Spirit is love, joy, peace, patience, kindness, goodness, faithfulness, gentleness, self-control; against such things there is no law. Now those who belong to Christ Jesus have crucified the flesh with its passions and desires. If we live by the Spirit, let us also walk by the Spirit" (Gal. 5:22–26).

Even though these qualities can be attributes of our human nature, created in the image and likeness of God, the spiritual gifts are the fruit of the Holy Spirit's presence within our spirits. Then they can express themselves in our emotions and behavior.

When we are in pain, experiencing persecution, or touched by the suffering of others, we can't expect to feel joyful or peaceful. But if we live from the foundation of Christ's reality in us, exterior circumstances can't shake the Rock that is our dwelling place. Over many years, still a long way from the seventh mansion, I would recall the mystery of unfelt peace and joy in the midst of troubles. At that moment, I had to decide whether the outward circumstances or the Truth within me would control how I responded.

In the seventh mansion, Teresa tells us that we experience "relative perfection" as Christians. However, neither Teresa nor John of the Cross believes that true perfection can be obtained until we are in our heavenly bodies; only relative holiness is experienced in this life. It is interesting that Teresa describes perfection not in terms of personal qualities but in terms of our obedience in love to Jesus: "The whole aim of any person who is beginning prayer . . . should be that he work and prepare himself with determination and every possible effort to bring his will into conformity with God's will. Be certain that, as I shall say later, the greatest perfection attainable along the spiritual path lies in this conformity [of our will to that of Jesus]."[8]

Dubay describes perfection in this way: "In this final development of prayer we find the relative perfection of Christian life that the Gospel lays upon us as both privilege and precept: we are to love the Lord our God with our whole heart, soul and mind, nothing less. We are to be perfect as the heavenly Father is perfect and to be completely one. While growth is always possible in our pilgrim state, the person in the transforming union has indeed been transformed from one glory to another into the image that he reflects. A relative perfection is now reached."[9]

You may be wondering, "In light of 'relative perfection,' what does spiritual growth look like in the seventh mansion?" There are a number of developing attributes or effects that this union with God has on us. One, which relates to the way we live our lives, is "forgetfulness of self."[10] I remember a comment about this forgetfulness made by one of our great modern evangelical theologians. James Houston, the founder of Regent College and a prolific writer on the spiritual journey, was asked, shortly after his eightieth birthday, about the meaning of personal significance for him. He answered simply, "Unintentional self-forgetfulness."[11]

So deeply impacted by our experience of union with the Trinity, we trust at a new level. We know, in complete confidence, that if we take care to follow Jesus faithfully He will take care of our circumstances in the ways that are best for us; we simply needn't be concerned about it. Jesus is enough. Teresa is quick to point out that this doesn't mean forgetfulness of such things as food, sleep, or exercise. We want to remain as fit as possible to serve our Lord with the best we can give. But we are willing to live in whatever circumstance He has placed us for the service of our Lord.

Another developing attribute is "the desire to suffer."[12] Because we have so identified with our Lord, seeing clearly His sufferings for us on the cross and daily patience with us and the world, we long to express our love for Him by sharing those sufferings. We may suffer through hard work. There are also often very real opposition and persecution that burden those who follow Jesus. Our faithfulness in love to God may actually bring out jealousy and spite in others who are threatened by our authentic love and humility. This desire to suffer transcends our desire for consolations or spiritual delights.

"Changing Patterns of Prayer" in Communication with God

In the seventh mansion, prayer has primarily become trusting silence, an adoring attentiveness to the Holy Trinity. In this silence, there is full union with the Trinity, an experience of the spiritual marriage that happens at our deepest soul center. Remember that Jesus in His humanity, and the Trinity in their community, have been revealed to us. We don't still "see" those visions, but we nevertheless now live within their reality. Our prayer reflects Their prayer, and Their prayer becomes ours. We live together, love together, and intercede together. Teresa says of the experience of prayer: "The difference in this dwelling place is the one mentioned: There are almost never any experiences of dryness or interior disturbance of the kind that were present at times in all the other dwelling places, but the soul is almost always in quiet."[13]

Teresa calls this prayer, which brings us the mind of Christ and expresses our fullest devotion, "transforming union." One can only use the language of marriage, both in physical intimacy and in times of quiet togetherness, to describe these depths of prayer. For John of the Cross, this prayer of union is the summit of "Mount Carmel," his description of what corresponds to Teresa's seventh mansion.[14]

Earlier in our spiritual journey, we may have experienced touches of union in times of contemplative prayer; now it has become a condition of life, pervading formal prayer and daily life.

Teresa says that when we might become distracted in prayer or in daily life, the Lord Himself reawakens us through flames of love that immediately focus our attention on Him. In the earlier mansions, our distraction might go on for some time until some memory or experience recalled us to focus on our Lord. Now God enables the eyes of our heart to behold Him ceaselessly.

Contrary to what we might expect, because of the inner experience of God's presence, the raptures that were once so wonderful and encouraging are now taken away. Teresa says that "only once in a while they are experienced and then without those transports and that flight of the spirit . . . and almost never in public."[15] The disappearance of these spiritual blessings would have been troubling before, but they have now become unnecessary. The story is told that Teresa was asked by a traveling companion,

Father Julian of Avila, while they were traveling from city to city, why her raptures had ceased. "One day when we were traveling and discussing many things I said to her: 'Mother, how is it that' your Reverence used to be in rapture very frequently, yet it is a long time since I saw you in ecstasy?'" She replied: it was true that she no longer had any ecstasies, but the prayer she had now was greater than the prayer she used to have in her raptures.[16]

She went on to say that earlier her experiences of God were so startling and caused such great amazement that she was "carried away and unconscious in the excessive pleasure that her soul experienced within her."[17] Now she had become more used to it. In another conversation with her carriage coachman on a similar trip, the same question was asked. She responded that she guessed that God was "simply enough."

LIFE IN THE PRESENT MOMENT

There is a mystery that has always been true for those who know Jesus as Lord and Savior but is fully tasted only in the seventh mansion. Jesus is the Alpha and Omega, the beginning and the end of all things, present in all time and space, the One who is, was, and is to come. (See Rev. 1:4; 4:8.) As we live "in Christ" and "Christ lives in us," we share this time and space reality with Him (cf. Eph. 1:3; Col. 1:27). The mystical experiences of the fifth and sixth mansions are experiential touches of this reality; we now find that each present moment is a full participation in this fullness of Christ. Here are some biblical examples that reflect this amazing truth.

Matthew 13:11: Jesus answered them, "To you it has been granted to know the mysteries of the kingdom of heaven.

John 14:3: . . . that where I am, there you may be also.

John 14:23–24: If anyone loves Me, he will keep My word; and My Father will love him, and We will come to him and make Our abode with him.

Ephesians 1:3–14: Blessed be the God and Father of our Lord Jesus Christ, who has blessed us with every spiritual blessing in the heavenly places in Christ. . . .

(Continued)

Ephesians 2:6–7: . . . and raised us up with Him, and seated us with Him in the heavenly places in Christ Jesus. . . .

Ephesians 3:19: . . . that you may be filled up to all the fullness of God.

2 Corinthians 4:18: So we fix our eyes not on what is seen, but on what is unseen. For what is seen is temporary, but what is unseen is eternal.

2 Corinthians 12:1–2: But I will go on to visions and revelations of the Lord. I know a man in Christ who fourteen years ago—whether in the body I do not know, or out of the body I do not know, God knows—such a man was caught up to the third heaven.

Matthew 5:8: Blessed are the pure in heart, for they shall see God.

This new awareness shows us how every event is tied into the eternal plan of God and is filled with His love, power, and wisdom.

Yet the level of awareness of God's presence in us still varies. There is no "dryness" in the way we experienced it in the previous mansions, but we don't experience constant awareness of our Lord in His inner dwelling place within us. There are times, says Teresa, when God leaves us in our natural state. This usually happens in some way connected to an event in our lives and results in a tumult of spiritual warfare. It usually lasts only for a few days, but she says that it is important for us to receive support from our spiritual community.

"Jesus' Initiatives" to Draw Us into a Deeper Intimacy with God

We have already described the experiences of the intellectual vision of the Trinity, the spiritual marriage, and the revelation of the new center where the Trinity resides within us. These revelations are a great work of God within our hearts. Remember, using Teresa's "Waters" analogy, we described our increasing growth in the last four mansions as an increase in God's initiative and corresponding decrease in our "work" at spiritual growth. In the seventh mansion, virtually all of life has become a response to Jesus' initiatives. The transforming union is constantly drawing us into deeper intimacy, and it is this intimacy that transfigures, heals, and beautifies us.

In the earlier mansions, Jesus was always initiating, but we were blind and deaf to most of it and went our own way the best we could. Now, His divine initiatives are received in our hearts and minds and we literally "do what we see the Father doing."[18]

"Schemes of the Enemy" to Try to Destroy Our Growth in God

As we discussed in Chapter Nine, the Dark Night of the Spirit can be an occasion for the attack of the enemy. He tempts and bites us in the midst of it, to confuse us. But despite his lies and attempts to make us give up, the result is a life that is more conformed to the life of Jesus, with increasing manifestation of the fruits of the Spirit.

The devil does not abandon his schemes against us in the seventh mansion. However, the ongoing temptations, accusations, and lies are automatically repulsed and resisted. Teresa says, "His Majesty reveals Himself to the soul and brings it to Himself in that place where, in my opinion, the devil will not dare enter, nor will the Lord allow him to enter."[19] In the full light of Christ, the enemy's schemes are obvious and Jesus' beloved, well suited in the full armor of God, repulses the attack as it is being launched.

Nevertheless, our human nature is still tainted by sin, and so we must be constantly vigilant to avoid deception or pride that would cause a fall. For example, we may know "enlightened" people who have been so struck with the love of God that they have dismissed His justice, ignoring Jesus' own admonition that He is the only way to the Father. There always remains the temptation to become so enthralled with the transcendent mystery of God that we ignore the imminent presence of God in a sister or brother, and thus fail to love in the way Jesus would have us love. These errors are certainly not unique to the seventh mansion, but they are examples of the subtle temptations that we may experience there.

Teresa believes that continued diligence is necessary so that we are not seduced by the world or the enemy to turn from God. After reading about the glorious intimacy that is experienced in the seventh mansion, it is hard for most of us to imagine that a person could now turn from God. C. S. Lewis gives us an important perspective when he says, "There is but one good; that is God. Everything else is good when it looks to Him and bad when it turns from Him. And the higher and mightier it is in the natural order, the more demoniac it will be if it rebels. It's not out of bad mice or bad fleas you made demons, but out of bad archangels."[20] So, what would become of a seventh mansion Christian who "turns to the dark side" is much more diabolical than the second mansion Christian who returns to his booze or pornography (as tragic as that is). The *likelihood* of falling may be less, on the one hand, but the *consequence* of the fall would be greater, more dangerous. It may not be an obvious "fall" or conscious "turning," but a deception, a pride, that would "undo" all the growth and the light given "even as Judas brought about the thing he least intended."[21] It is impossible to exactly discern a mansion level for biblical characters, but there are many examples of people who turned from God after experiencing great intimacy. Adam and Eve might be the most extreme examples of someone who turned from profound intimacy with God. Saul, Israel's first king, had received the Lord's anointing and yet ultimately became demon-possessed through his own pride. Solomon began his reign with great faith, God-given wisdom, and profound experiences of worship, but later he allowed Israel to become polluted by the gods of his many wives. The apostle Paul provides a frightening warning for those who have "tasted of the heavenly gift" and then "have fallen away" (cf. Heb. 6:4–8).

"Keys for Growth" That Help Us Cooperate with God

The most significant condition for our growth in union with God is the prayer of attentive trusting silence. We have discussed the nature and benefits of this prayer of union, but it is helpful to remember here that we must still be intentional. Because we have become even more focused on living out our love for Jesus through service, we must all the more guard our times for total attentiveness to our Lord. He has become our food, our guidance, our life. It is focused time in His presence that sustains us and enables us to follow Him faithfully.

An important part of this silent communion with God happens in extended solitude. We have seen in the lives of Abigail and Michael that they needed prolonged periods alone with the Lord. Maybe more than ever in history, the pressure of our world, the flood of information, and the violence to which we are daily exposed can exhaust us. As we live more and more in the heart of God, the sins of others grieve us and cause us pain. So we, like our Lord, must come away to a quiet place and rest.[22] At one time we may have taken our retreats with others and made extensive plans for how we will spend our days. Now we must go away and be alone with God.

Ongoing daily obedience to Christ constitutes another avenue of growth in the seventh mansion. It might seem as though a full circle is happening here. In the third mansion, our life with Jesus was expressed mainly through our service. In the fourth and following mansions, we were called to focus more on Jesus, to fall in love with Him, to yearn for deeper intimacy with the Lord. Now in the seventh mansion, as this intimacy has been established, our focus turns fully toward loving Jesus in others; loving God and loving neighbor have joined. Like the original disciples, who walked daily with Jesus, our ministry with Him brings us into closer harmony of mind and actions. To those who feel that the seventh mansion can only be reached by contemplation, Teresa states: "You may think that as a result the soul will be outside itself and so absorbed that it will be unable to be occupied with anything else. On the contrary, the soul is much more occupied than before with everything pertaining to the service of God; and once the duties are over it remains with that enjoyable company."[23]

Another seventh mansion movement of growth occurs with diligence in the spiritual disciplines that have proved helpful in maintaining a life of intimacy with God. Teresa says, "I repeat, it is necessary that your foundation consist of more than prayer and contemplation. If you do not strive for the virtues and practice them, you will always be dwarfs."[24]

A significant movement of our growth continues to take place in spiritual community. In each mansion, we have talked about the importance of Christian community, to sustain and encourage us. Even at this final phase of spiritual growth, it is no less important. We were baptized into the church, the Body of Christ, and no degree of spiritual growth changes our interdependence.[25]

But spiritual community may not be easy to find. As was increasingly true in the fifth and sixth mansions, there are few spiritual directors who have gone before us into the seventh. But God can use almost anyone to minister to us, if we are attentive. We see that the apostle Paul was continually encouraged and supported by other believers. Now, particularly, when we know fully that we are accepted and understood and affirmed by our Lord, we are free to receive the love and prayers of brothers and sisters, who may even be beginners in the Lord. People will quite naturally come to us for help from those who reside in the seventh mansion. So it is important for us to share our weaknesses and needs with others, and in that way we all are encouraged.

Immersion in the Scriptures continues to be an important avenue for growth. It is always possible to learn new information, but now we experience far more in His written Word. We are able to travel with our Lord into His history, recorded in the Bible, to love Him and learn from Him there. The Scriptures become for us, even more fully, the inspired Word of God, not because they are the only way we hear Him but because He is present and always speaking to us through them.

We may talk about "relative perfection" and "full union" as descriptive of our journey in the seventh mansion, but we must remember that it continues to be just as much a journey. On the one hand, God has given Jesus to us so that we might know God personally, and experience Him intimately, but God remains the Infinite One, the Alpha and Omega, the One that fills all time and space. We will never, at least in this life, experience or know all of Him. The Trinity remains Mystery and is far beyond all that we could ever think or dream of. The intimacy and knowledge we experience in the seventh mansion may be profound, but from our perspective we still remain in the dark from the infinite and eternal perspective. These words of the apostles Paul and John are a great encouragement as we look to our knowledge of God in Heaven:

> For now we see in a mirror dimly, but then face to face; now I know in part, but then I will know fully just as I also have been fully known.
>
> —1 CORINTHIANS 13:12

> Beloved, now we are children of God, and it has not appeared as yet what we will be. We know that when He appears, we will be like Him, because we will see Him just as He is. And everyone who has this hope fixed on Him purifies himself, just as He is pure.
>
> —1 JOHN 3:2–3

But even in heaven, we remain finite created beings. God, however, is King of Kings, Lord of Lords, Everlasting Father, Prince of Peace, Ancient of Days. There will be a fuller knowing and experience of God in heaven, to be sure, but it is my guess that He will remain to us an awesome Mystery of Love. So, even in the seventh mansion, we know that our journey to the heart of the Father is still an infinite one. We are all beginners.

Transforming Union: The Goal of Spiritual Formation

As we reflect on this amazing journey through the Mansions of the Heart, let's look again at the goal of spiritual formation that we identified in Chapter Two. Relationship with God in Jesus Christ is where we begin, and it is where we end. For Teresa of Avila and John of the Cross, the goal of spiritual formation is clearly relationship with God through faith in Jesus Christ. Thus, to follow the lead of Teresa and John and the clear teaching of Scripture, our goal in spiritual formation must be God Himself. It was a deepening relationship and its resulting transformation that we glimpsed in Abigail and Michael. We could go on telling their stories of their deepening love for God, and their unique ministries to others well into their senior years. But suffice it to say that, as before, their stories remain different and unique to whom God made each of them. Yes, they faced many struggles over the years. However, we can be assured that each day was an amazing adventure with their beloved Creator of the Universe, until the day they stepped across the threshold from death to life and received the fullness of Jesus' promise: "In My Father's house are many mansions; if it were not so, I would have told you; for I go to prepare a place for you. And if I go and prepare a place for you, I will come again and receive you to Myself, that where I am, there you may be also" (John 14:2–3). Then they will experience in its fullness the vision of the apostle John that awaits all who have come to know Jesus as Lord and Savior, no matter which mansion they have reached:

> Then I saw a new heaven and a new earth; for the first heaven and the first earth passed away, and there is no longer any sea. And I saw the holy city, new Jerusalem, coming down out of heaven from God, made ready as a bride adorned for her husband. And I heard a loud voice from the throne, saying, "Behold, the tabernacle of God is among men, and He will dwell among them, and they shall be His people, and God Himself will be among them, and He will wipe away every tear from their eyes; and there will no longer be any death; there will no longer be any mourning, or crying, or pain; the first things have passed away.
>
> —REVELATION 22:1–5

> Then he showed me a river of the water of life, clear as crystal, coming from the throne of God and of the Lamb, in the middle of its [the city of God] street. On either side of the river was the tree of life, bearing twelve kinds of fruit, yielding its fruit every month; and the leaves of the tree were for the healing of the nations. There will no longer be any curse; and the throne of God and of the Lamb will be in it, and His bond-servants will serve Him; they will see His face, and His name will be on their foreheads. And there will no longer be any night; and they will not have need of the light of a lamp nor the light of the sun, because the Lord God will illumine them; and they will reign forever and ever.
>
> —REVELATION 21:1–4

The final destination will be the same for all who have put their faith in Jesus, the Son of God, as their Lord and Savior. We all go through the same fundamental process toward maturity in that relationship. However, each of us is a unique individual, and each one of us has a unique story. God delights in using our uniquenesses to guide our journeys. In the following chapters, we'll look at how God uses our individual differences to help us relate to Him. Then we will discover why understanding our individual journeys, in the context of the Mansions of the Heart, can make our life together in the church an amazing adventure.

REFLECTION

- What is your goal in your relationship with God? Is it intimacy with God, or is it what you can get from Him?

- What attachments do you think God still needs to weed out of your life that may be blocking full union with Him?

- Which of the Keys to Growth listed above seem most important for you at this point in your journey with Jesus?

CHAPTER 12

Your Unique Journey

*But we have this treasure in earthen vessels, so that
the surpassing greatness of the power will be of God
and not from ourselves; we are afflicted in every
way, but not crushed; perplexed, but not despairing; persecuted, but not forsaken; struck down, but
not destroyed; always carrying about in the body the
dying of Jesus, so that the life of Jesus also may be
manifested in our body.*

—2 Corinthians 4:7–11

"But what about me?" you may be saying. "I'm not like
Michael or Abigail. My history is different from theirs, and
I don't relate to God that way." This might well be the way many
of us feel after reading through the Teresian Mansions and the
stories of Michael and Abigail. The fact is that each of us is different. It's a mind-boggling truth that God created each one of
us uniquely; we may have similarities with others, but we don't
look, feel, think, or act like a single other human being on the
planet. We each have our own history that affects us radically.
Even brothers and sisters, raised in the same home, are quite
unique and are affected differently by the environment in which
they were raised.

How does our individuality factor into our spiritual formation
journey? We have seen that God's basic roadmap for our growing

relationship with Him is the same for all of us. His goal for us is a deep love relationship with Him and with others. We are all created to grow and develop physically, emotionally, and spiritually. Created in God's image, we are designed to love and be loved; it's part of what makes us human. Therefore, the general process of our spiritual formation, outlined in the Seven Mansions, will be the same for each of us, no matter how far along we travel. It is amazing, however, that God loves us so much that He relates to us and grows us in ways that are unique to who we are. A look at prominent characters in the Bible shows us that this is true. God relates consistently, but there are no two stories the same. Abraham, Moses, David, Elijah, Peter, and Paul each responded to God in their own way, and we see that God related to them in ways that were unique to each one's personality and situation. Let's take a deeper look into our uniquenesses, as they relate to our spiritual formation. By looking at dimensions of our own history and personal development, our own personality characteristics, and our unique temperaments, we can better understand how God is leading us and transforming us. God wants you to experience His love in ways that are perfectly suited to you.

There's a further complication, however. Not only are we uniquely created, but we are uniquely wounded. We were designed by God to be sinless, perfect in every way. We were also created by Him to live in a perfect world, with perfect parents, perfect brothers and sisters, perfect communities, friends, and so on. Yet the sad truth is that, because of the Fall, sin has infected each of us and distorted the world around us. We have therefore been wounded by the sin and evil that has touched us. We have not loved and been loved perfectly. Nor were we raised in the purity of God's holiness.

Our wounds may be physical. We may struggle with some disease or injury; we are all experiencing the decaying process of death. Our wounds may also be emotional. How we think and feel have been distorted, to some extent, by things that have happened to us and the influence of the world around us. Certainly, our wounds are also spiritual. Our spirits, uniquely like God among all living things, have been touched by evil and deformed.

The story of the prophet Isaiah gives us a good biblical example. In Isaiah 6, Isaiah records the story of his call to become a prophet.[1] He is probably performing his annual duty in the temple when he has a vision of God on His throne, surrounded by angels. In the midst of this amazing experience of God's holiness, Isaiah becomes fully aware of his own sinful nature and its relationship to his own history: "I am a man of unclean lips and I live among a people of unclean lips." Isaiah's "lips" had expressed the sinfulness of his heart, and he became profoundly aware that he was not able to live in the presence of God. God acts powerfully with forgiveness and healing. An angel takes a live coal from the altar and touches Isaiah's mouth with it. "Behold, this has touched your lips; and your iniquity is taken away and your sin is forgiven" (Isa. 6:7). We understand that God's act prefigured the atoning death of Jesus and the forgiveness and healing He would bring through the cross. "And by His scourging we are healed" (Isa. 53:5). After Isaiah's forgiveness and healing he was able to hear and respond to God's invitation to become His prophet. "Whom shall I send, and who will go for Us?" Then Isaiah said, "Here am I. Send me!" (Isa. 6:8–9)

For our ongoing transformation to continue, God must uncover and heal many wounds that result from our own sin and from growing up in this sinful world. The apostle Paul described the situation this way:

> For the anxious longing of the creation waits eagerly for the revealing [through conversion and transformation] of the sons of God. For the creation was subjected to futility, not willingly, but because of Him who subjected it, in hope that the creation itself also will be set free from its slavery to corruption into the freedom of the glory of the children of God. For we know that the whole creation groans and suffers the pains of childbirth together until now. And not only this, but also we ourselves, having the first fruits of the Spirit, even we ourselves groan within ourselves, waiting eagerly for our adoption as sons, the redemption of our body. For in hope we have been saved, but hope that is seen is not hope; for who hopes for what he already sees? But if we hope for what we do not see, with perseverance we wait eagerly for it.
>
> —ROMANS 8:19–25

Consequently, we see that our hope is focused on Jesus and His work, both in our spiritual formation in this world and in the complete new "formation" of all of creation, in the new heaven and earth. Likewise, the world around us is waiting for us, as sons and daughters of God, to shine His light and love into the dark and broken places of society. It is our ongoing spiritual formation that increasingly allows the light of God's love to shine through us.

We're Unique in Our Mental and Emotional Development and Health

Our mental and emotional development and health must be taken into account in our spiritual formation. Psychology offers many insights into the development of our self-perception, motivation, and personality. Issues of mental health are intertwined with our perception of reality and spiritual experience. Therefore, our spiritual formation roadmap must account for our physical and emotional development, as it relates to our spiritual perception and faith. Recall that both Michael and Abigail struggled with "personal issues" that God surfaced at key times in their spiritual formation process. Until the issues were dealt with, our pilgrims became stuck and frustrated.

Human Development and Faith

Human maturation and personality development are obviously important dimensions of spiritual formation. God created us to mature in a particular fashion, even though this development is lived out uniquely as a function of individual history and experience. Faith also develops as part of this overall maturation process. James Fowler's *Stages of Faith: The Psychology of Human Development and the Quest for Meaning*, written in 1981, is a thorough analysis of the development of general, though not necessarily religious, faith.[2] In *Faithful Change: The Personal and Public Challenges of Postmodern Life*, Fowler offers insight into the nature of change and its impact on faith.[3] He also shares his expanded thinking on the stages of faith and addresses the stages of faith in early childhood, comparing the psychology of the emotional life with the concepts of conversion and transformation. Fowler's contribution is significant in understanding the relationship between faith development and progression in an adult relationship of love with God. Fowler's stages of faith do not correlate directly with Teresa's Seven Mansions, but we can see that adult faith maturity must take place before we can progress significantly beyond the third mansion.

I remember a young teen in the youth group of our church. Phillip was invited to one of our confirmation camps. Though he had grown up in a culturally Christian family, Phillip had little church background and only a distant belief that Jesus was a historical figure. In the process of the camp experience, he was touched by the faith of his friends and moved by the enthusiastic worship. In a late night session with his cabin counselor, Phillip prayed the sinner's prayer and gave his heart to Jesus. Initially, he made it known that "this is all only experimental," but in the following months he became very vocal about his love for Jesus. Many things did change in Phillip's life, and it was obvious that a profound relationship with God was emerging. He even shared his testimony in church on Sunday, and many people were touched by his passion for Jesus and desire to serve Him with his whole life.

Knowing the Teresian Mansions and the influence of personal development, what might we say about Phillip's spiritual maturity? Could we say that he jumped quickly into the fourth mansion? No. Despite the fact that he was madly, passionately in love with Jesus, we also saw that he felt much the same about one of the cheerleaders at school. We remember that he was only fifteen years old, living in a huge transitional time in his developmental process. Is his love for Jesus real? Of course it is. Does Phillip have a mature love for Jesus? Probably not. We can expect the same highs and lows that any teenager experiences with life to characterize his relationship with Jesus. We know that Jesus loved and accepted Phillip right where he was, in process. It is important that we do too. We won't be surprised or crushed if Phillip does something "stupid" that would seem to deny his faith, or that he might later expresses doubts about the very flag he waved so highly in the church service. Phillip is in process, developmentally and spiritually, and so are we.

There are a few modern authors you may want to read if you are interested in studying further to better understand this relationship between our developmental maturity and spiritual growth. For example, Benedict J. Groeschel, in *Spiritual Passages: The Psychology of Spiritual Development*, discusses the psychology of spirituality and the interrelationship of psychology, spirituality, and human development.[4] He then applies these insights to the three-step-ladder understanding of spiritual formation: purgation, illumination, and union (contemplation). Groeschel's insights come close to a correlation with the Seven Mansions. Larry Crabb has also done excellent work that correlates our emotional health and our spiritual growth.[5] Peter Scazzero published a recent work that addressed the importance of this integration.[6] Scazzero, a pastor in an inner city church in New York, describes his deep need for emotional health in his marriage and church, after discovering that both mirrored his own developmental dysfunction. Although he says he made some progress, his real breakthrough came as he realized that his developmental dysfunction had also negatively affected his spiritual growth and how he pastured his church. Not only did his developmental issues affect his relationship with God, but he found that the power to deal with his emotional life lay in a new and deeper relationship with God. His books are insightful and well worth reading.

To gain a close insight into the relationship between our emotional development and our spiritual growth, let's recall some developmental examples from Michael and Abigail. We tuned in to both their stories during their late adolescence, but their histories were significantly different. Abigail was raised in a Christian home, and her basic values and faith perspectives were formed by that environment. Adult commitment to faith in Jesus was only a small step for her. Michael, in contrast, was not raised as a Christian.

Both of our pilgrims dealt with wounds caused by family dysfunction in their childhood. Michael's family environment significantly scarred his value system, and his inappropriate responses to unmet needs remained obstacles throughout much of his faith journey. Abigail found that she transferred her experience of her father's inability to express his love for her "perfectly" to her perception of God. Yet we saw in both that these very same wounds and developmental difficulties became important resources in their relationships with God, and their ability to reach out to others. Michael's own addictive history became a platform of compassion for hurting people, and it afforded significant insight into how Jesus wants to deliver us from attachments that control and destroy our lives. Abigail, once she experienced the depth of authentic love in God the Father, was able to love her husband, Bill, and others in a sacrificial way.

One of my readers, in the early development of these chapters, wrote to me to express sadness at my sharing that Abigail had "fallen" sexually, in her early faith journey, and that Michael continued to struggle with pornography and drugs even into his third mansion years. We want—even expect—our journeys to run more smoothly. Yet we each have our own history of regrets. Every one of us would be tempted, if we could, to erase from our history some of our painful and sinful experiences. But the wonderful truth of the Gospel is that Jesus not only forgives our sins and heals our wounds, but He *redeems* them. The apostle Paul says it most clearly in Romans: "And we know that God causes all things to work together for good to those who love God, to those who are called according to His purpose" (Rom. 8:28). Our ability to know the love of God and to share that love with others is uniquely greater *because* of our brokenness and woundedness.

But the painful feelings from our experiences often remain. We might think that, once sins were confessed in repentance, forgiveness extended and received, and healing accomplished, the pain of our memories would go away. God does deliver us from the control of these experiences, but the memories may still remain places of tenderness and pain. Why? We are called to share not only the resurrection joy of Jesus but His suffering as well. Those places in our lives caused His suffering and death on the cross. Jesus continues to suffer, as the Lamb of God, because He so profoundly loves those who continue to choose death over life, those who hurt and wound themselves and others through sin. If all feeling of our pain were gone, we might easily look at others with pride and judgment. Instead, our hearts become soft, loving, and compassionate—like Jesus. We are conformed into the image of Christ, even in the uniqueness of our sin experience. What a wonderful and amazing Lord we have.

Unique in Our Need for Healing and Spiritual Formation

We can see, therefore, that healing is another important factor in our spiritual formation. God reveals past spiritual and emotional wounds that keep us from growing and maturing. Healing for our spirits has already been accomplished and made available to us through Jesus' death on the cross. But He does not force it upon us; it must be received.

As we saw in our discussion of the mansions, God often surfaces our need for healing as we progress. I have noticed that people who are entering the fifth mansion, who are longing for a deeper intimacy with God, find that their old intimacy wounds begin to resurface. As our Lord draws closer, our intimacy-wound buttons are pushed, and we may find ourselves frightened or wanting to pull away. We may well be confused by the resurfacing of our "old issues"; we thought we had dealt with them years ago. But now God is taking us deeper and closer, and further levels of healing are required. Now, we are ready; before, we could only go so far.

There are many authors who have written about this kind of healing. Understanding their insights can be helpful for us to recognize our own issues related to healing and spiritual growth, as well as prepare us to be of help to others. Agnes Sanford's work is foundational, and her book *Healing Gifts of the Spirit* is the most concise.[7] Sanford is one of the first modern writers to provide insight and training related to the interconnected aspects of physical, emotional, and spiritual healing. Another foundational work on inner healing was written by John and Paula Sandford.[8] The Sandfords extensively review the biblical and theological foundations for healing with specific instructions related to common issues that face many of us as we mature physically and grow spiritually. A more recent author who has written in this area is David A. Seamands. His *Healing for Damaged Emotions* is a good integration of the understanding of psychology and the power of God to heal.[9] Leanne Payne is another author and teacher who has offered profound insights into the nature of inner healing. Her book *Restoring the Christian Soul* provides the most concise insight into her work.[10] These authors and teachers, and many others, have demonstrated the connectedness of mind, body, and spirit. When one part of us is wounded, the other parts are also affected. Their work is an important resource for understanding our own spiritual growth, as well as equipping us to support others in their growth. In several cases with each of these authors, significant personal insights have come as I studied to be able to help "others." On more than one occasion, a tear running down my cheek alerted me to the fact that there was more than an academic connection happening. Looking at a timeline of my own spiritual history, it is easy for me to correlate important incidents of healing of my own wounded spirit with significant moves forward in my relationship with God.

Unique in Our Personality and Spiritual Formation

Have you ever read or listened to an account of someone's spiritual victory story and thought to yourself, "I'm just not wired that way; that doesn't sound very attractive to me"? Well, there is good news. Another important contribution to our understanding of spiritual formation comes from the description of personality types and their effect on our spiritual development and the practice of the spiritual disciplines. The best known personality assessment tool used in relationship to spirituality is the Myers-Briggs Type Indicator (MBTI). The MBTI describes sixteen personality types and four temperament indicators. The type system comes from the work of Jung and Myers and Briggs. The temperament system was then compiled by David Keirsey.[11] Familiarity with the dynamics of these personality types can help us understand how we relate to others and to God. It can inform what aspects of spiritual growth might come naturally to one individual and be quite a challenge to another. For example, and maybe to our surprise, spiritual disciplines that are not natural to us often facilitate greater spiritual growth. Chester Michael and Marie Norrisey present an in-depth discussion of the relationship between temperament and spiritual formation.[12]

Let me use myself as an example. As an activist, driven to accomplish and gain approval, stillness with God in abiding prayer was very difficult. I was happiest when the work was getting done, and therefore my prayers tended to center around my work. Sitting quietly with God, to just be with Him, felt like a waste of time, even though intellectually I knew it wasn't. Quieting my mind of thoughts and distractions was almost impossible. Yet, probably more than any other spiritual practice, God has used abiding prayer to draw me into His heart and to enable me to experience His love. Realization that my personality made this practice difficult for me gave me courage to persevere, and now abiding prayer is a precious part of my daily life.

My personality "type" on the Myers-Briggs is an NF (Intuitive and Feeling). I relate to the world around me more through feeling and intuition than through what I think about things. Some of my closest Christian brothers and sisters can get spiritually high from reading profound theology, but I am more apt to be touched by God through personal interaction with others. The writings of others have played a significant role in my life; correct theology (the way we think about God) is important to me, but solitude with God or sharing with spiritual friends is where I am more apt to touch the Infinite and become transformed. The discovery about how I am wired has set me free to be myself, enjoy my natural proclivities, and allowed me to push into spiritual disciplines that aren't as natural and fulfilling for me.

Knowing Our Uniqueness

What is important to us here is our self-knowledge. As we saw in our discussion about movements of growth in each of the mansions, self-knowledge is an important part of growth, both in emotional as well as in spiritual maturity. When we view ourselves or the world falsely, we make significant mistakes. Self-knowledge is critical for those of us who want to walk with Jesus. God loves and relates to the real person, not to our illusions or projections. He communicates with us and guides us on the basis of who we really are and how we're wired.

Remember, however, that the *real you* is not simply a matter of genetic wiring and personality formation. How we relate to the world around us is only the first dimension of self-knowledge. Our relationship with Christ defines us more profoundly. We are sinners, loved, forgiven, and redeemed by the Creator of the Universe. His indwelling Holy Spirit removes the limits of the first dimension of self-knowledge.

As we grow in our faith and relationship with God, we discover the third and most important aspect of our self-knowledge: we have become a new person, in Christ. We are sons and daughters of God whose whole personhood has been caught up in the Trinity, whose very being is in transformation, from the inside out, into the likeness of Christ. It is this identity that must undergird our ongoing spiritual growth. Most amazingly, we are not being stamped out, in cookie cutter fashion, into automatons, but set free to become who we really are in intimacy with God, in all our uniqueness. Therefore, to truly understand ourselves we must know ourselves well in these three dimensions, all defined by the last, the Center.

A significant problem that we face, relative to self-knowledge, however, is fear. Many of us, particularly we Christians, have labored to craft a positive image. We've worked hard to be successful, likeable, caring, wise, and so forth. Many of us have become so focused in creating this image we project to others that we begin to believe it ourselves. Behind this false image (never totally false, of course) lurks the fear that if the real us were to be fully exposed, people wouldn't like us, and worse, we wouldn't like ourselves. Recognizing and affirming our true self can be one of the most painful struggles of Christian maturity and our spiritual formation. Yet it becomes one of the greatest victories.

A personal example might show what I am talking about. In my own youth, I unknowingly made two promises in response to my family setting. First, I promised myself that I would never become the failure that my father had become because of his alcoholism, and second, I would become the success my mother had always wished for herself. Therefore, I worked hard to do well and to project a successful person. Inside, I was really a scared and lonely little boy who desperately needed to be loved and affirmed. Many years later, I was talking to a close Christian friend, complaining that I seldom felt cared for by the people around me. My friend looked at me with astonishment and responded, "Tom, why do you need to be cared for? You always seem to have it together." Even this close friend was not able to see through the façade I had erected, even though I would have told you that I was a transparent and vulnerable person. It took many years for me to learn to let the scared little boy show, even to God. When I did, to my amazement no one criticized me, told me to shape up, or grow up. They simply loved me where I was. My true needs began to be met in healthy ways, and I was freer to be myself. More important, I began to let God love me in the ways I most needed, and I grew spiritually and emotionally.

A wonderful novel that describes this self-discovery process was written by Susan Howatch: *Glittering Images*.[13] Her main character, an Anglican priest, once recognizing that he was projecting a "glittering image," realized he thought of his hidden true self as "the beast." The story is a marvelous example of discovery and the kind of help we often need.

The Process of Discovery

Although most, if not all, of us grow in self-knowledge over the years, few are really intentional about it. We have all known people who go to their grave, tragically still living with major delusions about themselves and the people around them. If we are to grow spiritually and cooperate with God fully in the process of becoming like Jesus, we must be intentional about our process of discovery, about who we are, and how we relate to God and others. It is vital for us to understand what drives us, where our needs come from, and the helpful and unhelpful ways in which we attempt to navigate life. The unfortunate process of hitting the walls of our misperceptions can bring significant insight to those who are willing to learn, but it is possible for us to be intentional in our discovery process. In fact, it is critical that we do so.

Let's look briefly at some of these methods of discovery that have come up in our discussion of the mansions, and reflect a bit further on how we can be intentional about our own learning.

Biblical perspective: The world around us attempts to define as normal a life that is broken and dying, estranged from God. Only in Scripture can we gain the real perspective to honestly see ourselves as sinners, in the light of God's love, forgiveness, and reconciliation. Without this perspective, life will continue to confuse us and we will never grow spiritually.

Authentic spiritual friendships: Most of what we know about ourselves, truth or falsehood, has been reflected back to us from others. It is vital that we have close brothers and sisters in Christ with whom we can be open and vulnerable and who love us enough to tell us the truth.

Christian community: Individual relationships are important, but we truly come to understand ourselves in the context of a safe, loving, and honest Christian community. There our uniqueness rubs up against that of others and our spiritual gifts can be revealed and affirmed. It is in the context of such a community where our use of personality inventories such as the Myers-Briggs can be most helpful and tested by others.

Spiritual direction, coaching, and counseling: There are many times when it is helpful to have the assistance of a person trained to listen to our experience with God, and help put it into context and give guidance where needed. Unfortunately, just as we do with our physical health, we tend to seek out this expertise only if the normal remedies have not worked and we are desperate. Wisdom would encourage us to take advantage of this kind of help regularly.

Journaling: Often it is easier to understand what we are feeling when we put words to it. Most of us have experienced new insights as we shared with others what has seemed a swirl of thoughts and feelings with no real connection. In the same way, writing about our spiritual experiences can bring clarity. Some of us find it helpful to actually write out our prayers and conversations with God. The added advantage of keeping a journal, whether it is regular or occasional, is that a review can allow us to see the continuity in our spiritual journey. In retrospect, we can see both how we have grown and how some issues remain a struggle for us. I have often found it helpful to share my journal with a spiritual friend and ask for feedback.

Solitude: The busyness of daily life often obscures self-knowledge because we don't take time to be reflective. Day after day, we plow through life's demands and activities without stopping to take count of what is happening in our hearts. It is often only when we get away by ourselves, for an extended time, that our inner conversation with God can be heard. Without the protection of the distractions of our harried schedules, we are forced to face what is going on within us, and then have the time to seek God about it.

Spiritual formation discovery retreats: Many of us have had significant breakthroughs in our spiritual journey by participating in a guided spiritual retreat. A leader who understands how to facilitate a process of solitude, community, worship, personal reflection, and sharing can help set a context in which the Lord can speak to us profoundly. We'll look at one of those opportunities provided by *Imago Christi*, as an example.

As you may remember, *Imago Christi* is the community and ministry of which I am a part. One of the significant contributions of *Imago Christi* is Spiritual Formation Discovery for Leaders.[14] This three-day guided retreat takes maturing Christians through a discovery process designed to help them discover where they are in their spiritual formation journey and how to cooperate more fully in the spiritual formation process. The Discovery helps participants understand God's goal in their lives and reflect on their journeys in the context of the Teresian Mansions. They are able to discern their practical or operative view of God, in contrast to their theologically correct view. The Discovery helps participants experiment with abiding prayer and explore their experience with authentic spiritual community. The process concludes with development of a personal spiritual formation plan, based on what they have discovered. At this writing, hundreds of leaders have found that the Discovery experience clarified many misunderstandings about what God was doing in their lives and launched them ahead in their spiritual growth. You can explore the *Imago Christi* website to find out about Discoveries that are being offered in various parts of the world, and other resources offered by *Imago Christi*. See www.ImagoChristi.org.

Uniquely, you and I are traveling the same journey toward the heart of God, using the roadmap described by the Seven Mansions, and we are each traveling that journey in our own way. God loves each one of us personally and guides us forward in ways that are specifically tailored to our personality, history, and needs. In the following chapter, we will look at how this unique journey can work out in the context of spiritual community, the church. What would it be like to be part of a vibrant and alive community where each person is intentionally engaged with Jesus in the mansion where He has them? What might it be like if that community was committed to one another to support our ability to fully love and be loved by God, and then share that love with the world around us?

REFLECTION

- Through what experiences has God enabled you to discover the most about yourself?

- What parts of your personal temperament and history do you find most difficult to accept and share?

- What are the steps that God is asking you to take now to both discover and affirm your uniquenesses?

CHAPTER 13

Spiritual Formation and the Church

*You are the light of the world. A city set on a hill
cannot be hidden; nor does anyone light a lamp and
put it under a basket, but on the lamp stand, and it
gives light to all who are in the house. Let your light
shine before men in such a way that they may see
your good works, and glorify your Father who is in
heaven.*

—MATTHEW 5:14–16

BY NOW I HOPE THAT YOU HAVE COME TO UNDERSTAND the goal
and the process of spiritual formation. In looking at your own
journey of growing intimacy with God, you've used the roadmap
described in the Teresian Mansions, seen your own story in that
context, and looked at your uniquenesses; you are excited about
moving forward with Jesus into the wonderful adventure He has
in store for you.

There is, however, a critical part of our journey that we need
to discuss: church. Strangely, a large number of us who are journeying in what Teresa called the "Passive Mansions" (the fourth
mansion and above) struggle with our lives at church. Many of us
find little support for our journey and in fact are often frustrated
by the total lack of preaching or teaching that would indicate

there is anything more than the third mansion of working for God. Yet we have seen that spiritual community is essential to our ability to follow Jesus and mature in our relationship with the Trinity. Spiritual formation coaches, friendships, camps and retreat centers, and opportunities to minister together formed key milestones for Abigail and Michael.

As we mentioned earlier, recent studies by Willow Creek Church demonstrate this frustration. Remember that more than 60 percent of the "Christi-centered" members interviewed (probably fourth mansion and beyond) found virtually no aspect of church life that supported their spiritual growth. These studies indicated that this group was so discouraged with church life that a considerable number were considering leaving the church. George Barna, an eminent Christian sociologist and researcher, indicates that an increasing number of serious followers of Jesus are doing just that.[1] Barna doesn't quite encourage abandonment of the local church as a helpful place for serious Christians, but he expresses little hope that churches will fully embrace the Good News that Jesus wants to transform us and that church communities will dynamically affect the world.

Personally, I am much more optimistic. Despite significant indications of decline in church attendance, the Holy Spirit is at work in new ways. Jesus is head of the church and clearly central to God's plan to bring the Kingdom. Although it is certain that the "way we do church" will need revamping in the years to come, there are already encouraging signs. The words *spiritual formation* are emerging in significant numbers of churches today. Leaders are recognizing that immature members cannot be expected to follow Jesus into the tough places of our culture. Many of these churches may have faddishly substituted "spiritual formation" for the older title "Christian education," but many others are seriously asking questions about what it would mean to move past discipleship of new believers and members and fully support the lifelong transformation of its members. As you and I grasp what an authentic, spiritually forming community looks like, we can become powerful influences for change in our local churches and the world.

Imagine with me. Can we picture a church where loving God and taking that love to our neighbors is simply what church is about? What would it be like to have Sunday morning worship radiate our dynamic love for Jesus, and the preaching and teaching guide us to discover and live out that love more fully? Can we imagine a church of spiritual pilgrims, recognizing their unique journeys to the heart of God, dependent on one another for help and encouragement in that adventure? What if small groups and spiritual friendships were intentionally facilitated to focus on helping us grow spiritually, and live out the love of Jesus in the world around us? What might happen if the leadership of the church was formed by a community of men and women whose intimacy with God was so deep that they were able to discern His specific leading for the body, rather than have to rely on canned programs and traditions? What if, one day, you were reading about Jesus and His disciples' overnight trip to the mountain to pray together, followed by their journey to the valley to work miracles among people who desperately needed God's love, and we were able to say, "Of course; that's what happens every week at our church"?

I recently received two beautiful images for this kind of church. It was still dark as I sat in my usual chair for prayer. A candle was lit on the table next to me. In a time of deep stillness with the Lord, I felt prompted to look at the candle. This three-inch-diameter candle was almost spent, and the wick was deep inside, near the bottom. The whole candle glowed beautifully and flickered with life, but I could not see the flame. As I stared at the candle, the thought came to me, "It's not the candle that is beautiful, but the light within." Later in my time of prayer, I again opened my eyes and the whole room was lit up with a warm yellow light. The window in my room faces north, so it couldn't be the sun. As I looked out the window, I saw the winter tree in the backyard, ablaze with light from the sunrise. It was so bright that it radiated light into my room. Both images spoke to me about the church. It can be a "light upon the hill" only insofar as it radiates the light of Christ from within it. This light shines through us, as we are transformed into the likeness of Jesus. A community of maturing Christ-filled people does shine like a light to everyone around it. I think you'll agree with me that this is the kind of church the New Testament calls us to be and become. How did we get stalled?

Of course, personal spiritual formation has always been integral to the life of the local church. The biblical imperatives for us to be spiritually forming churches are undeniable. From the earliest Hebrew traditions, it has been taught that it is the role of the community to instruct and train the young so they will discover how to live in covenant relationship with God. Proverbs teaches, "Train up a child in the way he should go, even when he is old he will not depart from it" (Prov. 22:6). God speaks to Aaron about his responsibilities to teach the people: "teach the sons of Israel all the statutes which the LORD has spoken to them through Moses" (Lev. 10:11). The apostle Paul charges the church with the same responsibility in naming some as apostles, prophets, teachers, and so on (cf. 2 Tim. 4:1–2). These passages, addressed to the community of faith, all point to the church's role in instruction and spiritual formation, in both old and new covenants.

This practice of intentional instruction in spiritual growth continued in the early church with the practice of confirmation prior to baptism, and the use of homilies at church gatherings. Because of the small house churches and the closeness of the community, the spiritual education in the early church was not only taught but also experienced. Children and new believers were not only instructed in the Scriptures and creeds but learned by observation how to pray and live the Christian life. Through the expressed faith of others and their example of spiritual growth, less mature Christians were shepherded by the more mature (cf. 1 Tim. 4:11–15; Eph. 4:14–16).

As the church became more focused on the sacraments as the center of church life, teaching became less important, except for the training of clergy.[2] In the Reformation era, with the Scriptures in the common vernacular, Christian education (mostly accomplished through Sunday morning sermons) was again restored as a focal point of Protestant community worship.[3]

However, as the Western church became more clergy-centered, and intellectually and doctrinally focused, intentional spiritual training was often limited simply to communication of information. Character formation and transformation may have been preached and taught as goals, and even laws, but that was often as far as it went. How spiritual formation was to be accomplished personally was left to the individual.

Yet the tradition of spiritual formation training was kept alive, in both East and West, in monasteries and lay movements.[4] The monks and nuns became the spiritual directors for the clergy and those few others who sought it out. Concern about spiritual formation was also preserved among the Moravians, Quakers, Methodists, Puritans, and at some level in all of the Protestant traditions. The modern missions movement and the Sunday School movement are examples. The missionaries of many traditions have sought not only to evangelize unbelievers around the world but to teach them how to live in a Christian manner. Sunday schools have sought to teach both youths and adults the truths of Scripture and help them explore practical applications in their lives. There have been many faithful and holy people, in every tradition, whose lives exhibited significant spiritual growth, who became beacons for others in their settings. Unfortunately, much of our church life has focused on preserving doctrinal positions, enjoying familiar community, and promoting basic evangelism for the unchurched.

Although spiritual direction is now becoming somewhat more accepted among Protestants, it is often pursued outside the congregation, often through a number of parachurch organizations offering spiritual retreats, direction, and so on. There is even a movement to establish "spiritual direction" as a subspecialty of pastoral care, implying that it is beyond the scope of pastors and elders. John Ackerman, a pastor and church consultant commenting on spiritual awakening in the church, writes, "Pastors need not and probably should not be trained as spiritual directors and should not be spiritual directors for parishioners."[5] He believes that spiritual direction requires a knowledge of spiritual formation and psychology that goes far beyond the training (and possibly interest) of most parish pastors.

The problem, however, is obvious. If we compare the huge number of Christians in the world to the few trained spiritual directors, we see that the task would be impossible. Most Christians will get only whatever spiritual formation training and coaching they find in local churches. Few will seek out specialized learning opportunities or retreat experiences, because people don't know they are available or don't realize they need them. If today's Christians are to become spiritually mature, the local congregation must make spiritual formation its intentional focus.

In the preceding chapters, I explained how important and vital it is, at every stage of spiritual growth, to have a constellation of mentors, teachers, and encouragers for spiritual growth to progress normally. It is clear from Scripture that God intends the majority of these resources to reside in the local church. We are, as the apostle Paul says, "baptized into the Body of Christ" (cf. 1 Cor. 12:13; Gal. 3:27). We are intended to live interdependently, so that our Lord can shepherd us as a flock as well as individuals. But for this to happen, pastors and church leaders—whether in a leadership role or godly influencers—must be aware of the goal of spiritual formation and the stages of growth along the way. We must understand that the process of spiritual formation starts with seekers and continues throughout life. We must also be able to recognize where a believer is in process and know how to coach the person in further growth.

Discipleship and Spiritual Formation

The problem, however, is that spiritual growth thinking, in most of our churches, has considered the journey only through basic discipleship, or to the third mansion. The goal of spiritual formation, in many cases, has been shortsighted. Many churches have narrowly focused on conversion as the primary ministry of the church. As we'll see in some examples that follow, they have been mainly concerned about the growth of members to the point where they are effective in witnessing to unbelievers, and then working in the church so that more unbelievers can be saved. Evangelism, motivated by the Great Commission, is certainly a vital mission of the church, but we must pay just as much attention to the Great Commandment: to love God and neighbor. It is only as Jesus lives in us, in practical and experiential ways, that the church will be the evangelizing and loving presence of Jesus in the world.

Let's look at some of the limitations of contemporary discipleship programs to illustrate the problem. No two churches are exactly the same, but it is possible to describe a typical disciple-ship program by reviewing some prominent examples that many churches are using. Rick Warren's Purpose Driven Church at Saddleback Valley Community Church, for example, puts greater emphasis on spiritual growth than many congregations and has become well known for its encouragement to be intentional and purposeful about maturing believers. Saddleback uses four basic components in discipleship training: (1) conversion, or knowing Christ; (2) turning attenders into members, or growing in Christ; (3) developing mature members, or serving Christ; and (4) turn-ing members into ministers, or sharing Christ.[6] Warren has an excellent program to develop Christians—up to the third man-sion. But there is little mention about the adventure of love with Jesus and a life of walking with Him personally and intimately.

Ron Bennett describes discipleship training from the Navigators' perspective.[7] He delineates four categories in his Spiritual Maturity Profile: commitment, competence, character, and con-viction. Bennett's profile goal is a well-functioning Christian in the life and ministry of the church. Like Rick Warren, his disci-pleship model goes only as far as the third mansion: a Christian active in the ministry of the church.

There are a number of other excellent discipleship programs we could cite, but the vast majority identify what we know as the third mansion as being the ultimate in Christian experience.

Some discipleship models come a little closer. For example, Howard Rice, former national moderator of the Presbyterian Church, USA, suggests that spiritual guidance is the lens through which all of pastoral ministry should be seen.[8] His eight disciple-ship activities are certainly a great place to start, especially with the aid of a spiritual mentor or coach. But how much more pow-erful this approach could be if it included a clear roadmap for spiritual formation and the discernible markers for progress we have already discussed. Not all practices are equally appropriate everywhere on the journey. Meditation, for example, is certainly a good thing to do, but it is probably more helpful in the fourth man-sion and beyond, where meditation and contemplation become essential practices for spiritual growth.

An example of someone who is still a step closer might be Bill Hybels, pastor of Willow Creek Community Church. Like Teresa of Avila, he teaches that the key to our relationship with God is prayer.[9] Certainly for a seeker-church pastor, Hybels's teaching goes one step further than many churches, by calling the Christian to listen to God and obey Him. Like many of the other approaches to discipleship, the Willow Creek model offers a good primer for new Christians as they advance into the third mansion, but it does not prepare them for the fourth mansion of falling in love with God, and the adventures beyond.

The goal of discipleship in so many of our churches is to produce an enlightened, well-behaved, and organizationally effective church member. We can see that even though a typical Christian education program can give a person a good start, it tends to stop short of preparation for the depths of a love relationship that truly "transforms the mind" (cf. Rom. 12:2). Imagine what could happen in our churches if we used our understanding of the complete journey and developed a way to guide one another along that journey.

Transformation of the Church

What we need is a spiritual formation ministry that builds on our basic discipleship. There are probably no two churches whose programming and needs are exactly the same. However, a good spiritual formation ministry for a local congregation could be constructed using the best of the discipleship models discussed here, and the movements of growth for each Teresian Mansion. Because spiritual formation is fundamental to everything the church does, the task can feel overwhelming; one could mention every ministry a congregation could possibly have and relate it to spiritual formation. But there are some relatively simple steps we can take to facilitate transformation in our congregations.

The components listed here do not have to be considered formal "classes," but activities that are intentional and available to all members of the congregation. It could even be possible for several congregations to team together to provide a full range of resources that it might be difficult for one congregation to accomplish.

We need to emphasize, however, that we are clear about the scriptural foundation on which each component is built.

It is important that we distinguish between the clear teaching of Scripture and speculation about some element of spiritual growth. There are many circumstances in which we must speculate, where Scripture is either unclear or does not address the topic or context; but we must always be able ensure that we are at least consistent with the clear teachings of Scripture.

It is also important to remember we are personally responsible for growth in our relationship with God. It is not the job of the church to grow mature Christians, but rather to foster an environment that supports what God wants to do in each person's life.

From our understanding of the spiritual formation journey, we can say that the exciting church we envision needs to include at least these dimensions (I'll say a few words about each just below):

1. Vision values for spiritual formation
2. Spiritual leadership
3. Authentic community and spiritual formation groups
4. Whole journey discipleship education
5. Spiritual formation mapping
6. Abiding prayer
7. Support in spiritual warfare
8. Resource center for reading and study
9. Counseling, healing, spiritual direction and coaching
10. Rule of life and spiritual disciplines
11. Spiritual formation retreats
12. Evangelism and missions from a spiritual formation perspective

Spiritual Formation Vision and Values for the Congregation

The role of vision and values for the church is becoming increasingly important for congregations in the postmodern era. At one time there may have been a shared understanding within most congregations about the purpose and strategy of the church. But in our rapidly changing culture, the old norms are being dispensed with and people are searching for new alternatives.

The biblical exhortation is truer than ever: "Where there is no vision, the people perish" (Prov. 29:18).

In today's church, clear vision and values are what will draw members together around an agreed-on and God-given goal. Many times, church visions have more to do with exterior outcomes than with the interior nature of the church. But both are important. As the congregation agrees on the outward mission of the church, it also needs to recognize that the spiritual transformation of the membership is God's vision as well, and a deeply engrained value among us, not just a means to the outward end. Therefore, it is important to establish a clear congregational vision for the ongoing spiritual formation of unbelievers into believers, and for believers to grow in their relationship of love with God. Spiritual formation of our membership is the key to all we envision. We cannot relegate it to one of the "aisles in the consumer market."

Spiritual Leadership

Although we are listing elements that can be part of a spiritually forming congregation, we need to be careful not to make the mistake of thinking that we can simply plug and play a set of programs. Jesus is head of the church, and if we are to truly have a spiritually alive community then Jesus must build it: "Unless the LORD builds the house, they labor in vain who build it" (Ps. 127:1). Each congregation is unique. It has a unique history, setting, membership, and challenges. If our desire is to help a community of people mature spiritually so that they can love God fully and follow Jesus specifically, then this has to start with the leadership of the church. No lasting change can take place in a church, or any organization, unless it first happens in the leadership. We cannot lead others where we ourselves have not yet been. However leadership is defined in a given congregation, the members of that leadership community must be intentionally on the journey of spiritual growth before they can lead the congregation into spiritual growth.

A pastor recently told me, "Our elder board fully approves of our move toward spiritual formation." It may seem easy to gain "approval" from a leadership board and staff to implement spiritual formation programs. Who could argue with spiritual growth? But there is a difference between assent and true leadership. Any change is difficult for a community. Worse, however, if leadership has not developed their own community of trust and mutual support for their own transformation, they cannot enable that kind of community to develop in the congregation. Further, unless leaders are living intentionally in their own spiritual formation, they have no spiritual authority to call the church to spiritual growth.

Several churches working with *Imago Christi* have taken their entire staff, elder group, small group leaders, and teachers and spouses through the Spiritual Formation Discovery for Leaders process. From that common foundation they have gone forward to experience wonderful personal growth, learned to listen to Jesus as a group, and then lead the congregation forward according to God's plan. It is an exciting thing to see.

Authentic Community and Spiritual Formation Groups

We have seen that our individual spiritual formation is greatly dependent on our life in the Body of Christ. We have also seen that, historically, it has been monastic communities actually living together that have fostered the greatest insights into the practical aspects of spiritual formation. However, even our local congregation can become a community that encourages and supports our spiritual growth; it has to become one of our core values.

There are two dimensions of our community life that must become intentional, as a minimum. First we need to instill a "climate" of openness, vulnerability, and journey. It is inadvertently possible to imply that "real" Christians should have attained some level of knowledge, church practice, giving, and so on. However, if we are to become encouraged to embrace our spiritual growth, we need to understand that everyone is in process; we have times that feel like growth and times that feel like backsliding. Such a climate requires transparency from leadership; this imparts not only permission to admit we are still in process but real joy in change and growth.

Second, if we are to provide an authentically transforming community, we need to be intentional about helping people establish meaningful relationships. We are not apt to share our deepest struggles with people we know casually, or seek help from mentors who seem to have it all together. The way we gather on Sunday mornings and conduct small groups, classes, and committees can either put business first or relationships first. We need to be intentional about the latter.

Although a congregational climate of community is essential, our spiritual formation needs a smaller place of intimacy and trust. Spiritual formation small groups are essential. Our ability to discuss our spiritual life, successes, and failures is an important resource in the spiritual formation process. Spiritual friendships can be developed that provide encouragement and insight for those who are intentional about continuing their spiritual growth. Much of the work of spiritual directors, mentors, and counselors might not be needed if church members had access to a spiritual formation peer group, to help them work through growth issues.[10]

Whole Journey Discipleship Education

We've talked a great deal about good discipleship programs that are available to guide members into the third mansion, so we won't repeat the necessary elements here. It is interesting, however, that these programs don't recognize the "growth" struggles of the second mansion. Remember that in the second mansion our basic faith in Christ was strengthened through the conflicting demands of our world and God's invitation to live a life of love and faithfulness. We faced increased temptations to conform to the world rather than follow Jesus faithfully. Simplistic discipleship approaches can imply that growth is a nice steady climb toward getting it all together, and fail to recognize this difficult "war of the worlds" season as an important growth process. But for the church to encourage and facilitate lifelong spiritual growth, these discipleship programs need to be augmented with teaching about the true goal of spiritual growth and the landscape of the journey. We need to make part of our educational offerings instruction that relates to all seven mansions.

To do this effectively, however, means that members need to have some idea about what is appropriate for them. For example, it would not prove fruitful for someone who has just become a Christian to attend a class about experiences in the sixth mansion. This need for people to be able to have some idea about where they are in the journey leads us to the next consideration.

Spiritual Formation Mapping

With a clear roadmap that describes the phases of spiritual growth, it is possible to gauge more precisely a person's point of growth in relationship with God. Once members understand where they are in the process, they can more intentionally and appropriately cooperate with God in the ongoing spiritual formation process. Reading about the rooms for each mansion can be helpful in giving us a general idea of where we are in our spiritual growth, but there is too much overlap between the mansions to discern between them with any certainty. It would be helpful to have a mapping tool to make the process somewhat more objective. Therefore I have constructed, and *Imago Christi* has substantially refined, a tool that uses the Teresian Mansions and the five descriptive markers for each to enable us to locate ourselves within the Teresian Mansions.

The Mapping Tool was developed by taking the first five descriptive markers, or rooms, for each mansion and preparing three statements for each marker. Our answers to these statements can indicate whether we are experiencing spiritual life in one mansion or another.[11] By answering all 105 questions, we generate a score in each of the seven mansions. The higher scores indicate the principle mansions in which we are currently experiencing our relationship with God. Remember, the mansions are progressive but not linear. A person may be "residing" in a given mansion but experiencing aspects of mansions ahead and behind her or his principal residence.

Spiritual formation mapping could be done at any stage of our development, but it is best for adults who have demonstrated some maturity and consistency in their relationship with God and the church. Waiting until this time may help to avoid a competitive and prideful attitude toward spiritual growth.

The process can be done with an introduction to the spiritual formation journey, explaining the summary of each mansion and the relationship between our effort and God's grace. This can be done individually, with a mentor, or in a class or small group setting. We can now develop an individually suited growth plan, using the Teresian Mansions' Movements of Growth. The Mapping Tool is currently available only through *Imago Christi*. Because the tool is complex and most useful for Christians at a more mature phase of their journey, it is released only as part of personalized training for its use. The Mapping Tool is also used as part of *Imago Christi*'s Discovery process, discussed above.[12]

Abiding Prayer

Our basic discipleship training should include instruction about prayer that enables us to learn a balanced way of talking to God, such as the ACTS method discussed earlier. "Ministry prayer," which includes intercession and requests of God's wisdom and power, is essential. But "relational prayer" must ultimately be its foundation. For us to progress in deepening intimacy with Christ, we need to learn more about prayer that is responsive to God's initiative, more listening than talking.

Although seldom used for this purpose, Jesus' teaching about our dependent relationship in John 15 is a wonderful way to understand this relational dimension of prayer. Jesus uses the analogy of the vine and branches to describe the "abiding" nature or our relationship, and therefore our communication, with God.[13] "Abiding Prayer" is a spiritual conversation, in the heart, that communes with our Lord, expressing thoughts too deep for words and intuiting the mind of Christ. Abiding prayer includes listening to God in scriptural meditation, contemplation, and silence.

One very helpful method to assist our transition from Bible "study" to reflective listening in Scripture meditation is the nineteenth annotation of the Spiritual Exercises of St. Ignatius. Coaching can be done in a group, retreat setting, or individually with a listener or coach. James Wakefield has slightly revised the nineteenth annotation of the Spiritual Exercises for Protestants, presenting clear instructions for journaling and use in a congregational setting.[14]

Journaling can be an important part of prayer. Though not everyone finds journaling helpful, it is important that growing Christians know how to retain their insights and experiences of prayer, through journaling.

There are some excellent resources available to help us develop our life of prayer. For example, Richard Foster provides a good introduction to basic prayer, along with some insights into advanced prayer.[15] Joyce Huggett's *The Joy of Listening to God* is a good introduction to responsive prayer, written from an evangelical perspective.[16] Basil Pennington's *Centering Prayer* is a good overview of contemplation and silence.[17] The spiritual formation coach should recommend readings relative to the stage of prayer that lies ahead, inviting experimentation with new forms of prayer and providing appropriate guidelines.

Support in Spiritual Warfare

Spiritual warfare is part of our spiritual experience, from before we come to know Christ personally through our last moments on earth. It is also an area where speculation is apt to become confused with the clear teaching of Scripture. Every believer should understand the fundamentals of the devil's identity, his purpose, and his tactics. Ignorance or presumption is a real danger. As we saw in our discussion of the individual mansions, the line of attack changes as we mature. It is important to understand that discernment is always necessary, and to know when assistance from other mature believers is needed. Because there is such a wide array of approaches to spiritual warfare, taken by many authors from various traditions, basic teaching from the Bible is important. Few books on spiritual warfare talk specifically about the enemy's attack on our prayer life. Therefore classical teachers such as Evagrios' *Texts on Discrimination in Respect of Passions and Thoughts* and Ignatius of Loyola's Rules of Discernment are foundational.[18]

Spiritual Formation Resource Center

Our spiritual growth is, by definition, an exploration into the mystery of God—traveling where we have not gone before. A given congregation may have many mature Christians with whom to discuss one's life experiences, but classical and contemporary Christian mystics and leaders are also an important part of the "communion of the saints" from which we can learn.

It is important for growing Christians to have access to a wide range of spiritual formation materials to augment individual and group teaching and mentoring. A spiritual formation resource center can be developed for the congregation that includes credible readings and media, in all areas and disciplines, for each mansion. This center, including books, journals, Internet sources, movies, plays, and the like, will allow us to move at an individual pace that is comfortable and aid the congregational leadership in choosing sources that are consistent with its doctrinal perspective. It is helpful, however, to include readings and materials beyond the particular denominational or doctrinal position of the congregation. One should include classical writers who will balance the perspectives of being and doing. Annotated bibliographies can be used, both to inform and to caution believers about particular sources where appropriate. The resource center should also provide resources for those who are more visual and tactile, right-brain learners. Music and art, for example, can help us grasp the transcendent dimension of spiritual experience and help us recognize subtle feelings and responses of our hearts. Renovaré publishes an extensive resource list, as do spiritual formation and direction Websites.[19] *Imago Christi* has an extensive reading list organized according to the Teresian Mansions.[20] Richard Foster's Renovaré materials describe a variety of resources.[21] Obviously the list could go on and on.

Counseling, Healing, Spiritual Direction, and Coaching

Crisis and life struggles are a part of every life. They are also an important part of spiritual formation. As a significant ministry of pastors and congregations, pastoral care can either support the spiritual growth of an individual in crisis or deter it. Our pastor can help us understand that every aspect of life is filled with God's presence, and difficulty can therefore become an opportunity for growth. Part of our overall spiritual formation education can include understanding that seeking help is a sign of maturity rather than weakness.

Because pastors often want to be helpful, we might sometimes use pastoral counseling as an opportunity to fix a problem or shape someone up. But addressing the underlying questions about what God might be doing, and what we might learn, could prove more important than solving problems. The pastor and counselor can attempt to understand where we are in our spiritual process, and encourage us to listen to God in the midst of problems.

A spiritual congregational coaching or mentoring ministry may be a better way to deal with difficulties in our spiritual journey, before they reach a crisis stage. As we have seen, spiritual formation is a unique journey for all of us, and one-size-fits-all approaches are seldom effective. Spiritual formation coaches can be identified and trained within the congregation and made available to the membership. As the pastor recognizes individuals with the gifting and adequate spiritual growth to help others, an intentional training program can be established to enable these maturing believers to become encouragers and accountability partners for other growing Christians. Intentional training provides both competence and credibility for the coach or mentor, and it can establish and communicate appropriate expectations and boundaries for mentoring relationships. People are often more willing to confide in someone who is a peer-in-process than in their pastor or elder, who they assume has it all together.

Spiritual direction has, in recent years, become a recognized specialty with specific training and certificated programs. Most of us may find pastors and spiritual mentors adequate to provide counsel and help, but there may also be others, either more advanced or struggling more intensely, who need expert assistance. Pastors who are seriously attempting to lead their congregation into deepening spiritual growth may want to spend some time in spiritual direction themselves. Since there has not been a commonly agreed goal or roadmap for spiritual formation, the practice of spiritual direction can vary widely. A pastor can, however, locate qualified local spiritual directors and establish referral relationships.

Although spiritual formation coaching and direction can help us deal with issues of spiritual growth, sometimes expert help is required. Spiritual growth often includes the healing of past wounds that have us stuck in unhelpful attitudes or behaviors. Many Christians struggle with addictions to chemicals, possessions, activities, or people. We observed in Michael, particularly, that his struggle with addictions was initially a huge obstacle to his relationship with God and his spiritual growth. Later, however, the same issues became important sources of strength and ministry. Abigail too made good use of counseling and prayers for the healing of past spiritual and emotional wounds.

Need for counseling and therapy often occurs well into the maturing process, as God sees that we are now ready to address certain issues with His help. Developmental issues associated with adolescence, midlife, and senior years can yield opportunities for spiritual growth or they can be obstacles, depending on whether they are dealt with appropriately and with the right help. Not every congregation can provide quality Christian counseling, so specific resources can be identified.

Rule of Life and Spiritual Disciplines

As we have discussed, transformation requires intentionality on our part. A big part of cooperating with God's work in us is reflected in how we live. Knowing that this is true, Jesus modeled, and the apostles recorded, a lifestyle of spiritual practices that made Jesus available to the Father and enabled Him to "do what I see the Father doing" (cf. John 5:19). Over the centuries, men and women have emulated Jesus' lifestyle through a Rule of Life. This rule simply described a rhythm of daily life that incorporated various spiritual disciplines that would help them resist the cultural norms of their era, and live in a way that faithfully loved and followed Jesus. There are a number of rules developed historically, and several contemporary ones, that can be used as a guide.[22] But if we are able to understand the journey of spiritual formation and our place in it, we are uniquely able to develop or adapt a Rule of Life that fits our unique place in the journey and our individual wiring.

To support members in developing such a rule for themselves, it is helpful in the process of spiritual growth to study and understand these classical spiritual disciplines. Teaching can include their sources in Scripture and history and how they can be practiced. Use of the disciplines will change somewhat as we mature through the mansions, but a basic understanding and experience of each will enable members to choose which ones are helpful at a given time, as they develop and revise their spiritual formation plan. A group setting is excellent for teaching spiritual disciplines so people can ask questions and learn from one another. It may be helpful to use a "laboratory" approach, to experiment with spiritual disciplines as a learning experience without fear of failure. Richard Foster and Dallas Willard give excellent introductions to the spiritual disciplines and reference many additional resources.[23] Also, Adele Calhoun's *Spiritual Disciplines Handbook* is comprehensive, offering both descriptions of the disciplines and related spiritual exercises.[24]

Personal and Group Retreat Opportunities

Most of our church discipleship programs have been modeled on educational institutions; we decide what people need to know and then design a curriculum to teach that information. But as we have seen, we grow spiritually more from experience than from information. Therefore, the Sunday school classroom, even though an important part of the church, is not the best venue to help people grow spiritually. Spiritual formation retreats that create opportunities for members to not only learn about aspects of the Christian life but experiment with them can greatly assist our spiritual growth process.

Time is another reason that retreats can be important. One of the greatest obstacles to spiritual formation for most Christians in the modern world is busyness. Life is filled with family, work, recreation, and ministry duties to the point that members often don't set aside quality time with God. Because of the fullness and hurriedness of our lives, even the times of prayer and meditation can be frustrated by distracting thoughts of agendas. Christians have always found it helpful to take extended times away for prayer and reflection; it probably has never been more important and necessary than for busy and distracted Western Christians today. It is amazing what God can do when we give Him some extended attention, away from distractions.

At least two types of retreat experience can greatly enhance our spiritual growth: group retreats and personal retreats. Group retreats that include teaching, worship, and extended times of solitude and prayer can promote deeper spiritual experience in a supportive and interactive community. Regular spiritual retreat opportunities for the congregation can enable quantum leaps for believers who struggle with regular quality prayer. For those who have developed self-discipline, extended personal retreats of silence and solitude can prove very meaningful. The congregation can locate retreat facilities with a spiritually nurturing atmosphere and ready availability. It is often helpful if the retreatant has the opportunity to debrief with a spiritual mentor or friend, possibly sharing the journaling done on retreat.

Evangelism and Missions from a Spiritual Formation Perspective

We have seen, throughout the spiritual formation process, that an authentic love relationship with God naturally results in loving one's neighbor. Conversely, as we love and care for others, we find ourselves drawn closer to Jesus and learn to depend on Him more deeply. Therefore we simply cannot separate the missional life of the church from the spiritual formation life. We are not talking so much about a special program or ministry in the church; it is more a matter of how we think and talk about these two vital aspects of church life. Spiritual formation teaching and coaching must encourage us to look beyond ourselves to those God has placed in our lives. Opportunities for evangelism and mission work must be created in the congregation, as important ways to cooperate with God in our own formation. Conversely, we can greatly help those who participate in mission experiences to reflect on what God was doing in them, not just through them, during the process. It is not uncommon to hear youths and adults who return from a mission experience say something like,

"I don't know if God used me, but I sure was blessed." We need to help them unpack what they have learned and discover how to live it out in daily life.

A Spiritually Forming Church

This list of congregational spiritual formation ministry components is certainly not exhaustive, but it does show that it is possible to design and implement an intentional spiritual formation ministry within a congregation when there is (1) a clearly understood goal for spiritual growth, (2) a roadmap for the journey, (3) a way to assess spiritual progress, and (4) congregational life that supports and encourages our deepening love for God and our life of love for others. Of course, we must remember that our spiritual formation is not the responsibility of our church or pastor. It is our responsibility to cooperate with Jesus as He invites us into a deeper, more loving relationship with the Trinity. But our church community life is essential to the process.

Intentional spiritual formation ministry can move us to become communities that more fully reflect the love of Jesus. Using the spiritual formation roadmap and Mapping Tool and the spiritual formation ministries described here, we can make spiritual direction, mentoring, and coaching an integral part of our church life. Conflicts and struggles can be seen as opportunities for spiritual coaching rather than merely problems to be solved. As authentic spiritual leaders within our congregations, we can encourage one another to grow in our faith through deepening intimacy with God. Our roles in ministry to others can emerge out of our personal sense of God's calling, rather than pressure to fill a slot in a church program. We can identify spiritual formation resources that ignite and fan the fires of love within us. As followers of Jesus, we can take full responsibility for our personal spiritual growth and avoid the presumption and blaming that can result when we think that someone else should be making our growth happen. The church can become an environment of freedom and vulnerability where we all see ourselves as pilgrims together in process. As we become more mature in our relationship with Jesus, the church can also mature in its mission and ministry. Most of all, Christ can be glorified in and through us, in new life giving. Our churches can become "cities set upon a hill" in new ways, as love for Jesus and for neighbor flourish in our hearts.

REFLECTION

- What dimensions of a spiritual formation church seem to be missing in your church? How is God inviting you to make a difference?

- Christian community often begins with just two people. Who might God be calling you to, as a spiritual friend?

- Are you willing to invest yourself in prayer for your church and its leadership, that together you all might become a spiritually forming congregation?

CHAPTER 14

Our Call to Action

*"For I know the plans I have for you," declares the
LORD, "plans to prosper you and not to harm you,
plans to give you hope and a future. Then you
will call upon me and come and pray to me, and
I will listen to you. You will seek me and find me
when you seek me with all your heart. I will be
found by you," declares the LORD, "and will bring
you back from captivity."*

—JEREMIAH 29:11–14 (NIV)

BROTHER BONIFACE ALWAYS USED THE WORD "ausculta" to
describe the nature of prayer and our relationship with God.
Ausculta is old Latin and literally means "give ear to." Bon used
the nuance of the word to mean "be attentive," implying that
God does not so much "speak" to us as He invites us to be attentive to His heart, to intuit His movements and our subtle heart
responses. I hope, in your journey through *Mansions of the Heart*,
you have been attentive to what the Lord has been saying to you.

The real point—maybe God's point—of reading this book
is not to gain information but to encourage you along your personal journey through the mansions of your own heart into His
heart of love. If you have read attentively, you found yourself
strangely drawn to some words or stories, maybe even with tears.
In other sections, you found yourself skimming. I'd suggest that

the sections where your heart seemed to move toward God, in the text, point out places of your own yearning for growth—places of learning, struggle, longing, and God's whispered calling.

Recently I was leading a Discovery retreat in which I shared a monologue describing our potential experience in the sixth and seventh mansions, much like what you read with Michael and Abigail. One of the participants was moved to tears and had to leave the discussion time that followed. Later he came to me and shared what a wonderful job I had done in the presentation. After thanking him for the compliment, I observed that maybe it was not whether I had done the narrative well that moved him, but rather the longing of his heart to experience what I described. Again, he teared up and responded, "This ache has been sitting in my heart for some years, and this is the first time anyone has ever put words to it. Now I know that what I long for is possible, and even more, something the Lord wants to give me."

It is my prayer that God has touched you at various points in your reading. God is at work in you in a wonderful way, right where you are, gently leading you on to discover His love more deeply. He enjoys your company as He guides you into the lives of others whose hearts also ache for Him. Let me review where we've been and explore where God might be taking us further in the years ahead.

Remembering Where We've Been

Suggesting that spiritual formation has not been clearly understood or taught in most of our churches today, I argued that we are often left without clear reference points for assessing spiritual maturity or processes by which we can make progress in our spiritual journey. Dead-end roads have frustrated and derailed many of us, as we felt drawn to know our Lord more personally but tried the wrong path. We need to understand the overall journey, to find ourselves in process, and therefore see how to better cooperate with God as He leads and forms us toward the destiny that He has planned.

By reviewing a number of spiritual formation writings, I pointed out that even the goal of spiritual formation has often been confused. I suggested there are three alternative goals for spiritual formation that are often used: personal holiness, usefulness to God, and wholeness. However, when used as a primary goal, these potential goals all threatened to lead us down dead-end roads, luring us to try to accomplish what ultimately only God could do. Review of the nature of the Trinity and core biblical passages showed that a love relationship with God is the spiritual formation goal most faithful to the Christian biblical, historical, and theological witness. God's purpose is to transform us into the very image of Christ. He desires that we may be able to fully receive His grace, love, and presence within us. His greatest delight is to enable us to live with Him, participating in the Trinity, with the fullness and freedom of who we are as His daughters and sons. He wants us to live so in tune with Him that we naturally join Him in His redeeming ministry to the world, not by some grand scheme but by simply doing what we see Him doing.

I argued that it is vital to identify a spiritual formation roadmap that describes our journey and helps us find our general place in the journey. Not just any scheme could do, however. Our roadmap would have to be faithful to Scripture; validated by history; detailed descriptively; and focused on the clear goal of a love relationship with God in Christ; it would reflect our human development; apply universally across gender, cultural, socioeconomic, physical, and emotional differences; and encompass the full range of lifelong Christian experience. Teresa of Avila's Seven Mansions has the goal of a love relationship with God and meets all the necessary criteria.

I then led you in an exploration of each mansion of this amazing journey, showing how Jesus invites us to visit its rooms of growth: spiritual activity, personal motivation, prayer, spiritual warfare, experience of God, and movements of growth. As we journey onward through the mansions, visiting here and there, the Holy Spirit transforms how we think and feel and behave. Most of all, He creates within us a heart that can fully love and be loved. Abigail's and Michael's stories provided some concrete examples of the kinds of experiences we can have in our ongoing pilgrimage, and they permitted insight into how we can cooperate with God more fully as He leads us onward.

Next I discussed the impact of our uniquenesses as individuals. God is *not* trying to turn out cookie-cutter followers; He delights in the unique and beautiful ways in which He has created all of us. He therefore relates to us and loves us so that we are able to understand and respond.

Finally, I addressed spiritual formation and the church, suggesting that you and I have a responsibility not to focus on our own spiritual growth alone, but also to allow Jesus to use us in transforming our congregations. Our spiritual formation is designed by God to happen in the context of Christian community, the church. The overall ministry of the church can guide people through the spiritual formation process, once the congregation has a clear, describable, and measurable model of spiritual formation. A comparison of the Teresian spiritual formation journey with "typical church discipleship programming" showed that most discipleship models took us only as far as the Third Mansion. Yet we must help people continue their growth at all stages, furnishing necessary teaching and mentoring. A spiritual formation mapping tool can locate or "map" our progress within our spiritual formation journey, giving us a better idea about the particular nature of the help we need, and facilitate development of a spiritual formation plan by which to journey forward.

Spiritual Formation Is Not an Option for the Christian Community

The full spiritual development and formation of followers of Jesus is not an option for our local churches. Maturing members undergird a mature church and make it a safe and powerful place for new believers and seekers. You and I can be instrumental in developing and implementing a spiritual formation ministry that enables every one of us to live out our full calling in Christ. It is not enough to focus merely on getting members, winning souls, or survival. It is not sufficient to provide discipleship training that exposes us to only a portion of the possibilities of relationship with God through Jesus Christ. God is calling the church to a far greater task. George Barna writes: "America's superficial spirituality demands that we rededicate ourselves to proclaiming the gospel in new ways that are relevant to people's lives. The skin-deep commitment of most Christians to their faith requires that we first get our own house in order before we can hope to present a strong and attractive witness to a watching and skeptical world."[1]

God is crying out to us to follow Him into a bold new era in the Kingdom of God. We can discern this call from a number of perspectives.

We Have a Biblical Mandate

The primary reason for pursuing spiritual formation emerges from our Lord's clear instructions in the Great Commandment, in Matthew 22:37–40, and the Great Commission, in Matthew 28:18–20. All that God has prepared for us in the Old Covenant, and all that God has fulfilled in the New Covenant in Christ, culminates in boldly loving God and neighbor. At a minimum, the foundational scriptural passages identified in Chapter Three for each Teresian Mansion make it clear that a transforming relationship with God in Christ is God's way to live out this commandment and commission, enabling us to be a community of people who fully love God and neighbor. It is love for God and neighbor that mobilizes and motivates us to sacrificially share the gospel of salvation and new life with others. If we're truly growing in an intimate love relationship with Jesus, we can't help ourselves.

It's Time to Say Yes to Jesus

As I write this final chapter, I have a great hope, as well as a nagging fear. I am convinced that today we stand at the cusp of a new movement of God in history. We are being called in a new way to become *one* with God in His redemptive mission in the world. You and I are called, personally and specifically, to become an integral part of the final battle for the hearts and minds of God's beloved. We live in a time of mounting darkness into which our Lord plans to shine His glorious Light—through you and me. It can happen only if we become truly transformed into the image of Christ. The hand of Jesus is outstretched to each one of us: "Come to Me; become Mine; become like Me; follow Me into the lives of those for whom I died." My hope is that we will hear God's call and respond with our whole hearts.

My nagging fear? It is possible that the new interest in spiritual formation will be turned inward, made a plan for our personal happiness and comfort, or seen as a new tool to make our churches successful. It is possible that we will grab this manna, given to the whole world, for ourselves and gorge ourselves on it, until it rots. We can't let this happen. God has positioned us at a unique time in history; our response is critical.

God Is Calling the Church into a New Vitality

Today we are in a position to build upon the lessons learned from history as the church has grown from a fledgling mission to a massive institution to a worldwide community that has realized its call to function as the Body of Christ—an organism—locally and globally.[2] The Body of Christ has learned through the great historical emphases of rationalism, mysticism, and activism. Rationalism helped us think more objectively about our theology and practice. Mysticism helped us focus on our inner life with God. Activism encouraged us to mobilize great resources to address evangelism and care for the world. Spiritual formation is calling us further.

With this newfound emphasis in spirituality, we are realizing that we need to connect what is going on within us to the mission of the church. It is fundamentally who we are, rather than what we do, that makes us authentic children of God, the Body of Christ, the church (cf. 1 Pet. 2:9–10). We can give away only what we have received. We can proclaim only what we are authentically living.

God Is Moving in a New Cultural Context

The world is in desperate need of the authentic presence of Jesus in us personally and in our faith community. The world's potential for self-destruction is greater than ever before. Violence, crime, poverty, disease, and hunger continue to wound and even torture the majority of the world's population, despite the technological ability to deal with those issues. The church once set the standard for the ostensible moral values of the modern world, but sociologists agree that we have entered the post-Christian era, where the church and its values are no longer looked to for guidance.

On the contrary, much of the church is blatantly taking on the values of the world, with its relativism and narcissism.[3]

Our rapidly changing society is making it more and more difficult for the church to function internally as a real spiritual community and to reach out effectively in ministry. To navigate this new terrain effectively, we can no longer rely on old models. Even the question "What would Jesus do?" is no longer adequate to understand how to live authentically or take the Gospel to the world around us. We must be able to understand what Jesus *is* doing and cooperate with Him intimately. Jesus did what He saw the Father doing, nothing more and nothing less. As He was sent by the Father, He sends us in the same way.

There Is a New Spiritual Hunger Within and Without the Church

At the same time, interest in "spirituality" is increasing both within and beyond the church. It is particularly apparent when we study our rapidly changing generations. Across the board, spirituality is a growing interest. Wade Clark Roof, professor of religious studies at the University of California, Santa Barbara, offers an example of this new interest as he describes the baby boomer generation: "The new values emphasize self-fulfillment and self-growth, inner spiritual discovery and exploration."[4] George Barna talks about the spirituality of the next group, the "baby busters": "Busters possess an interest in religion because, in their transactional way of thinking, they see faith systems as potentially providing them with new insights or useful perspectives which would help them cope with life more effectively. But regular church attendance does not fit their life-style or correspond with the magnitude of the spiritual void they feel."[5]

Though we might say that much of this new interest in spirituality is misplaced, the fact is that at its heart it is a longing for what only Jesus can provide. Kenneth Boa, religious historian and president of Reflections Ministries, writes, "Thus religion is on its way out, while spiritualities that appeal to inner subjective and experiential authentication are on the way in. . . . Paralleling this growing interest in spirituality has been a pronounced increase in the church's appetite for spiritual renewal."[6]

John Westerhoff chronicles another example of this renewed interest. In telling about his own experience of the interest in spirituality while a professor at Duke University Divinity School, he says, "At first this concern was shared by only a few students and faculty. Courses in spirituality were seriously questioned. Today, spiritual formation is a major concern of faculty and students."[7] Christians, fed only the food of Third Mansion discipleship, are asking for something more.

A New Vision for the Future

In His prophecy in Joel 2:28, God says, "I will pour out my Spirit on all people" (NIV). It is not the job of the church to create a new heaven and earth, but it is the job of every one of us to fully live out the relationship to which God has called us. It is our task to "teach them *all* that I have commanded you" (cf. Matt. 28:20). We need to take seriously our responsibility to foster a community in which each Christian has the resources to grow in relationship with Christ to full potential. All followers of Jesus can come to understand the full range of potential spiritual experience in their journey of the heart into intimacy with God, toward transforming union. As we grow into the "fullness of Christ" (cf. Eph. 4:13), we will truly live out our destiny as the Body of Christ. The rest is up to Him. Jesus made this promise to us before His ascension into heaven: "Let not your heart be troubled; you believe in God, believe also in Me. In My Father's house are many mansions; if it were not so, I would have told you. I go to prepare a place for you. And if I go and prepare a place for you, I will come again and receive you to Myself; that where I am, there you may be also" (John 14:1–4, NKJV).

How will we respond—now, today—to Jesus' invitation? The whole Trinity is present, *in you* and *in the world*, moving forward mightily in His plan to save His beloved people. God is dwelling in the mansions of your heart, calling you into the deepest intimacy and joy in His love. He is calling you to know Him so completely that you will burn with His love for you and for the world. He is calling us to fully join Him in the adventure of the Kingdom of God.

Our response to His love and mission begins again every day, as we say *yes* to the quiet whispers of His Spirit in our hearts, as we intuit and obey His nods for us to follow Him into the lives of those around us. A new adventure awaits us in the mansions of our hearts.

NOTES

Chapter One: Is This All There Is?

1. Renované is a movement started by Richard Foster to encourage Christian leaders to grow in the spiritual life. See http://www.renovare.org.
2. Thomas Dubay, *Fire Within: St Teresa of Avila, St. John of the Cross, and the Gospel on Prayer* (San Francisco: Ignatius Press, 1989).
3. For information about the ministry of *Imago Christi*, see http://www.ImagoChristi.org.
4. James Wakefield, *Sacred Listening: Discovering the Spiritual Exercises of Ignatius* (Grand Rapids, Mich.: Baker Books, 2006).
5. Richard V. Peace, "From Discipleship to Spiritual Direction." *Theology, News & Notes*, Mar. 1999, *46*(1), 7.
6. Peace, "Discipleship," 7, 8.
7. Richard J. Foster, *Celebration of Discipline* (San Francisco: HarperOne, 1988).
8. Kieran Kavanaugh and Otilio Rodriguez, *The Collected Works of St. Teresa of Avila* (Washington, D.C.: ICS, 1986).
9. Thomas à Kempis, *On the Imitation of Christ* (Baltimore: Penguin, 1952).
10. Peace, "Discipleship," 8.
11. James M. Houston, "Spirituality," in *The Evangelical Dictionary of Theology*, ed. Walter A. Elwell (Grand Rapids, Mich.: Baker Books, 1984), 1046.
12. Peace, "Discipleship," 9.
13. Willow Creek Association, "Reveal: Where Are You?" (n.d.) http://www.willowcreek.com.
14. Brother Boniface went to his eternal reward on Feb. 8, 2006.

Chapter Two: Common Myths That Lead Down Dead End Roads

1. Willow Creek Association, "Reveal."
2. Cf. George Barna, *Virtual America* (Ventura, Calif.: Regal Books, 1994).

Chapter Three: Your Journey into the Love of God

1. A comparison of some alternative models of spiritual growth, surprisingly, shows that there are not many real models or journey descriptions available. Writers speak extensively about the experiences of spiritual formation and direction, but they seldom actually propose a descriptive model. However, there are a few historical models that have surfaced. As we review these possible alternatives, we find that some schemes are too simplistic, while others are far too complex. Some have a long history and others are recent models based on very limited experience.

2. Kavanaugh and Rodriguez, *The Collected Works of St. Teresa of Avila* (1986).

3. Kavanaugh and Rodriguez, *St. Teresa*; Kieran Kavanaugh and Otilio Rodriguez. *The Collected Works of St. John of the Cross* (Washington, D.C.: ICS, 1987).

4. Augustine, *The Confessions*, trans. Hal M. Helms (Orleans, Mass.: Paraclete Press, 1986).

5. Dallas Willard, *The Great Omission: Reclaiming Jesus' Essential Teachings on Discipleship* (San Francisco: HarperOne, 2004), 206–207.

6. Kavanaugh and Rodriguez, *St. John.*

7. Ibid.

8. Dubay, *Fire Within*, 78.

9. Ibid.

10. Kavanaugh and Rodriguez, *St. Teresa*, 1:263–452.

Chapter Four: New Beginnings: The First Mansion

1. Kavanaugh and Rodriguez, *St. Teresa*, Interior Castle, I: 1:286.

2. Ibid., 1:294.

3. C. S. Lewis, *The Great Divorce* (New York: Simon & Schuster, 1946), 96, 97.

4. Tom Clegg and Warren Bird, *Lost in America: How You and Your Church Can Impact the World Next Door* (Loveland, Colo.: Group, 2001), 34.

5. George Barna, *Virtual America* (Ventura, Calif.: Regal Books, 1994), 83, 84.

6. Kavanaugh and Rodriguez, *St. Teresa*, 2:287.

7. Ibid., 2:285.

8. Ibid., 2:293.

9. C. S. Lewis, *The Screwtape Letters* (New York: Macmillan, 1943), 27.
10. Lewis B. Smedes, *Shame and Grace: Healing the Shame We Don't Deserve* (San Francisco: HarperOne, 1993), 126.
11. Irving Harris, "Finding a Handle," in *Groups That Work*, ed. Walden Howard (Grand Rapids, Mich.: Zondervan, 1967), 11.
12. Kavanaugh and Rodriguez, *St. Teresa*, 2:270.
13. Dubay, *Fire Within*, 136–152. The term for addictions, in Teresa's time, was "attachments." Like addictions, they were sources of comfort, strength, security, and so on that substituted for God. Thomas Dubay gives an excellent discussion from the perspective of Teresa and John of the Cross.
14. Ibid., 80, 81.

Chapter Five: Between a Rock and a Hard Place: The Second Mansion

1. Kavanaugh and Rodriguez, *St. Teresa*, 2:298.
2. Dubay, *Fire Within*, 83.
3. Kavanaugh and Rodriguez, *St. Teresa*, 2:298.
4. Ibid., 2:301, 302.
5. Ibid., 2:298, 299.
6. This lack is apparent in the review of discipleship curriculum. Pentecostal and Charismatic churches are more apt to provide spiritual warfare teaching.
7. Kavanaugh and Rodriguez, *St. Teresa*, 2: 303.
8. Dubay, *Fire Within*, 84.
9. Kavanaugh and Rodriguez, *St. Teresa*, 2:301.
10. Lewis, *Screwtape Letters*.

Chapter Six: Following Jesus: The Third Mansion

1. Kavanaugh and Rodriguez, *St. Teresa*, 2:309.
2. Ibid., 2:304.
3. Ibid., 2:306.
4. Ibid., 2:313.
5. Ibid., 2:309.
6. Ibid., 2:311.
7. Ibid., 2:314.
8. Wakefield, *Sacred Listening*.
9. à Kempis, *On the Imitation of Christ*.
10. Kavanaugh and Rodriguez, *St. Teresa*, 2:309.

Chapter Seven: Discovering the Love of Jesus: The Fourth Mansion

1. Revelation 2:4.
2. Oswald Chambers, *My Utmost for His Highest* (New York: Dodd, Mead, 1935).
3. Dubay, *Fire Within*, 88.
4. Kavanaugh and Rodriguez, *St. Teresa*, 2:332.
5. Ibid., 2:327, 328.
6. Ibid., 2:317.
7. Dallas Willard, *The Spirit of the Disciplines: Understanding How God Changes Lives* (San Francisco: HarperOne, 1988), ix.
8. Richard J. Foster, *Celebration of Discipline* (San Francisco: HarperOne, 1988), 1.
9. Bernard of Clairvaux, *On the Song of Songs*, Cistercian Fathers Series, ed. Kilian J. Walsh and Irene M. Edmonds, vol. 40 (Spencer, Mass.: Cistercian, 1971–1980); *The Love of God* (Portland, Ore.: Multnomah Press, 1983).
10. Kavanaugh and Rodriguez, *St. Teresa*, 2:313.

Chapter Eight: Longing for Oneness with God: The Fifth Mansion

1. Kavanaugh and Rodriguez, *St. Teresa*, 2:335.
2. Dubay, *Fire Within*, 96.
3. Kavanaugh and Rodriguez, *St. Teresa*, 2:350.
4. Ibid., 2:351.
5. Ibid., 2:336.
6. Ibid., 2:346.
7. Ibid., 2:357.
8. Ibid., 2:351.
9. Ibid., 2:339.
10. Ibid., 2:348.
11. Ibid., 2:337.
12. Benedict J. Groeschel, *Spiritual Passages: The Psychology of Spiritual Development* (New York: Crossroad, 2000), 147, 148.
13. Ibid., 152.
14. Foster, *Celebration of Discipline*, 72.
15. Dubay, *Fire Within*, 129.
16. Ezekiel 11:19b–20.
17. Psalm 51:10.

Chapter Nine: The Long Dark Corridor: The Dark Nights of the Soul

1. Dubay, *Fire Within*, 159.
2. Kavanaugh and Rodriguez, *St. John*.
3. Ibid., 295.
4. The list is compiled from John's discussion, ibid., pages 313 through 329.
5. Gerald May, in *The Dark Night of the Soul: A Psychiatrist Explores the Connection Between Darkness and Spiritual Growth* (San Francisco: HarperOne, 2004), identifies "darkness" with the physical and psychological pains for life. However, John takes great effort to say that the Dark Nights are solely the work of God. Although they may be exacerbated by Satan's temptations and the absence of consolations in the face of trials, they are not caused by human experience.
6. *Imago Christi* is a covenant community of men and women from around the world who develop spiritual formation resources and provide spiritual formation coaching to Christian leaders. See http://www.ImagoChristi.org.
7. Kavanaugh and Rodriguez, *St. John*, 316.
8. Ibid., 321.
9. Ibid., 323.
10. Psalm 51:10f.
11. Oswald Chambers, *My Utmost for His Highest Devotional Calendar* (Bloomington, Minn.: Garborg's Heart 'n Home, 1986, Dec. 5).
12. Dubay gives a helpful comparison between mental and emotional problems experienced by believers and the true experiences of the Night of the Senses. *Fire Within*, 163, 164.
13. Kavanaugh and Rodriguez, *St. John*, 334.
14. See Romans 6:6, Ephesians 4:22, and Colossians 3:9.
15. Dubay, *Fire Within*, 169.
16. 2 Corinthians 12:2.
17. Kavanaugh and Rodriguez, *St. Teresa*, 2:364.
18. Kavanaugh and Rodriguez, *St. John*, 332–333.
19. Ibid., 160.
20. Kavanaugh and Rodriguez, *St. Teresa*, 2:386.
21. See Gerald May, in *The Dark Night of the Soul*, and Dubay, *Fire Within*.
22. Kavanaugh and Rodriguez, *St. John*, 311, 303.
23. Ibid., 29.
24. Ibid., 295–296.

Chapter Ten: The Passion of God's Love: The Sixth Mansion

1. 1 Thessalonians 5:17.
2. 2 Corinthians 5:15, 12:2f.
3. Kavanaugh and Rodriguez, *St. Teresa*, 2:359.
4. See Romans 8:26, 27.
5. Kavanaugh and Rodriguez, *St. Teresa*, 2:362.
6. Ibid., 2:272, 273.
7. Ibid., 2:372–426.
8. Ibid., 2:368.
9. Kavanaugh and Rodriguez, *St. John*, 354.
10. Ibid., 365.
11. John 3:8
12. Kavanaugh and Rodriguez, *St. John*, 375.

Chapter Eleven: A Life of Love in the Trinity: The Seventh Mansion

1. Kavanaugh and Rodriguez, *St. Teresa*, 2:428.
2. Ibid., 2:430.
3. Ibid., 2:432.
4. Ibid., 2:232.
5. Ibid., 2:433–434.
6. Brian Kolodiejchuk, *Mother Teresa—Come Be My Light: The Private Writings of the "Saint of Calcutta"* (New York: Doubleday, 2007). It is clear that Mother Teresa's Dark Night included those described by John of the Cross but had a greater meaning. Teresa of Calcutta realized that the Lord gave her a profound "spiritual poverty," to enable her to fully understand the physical and spiritual poverty within the people to whom she ministered. Unlike the transitory Dark Nights described by John of the Cross, hers lasted for the rest of her life.
7. Kavanaugh and Rodriguez, *St. Teresa*, 2:351.
8. Ibid., 2:301.
9. Dubay, *Fire Within*, 106.
10. Kavanaugh and Rodriguez, *St. Teresa*, 2:438.
11. James Houston, interview by the author, in Kovagoors, Hungary, Nov. 6, 2002, during the Follower Formation Fellowship's International Gathering on Spiritual Formation.
12. Kavanaugh and Rodriguez, *St. Teresa*, 2:438.
13. Ibid., 2:441.

14. Kavanaugh and Rodriguez, *St. John*, 44f.
15. Kavanaugh and Rodriguez, *St. Teresa*, 2:442.
16. Dubay, *Fire Within*, 103.
17. Ibid.
18. See John 5:19.
19. Kavanaugh and Rodriguez, *St. Teresa*, 2:441.
20. C. S. Lewis, *The Great Divorce*, 96.
21. C. S. Lewis, *Hideous Strength* (London: Macmillan, 1965, 1979), 290.
22. See Mark 6:31.
23. Kavanaugh and Rodriguez, *St. Teresa*, 2:430.
24. Ibid., 2:447.
25. 1 Corinthians 12:13.

Chapter Twelve: Your Unique Journey

1. Isaiah 6:1f.
2. James W. Fowler, *Stages of Faith: The Psychology of Human Development and the Quest for Meaning* (San Francisco: HarperOne, 1996). Fowler addresses the developmental stages by which we progressively establish a fundamental set of meanings and values. Although he does not address spiritual formation (in the sense in which we are using it), he offers important insights for understanding how the human mind works in relationship to faith.
3. James W. Fowler, *Faithful Change: The Personal and Public Challenges of Postmodern Life* (Nashville, Tenn.: Abington Press, 1996).
4. Groeschel, *Spiritual Passages*.
5. Larry Crabb, *Inside Out* (Colorado Springs, Colo.: NavPress, 1998). Crabb has written numerous books about the spiritual life that surface important insights about our individual nature and spiritual formation. Also see http://www.newwayministries.org relative to his school of spiritual direction.
6. Peter Scazzero, *Emotional Healthy Spirituality: Unleash a Revolution in Your Life in Christ* (Nashville, Tenn.: Thomas Nelson, 2006).
7. Agnes Sanford, *The Healing Gifts of the Spirit* (Old Tappan, N.J.: Revell, 1966).
8. John and Paula Sandford, *The Transformation of the Inner Man* (Tulsa, Okla.: Victory House, 1982).
9. David A. Seamands, *Healing for Damaged Emotions* (Wheaton, Ill.: Victor Books, 1981).
10. Leanne Payne, *Restoring the Christian Soul* (Grand Rapids, Mich.: Baker Books, 1991). See also http://www.leannepayne.org or http://www.pcmschool.com for further resources.

11. Excellent resources for in-depth understanding of the MBTI are Carl Jung, *Psychological Types* (New York: Harcourt, Brace, 1923); David Keirsey and Marilyn Bates, *Please Understand Me* (Del Mar, Calif.: Prometheus Nemesis Books, 1978); Isabel Briggs Myers and Mary H. McCaulley, *Manual: A Guide to the Development and Use of the Myers-Briggs Type Indicator* (Palo Alto, Calif.: Consulting Psychologists Press, 1985). For a correlation of the MBTI with spirituality and religious leadership, see Roy M. Oswald and Otto Kroeger, *Personality Type and Religious Leadership* (Washington, D.C.: Alban Institute, 1988).

12. Michael and Marie Norrisey, *Prayer and Temperament* (Charlottesville, Va.: Open Door Press, 1984).

13. Susan Howatch, *Glittering Images* (New York: Ballantine Books, 1987).

14. *Imago Christi* is an international and covenant community of spiritual formation ministry. This community is dedicated to helping Christian leaders shepherd from a strong foundation of personal intimacy with the Trinity, and thereby enable the church to become a spiritually forming community that lives as the transformational presence of Christ throughout the world. *Imago Christi* understands its calling prophetically, pastorally, and missionally. Our vocation is to call the church back to her first-order calling to love God above all else. Toward that end, it aims to coach and resource leaders in their own personal spiritual formation, and to extend this ministry of transformation through new covenant communities around the world. The goal of its ministry is to glorify God through the beautification of the church (Matt. 22:38; Eph. 3:19–21; Col. 1:27–28; 1 John 1:3).

Chapter Thirteen: Spiritual Formation and the Church

1. George Barna, *Revolution* (Carol Stream, Ill.: Tyndale House, 2006).

2. Ibid., 31.

3. Ibid., 145.

4. Ibid., 83–97.

5. John G. Ackerman, *Spiritual Awakening: A Guide to Spiritual Life in Congregations* (New York: Alban Institute, 1994), 74.

6. Rick Warren, *The Purpose Driven Church: Growth Without Compromising Your Mission* (Grand Rapids, Mich.: Zondervan, 1995), 130.

7. Ron Bennett, *Intentional Disciplemaking: Cultivating Spiritual Maturity in the Church* (Colorado Springs, Colo.: NavPress, 2001).

8. Howard Rice, *The Pastor as Spiritual Guide* (Nashville, Tenn.: Upper Room, 1991), 36.

9. Bill Hybels, *Too Busy Not to Pray: Slowing Down to Be with God* (Downers Grove, Ill.: InterVarsity Press, 1988).

10. Again, Richard Foster's material is a useful resource of devotional readings and discussion questions for spiritual formation small groups. John Ackerman (Ackerman, *Spiritual Awakening*) also gives helpful insights on using small groups for spiritual formation. Danny E. Morris and Charles M. Olsen, *Discerning God's Will Together: A Spiritual Practice for the Church* (Grand Rapids, Mich.: Zondervan, 1997) present insights in the use of spiritual formation groups for the process of discernment. Rose Mary Dougherty (Ackerman, *Spiritual Awakening*) offers a good guide for group spiritual direction.

11. The sixth marker, Movements of Growth, tends to relate more with how to advance to the next mansion and therefore is not as helpful in assessing one's current position.

12. See http://www.ImagoChristi.org.

13. See John 15:1–11.

14. James Wakefield, *Sacred Listening: Discovering the Spiritual Exercises of Ignatius.* Sacred listening is an adaptation of the Spiritual Exercises of St. Ignatius of Loyola, in a twenty-four-week daily prayer format.

15. Richard J. Foster, *Prayer: Finding the Heart's True Home* (San Francisco: HarperOne, 1992).

16. Joyce Huggett, *The Joy of Listening to God: Hearing the Many Ways God Speaks to Us* (Downers Grove, Ill.: InterVarsity Press, 1986).

17. M. Basil Pennington, *Centering Prayer* (New York: Image Books, 1982).

18. *The Philokalia—The Complete Text*, Vol. I, 20; Wakefield, *Sacred Listening*, Part Three.

19. For example, the Spiritual Director, http://thespiritualdirector.org; http://www.renovare.org.

20. See http://www.ImagoChristi.org.

21. Richard Foster (ed.), in *Renovaré: Devotional Readings* (Wichita, Kans.: Renovaré, 1990).

22. Two helpful resources are *Imago Christi*'s extended community rule, which can be found at http://www.ImagoChristi.org, as well as a rule developed by Pete Scazzero and available at http://www.newlifefellowship.org.

23. For example, see Richard J. Foster, *Celebration of Discipline* (San Francisco: HarperOne, 1988), and Dallas Willard, *The Spirit of the Disciplines: Understanding How God Changes Lives* (San Francisco: HarperOne, 1988).

24. Adele Calhoun, *Spiritual Disciplines Handbook: Practices That Transform Us* (Westmont, Ill.: InterVarsity Press, 2005).

Chapter Fourteen: Our Call to Action

1. George Barna, *The Frog in the Kettle: What Christians Need to Know About Life in the 21st Century* (Ventura, Calif.: Regal Books, 1990), 28.
2. For an overview of this history related to spirituality, see Robin Maas and Gabriel O'Donnell, *Spiritual Traditions for the Contemporary Church* (Nashville, Tenn.: Abington Press, 1990).
3. Douglas Hall gives an overview of this historical shift in Douglas John Hall, *Confident Witness Changing World: Rediscovering the Gospel in North America, the Gospel and Our Culture,* ed. Van Gelder, vol. 4 (Grand Rapids, Mich.: Eerdmans, 1999), 67–79.
4. Wade Clark Roof, *A Generation of Seekers: The Spiritual Journeys of the Baby Boom Generation* (San Francisco: HarperOne, 1993), 147.
5. George Barna, *The Invisible Generation: Baby Busters* (Glendale, Calif.: Barna Research Group, 1992), 153.
6. Kenneth Boa, *Conformed to His Image: Biblical and Practical Approaches to Spiritual Formation* (Grand Rapids, Mich.: Zondervan, 2001), 19.
7. John Westerhoff, *Spiritual Life: Foundation for Preaching and Teaching* (Louisville, Ky.: Westminster John Knox Press, 1994), ix.

THE AUTHOR

R. Thomas (Tom) Ashbrook is the director of spiritual formation for Church Resource Ministries, and he leads CRM's international spiritual formation ministry, *Imago Christi*. *Imago Christi* develops spiritual formation resources and coaches Christian leaders and churches to be able to live and lead with a spiritual authority grounded in loving intimacy with Jesus. He provides spiritual direction and coaching for pastors and missionaries in various parts of the world and leads spiritual formation discovery seminars. Tom has degrees in aeronautical engineering, management systems, pastoral ministry, and spiritual formation. He has served as a Lutheran pastor for twenty-six years. In addition to leadership for *Imago Christi*, he provides spiritual direction and coaching to Christian leaders and leads retreats around the world. He also served as adjunct faculty at George Fox Evangelical Seminary in Portland, Oregon. Tom also coordinates Rocky Mountain Spiritual Formation Partners, a covenant community of pastors, educators, and spiritual directors in the Denver area. He lives with his wife, Charlotte, in Centennial, Colorado.

INDEX

CRM EMPOWERING LEADERS

CRM (Church Resource Ministries: www.crmleaders.org) is a movement committed to developing leaders to strengthen and multiply the Church worldwide.

More than three hundred and fifty CRM missionaries live and minister in nations on every continent, coaching, mentoring, and apprenticing those called to lead the Christian movement in their settings. This results in the multiplication of godly leaders who have a passion for their work and who are empowered to multiply their lives and ministry. Through them, CRM stimulates movements of fresh, authentic churches, holistic in nature, so that the name of God is renowned among the nations.

Imago Christi is CRM's spiritual formation ministry to Christian leaders around the world. *Imago Christi* is a covenant community that develops spiritual formation resources and coaches leaders and churches to be able to live and lead with a spiritual authority grounded in loving intimacy with Jesus.